THE IRISH LAND AGENT, 1830–60

The Irish Land Agent, 1830–60

The case of King's County

Ciarán Reilly

FOUR COURTS PRESS

This book was set in 10.5 on 12.5 point Ehrhardt by
Mark Heslington, Scarborough, North Yorkshire for
FOUR COURTS PRESS
7 Malpas Street, Dublin 8, Ireland
www.fourcourtspress.ie
and in North America for
FOUR COURTS PRESS
c/o ISBS, 920 N.E. 58th Avenue, Suite 300, Portland, OR 97213.

A catalogue record for this title
is available from the British Library.

ISBN 978-1-84682-510-1 hbk

Printed in Great Britain
by TJ International Ltd, Padstow, Cornwall.

Contents

Maps and illustrations

Abbreviations

BCA	Birr Castle Archives
DP	Downshire papers
FJ	*Freeman's Journal*
KCC	*King's County Chronicle*
LE	*Leinster Express*
NAI	National Archives of Ireland
NLI	National Library of Ireland
OPKC	Outrage papers, King's County, 1837, NAI
ORC	Offaly Research Centre
PRONI	Public Records Office of Northern Ireland
R.I.A. Proc.	*Proceedings of the Royal Irish Academy*
RLFC	Relief Commission
S & KA	Stewart & Kincaid Archive
UCD	University College Dublin
WWM	Wentworth Woodhouse Muniments

NOTE ON TEXT

The modern counties of Laois and Offaly were known as Queen's County and King's County respectively following the plantations of the 1550s, carried out during the reign of Queen Mary, and remained so until the creation of the Irish Free State in 1922. Thus, throughout the text King's County is used. Several towns and villages in the county were also known by different names and included Frankford (Kilcormac), Parsonstown (Birr) and Philipstown (Daingean). In addition, contemporary spellings are used when referring to townlands and villages. The Parsons family, earls of Rosse, resided at Oxmantown Hall which is frequently referred to as Birr Castle. Indeed, the family used both names to describe their place of residence in King's County.

Preface

On 19 October 1852, having secured ejectment proceedings against a number of tenants, William Ross Manifold, a land agent for several King's County estates, was murdered by persons unknown near the townland of Pallas, in the barony of Ballyboy, eight miles from Tullamore. Manifold's death brought the total number of agents murdered in King's County since 1830 to seven. Even though the murder occurred in 'broad daylight', on the public road and opposite a number of houses, there were no witnesses. 'Few of the peasantry showed themselves and the few that did showed their apathy and indifference to what had just occurred' concluded the *King's County Chronicle*.[1] Such was the general attitude towards the land agent in mid-nineteenth-century Ireland. Over time little changed and land agents have been largely depicted in Irish history as being rapacious, dishonest and in general the villains of the Irish countryside. As William Crawford notes 'in the absence of any defence these ill-considered charges soon assumed the status of canon in Irish history'.[2] Moreover, the victory over the 'demonic' land agent, as was the case with Manifold, is a central feature of local Irish history. These 'victories', often in the form of murder, are still recalled today.[3] In modern Co. Offaly, the location where four land agents were murdered during this period, namely 'Manifold's hole', 'Pyke's tree', 'Gatchell's bush' and 'Cage's bridge', are popular landmarks in the communities where the incidents occurred. However, to a large extent much of what we have come to know about land agents has been based on the memoirs of only a handful of such men, particularly Samuel Hussey and William Steuart Trench, and little scholarly attention has been paid to the profession. Writing in his memoir in 1868, Trench was determined to portray to the English public, and indeed a much larger audience, the many perils which daily faced the Irish land agent. This book then aims to examine the world of the land agent in King's County during the period 1830 to 1860 and address an anomaly in Irish historiography.

* * *

It is a great pleasure to pen the acknowledgments section to this book as a means of publicly thanking a number of people who have made this work possible and who have contributed in numerous ways. Much of the research that underpins

---

[1] *KCC*, 27 Oct. 1852. [2] William Crawford, *The management of a major Ulster estate in the late eighteenth century: the eighth earl of Abercorn and his Irish agents* (Dublin, 2001), p. 1. [3] See, for example, Laurence J. Taylor, 'The priest and the agent: Social drama and class consciousness in the west of Ireland' in *Comparative Studies in Society and History*, 27:4 (Oct. 1975), pp 696–712.

this work emanates from my PhD thesis carried out at the Department of History, National University of Ireland Maynooth, under the supervision of Professor Terence Dooley. It is to Terence that I owe the greatest debt of gratitude. He has inspired and encouraged a study that had humble beginnings when the research was first discussed in late 2006. His door was always open for guidance and I thank him sincerely for such. It is with sincere gratitude that I thank for his inspiration and assistance throughout my undergraduate and postgraduate studies Professor Emeritus R.V. Comerford, former head of the Department of History, NUI Maynooth. Professor Marian Lyons, the present head of the Department of History, NUI Maynooth, has been constant in her support and advice regarding this work and my ongoing postdoctoral studies. Likewise, Professor Raymond Gillespie offered advice on the direction of this study and suggested areas that could be developed further. I wish to thank the Irish Research Council for the Humanities and Social Sciences for the postgraduate scholarship, 2008–10, which greatly facilitated research into the land agent as part of my PhD thesis. Dr Maura Cronin of the Department of History, Mary Immaculate College, Limerick, provided encouragement and advice that has greatly enhanced this study. I am also grateful to the anonymous readers for their comments, suggestions and insights from which the book has greatly benefited. My colleagues at the Centre for the Study of Historic Irish Houses & Estates over the past number of years – Dr Brian Casey, Dr Patrick Cosgrove, Ms Emer Croke, Dr Karol Mullaney Dignam, Catherine Murphy, Dr Kevin McKenna, Professor Christopher Ridgway and Dr Edward Tynan – have provided both scholarly insight and friendship. I have also been fortunate to supervise a number of postgraduate students in recent years at the Department of History, NUI Maynooth, and from whom I have gained immense knowledge.

The Offaly Historical & Archaeological Society have offered continued support over the last number of years. In particular, I thank Michael Byrne who has provided information on numerous sources. His colleagues John Kearney and Stephen McNeill have also been invaluable in the location of sources. The society and members have also offered the opportunity to present research findings on a number of occasions, for which I am very grateful. Similar thanks is expressed to the staff of the following libraries, archives and institutions: National Archives of Ireland; National Library of Ireland; Public Records Office of Northern Ireland; John Paul II and Russell Library, NUI Maynooth; Bedfordshire and Luton Archives; Edenderry Public Library; Offaly County Library; Offaly Research Centre, Tullamore; Roscommon County Library and Westmeath County Library. For permission to quote from the Strokestown Park Archive I thank the board of Westward Holdings and the staff of the OPW/NUI Maynooth Archive & Research Centre. For permissioin to quote from the Rosse archive at Birr Castle I thank Brendan Parsons, seventh earl of Rosse. My thanks also to Dr Mary Kelly, Department of Geography, NUI

Maynooth, for her assistance with the maps, which greatly enhance this study. For comments, support and advice the following people are to be thanked: Therese Abbott; Trevor & Ciara Bannon; Roisin Berry; Diarmaid Bracken; Oliver Burke; Fidelma Byrne; Cherry Carter; Regina Donlon; Mairead Evans; Pádraig Foy; Michael Goodbody; P.J. Goode; Professor Peter Gray; Professor Jacqueline Hill; Tim Insley; Professor Margaret Kelleher; Dr Jennifer Kelly; Ciara Joyce; Paula Lalor; Professor Colm Lennon; Michael Lennon; Ester Molony; Cathal McCauley; Stan McCormack; Dr Gerard Moran; David C. Murray; Declan O'Connor; Mary O'Connor; Amanda Pedlow and Dr Olwen Purdue. I am delighted to work once again with the staff of Four Courts Press and particular thanks is expressed to Martin Fanning and Anthony Tierney.

As always my brothers and sisters – Garrett, Niamh, Cathal, Donal and Briain – and their families have offered continued support, as have the Julian family. Similar thanks are expressed to the extended Reilly and Farrell families. In particular, I am indebted to my uncle, Sean Farrell, for his historical insights and reminiscences. However, none of what I do would be possible if it were not for the unwavering support provided by my wife, Tara. Her numerous sacrifices have made sure that this book has seen the light of day. And just as this book was completed our lives were blessed with the birth of our son, Donnacha. Already he has brought immeasurable joy and filled us with pride.

Lastly, I thank my parents, Tom and Mary. From a very young age I have enjoyed a love of history much of which is due to my parents. I can clearly remember my father taking me walking on the banks of the River Dee in his hometown of Ardee, Co. Louth, regaling me with the story of the epic battle fought there between Cú Chulainn and Ferdia, from whom the town gets its name. Likewise, my mother has been a constant source of information and inspiration on local history when writing about my native Edenderry. Indeed, her own ancestors, the Usher family, were among those temporarily evicted in the 1830s by Lord Downshire's agent, Thomas Murray, referred to elsewhere in this book. My parents continue to offer their support and love for which I will be eternally grateful. For all the sacrifices that they have made for me over the years, I dedicate this work to them. *Guím beannacht agus rath Dé orthu de shíor.*

November 2013

Introduction

I have to thank my excellent resident agent, Mr James Devery. He is an excellent man of business, sensible, interested and of the strictest integrity. He is beloved by the tenantry, a thing rare in Ireland in the instance of any agent, and much esteemed by all who know him.[1]

Social memory has cast a dark shadow on the character of the Irish land agent and few, if any, of the references to them were as glowing as that presented by Frederick Ponsonby when referring to his agent, James Devery, at Cloghan, King's County, in 1847. The oft-quoted nineteenth-century verdict that the 'landlords were sometimes decent men but the agents were devils one and all' is perhaps more typical of how the agents of landed estates were traditionally represented in Irish nationalist historiography or indeed by contemporary commentators and/or nineteenth-century travellers and writers of fiction.[2] Writing in 1812 the British politician Edward Wakefield believed that land agents were responsible for the backwardness of Irish estate management and that 'the most bare faced bribery and corruption are practiced by the class of people without the least sense of fear or shame'.[3] More than half a century later the journalist, James Godkin, was equally unimpressed with Irish land agents, noting that they were able, in most cases:

> to defy the confessional and the altar; because he [the agent] wields an engine of terror generally more powerful over the mind of the peasantry than the terrors of the world to come. Armed with the 'rules of the estate' and with a notice to quit, the agent may have almost anything he demands short of possession of the farms and the home of the tenant.[4]

The influential nineteenth-century writer William Carleton was even more condemnatory of agents, believing that 'a history of their conduct would be a black catalogue of dishonesty, oppression and treachery';[5] more recently, according to Gerard Lyne, Irish folk tradition would seem to reflect an innate prejudice against agents.[6] For example, he notes in his study of William Steuart Trench that both he and his son, Thomas Weldon, are remembered as 'ruthless

---

1 'Report on the inspection of the estate of Cloghan, King's County by the honourable Frederick Ponsonby for the Earl Fitzwilliam, June 1847' (NLI, MS 13,020). [Hereafter cited as 'Cloghan report'].   2 Quoted in Kathy Trant, *The Blessington estate, 1667–1908* (Dublin, 2004), p. 79.   3 Edward Wakefield, *An account of Ireland: statistical and political* (2 vols, Dublin, 1812), i, p. 297.   4 James Godkin, *The Land War in Ireland* (London, 1870), p. 240.   5 *The works of William Carleton* (2 vols, New York, 1880), i, p. 112. See also Margaret Chestnutt, *Studies in the short stories of William Carleton* (Gothenburg, 1976), pp 112–13.   6 Gerard Lyne, *The Lansdowne estates in Kerry under the agency of W.S. Trench, 1849–72* (Dublin, 2001), p. lii.

exterminators and tyrants'.[7] Taking account of such perceptions, K.T. Hoppen argued in the early 1970s that 'for too long historians and others have been content with breezy generalizations about the landlord–tenant relationship' and suggested the need to reappraise the role of the agent in Irish historiography.[8]

Undoubtedly, since the early 1970s the study of landed estates, landlordism and the land question in general has received a new impetus, although a comprehensive scholarly study of the land agent has yet to appear. Moreover, there are still certain watershed periods in Irish history for which the management of landed estates requires more systematic attention. Thus, for example, as Terence Dooley has noted, the management of individual estates has remained neglected with the exception of a number of works.[9] While a plethora of research pertaining to the causes and impact of the Famine have been published (especially coinciding with the sesquicentenary of the Great Famine in the mid-1990s) only those of Maguire, Donnelly Jr, McCarthy, Crawford and Lyne have begun to address the role of the land agent and the management of landed estates.[10] In his 1970s study of the Downshire estates Maguire argued that, apart from Trench, Hussey and Capt. Boycott, most nineteenth-century land agents lie buried in the archives of the estates that they served. Few agents wrote memoirs and thus had no avenue or platform to redress a slight on their character. That one of these men, Hussey, was referred to by a contemporary as 'the most abused man in Ireland' is perhaps evidence of the need to fully investigate and understand them further.[11] Moreover, as Maguire suggested, if we are to truly understand Irish agrarian history, then a proper appreciation of the role of the agent is necessary.[12] Land agents were central to the Irish rural world in the nineteenth century as they dealt with tenants on a daily basis and in most cases were aware of the inherent problems that existed in the countryside.[13] Indeed, the Co. Down landlord, Lord Dufferin, believed that if 'the landlord was the father of his tenantry' then the agent was their nurse.[14] Perhaps somewhat

---

7 Ibid., p. 718.   8 See K.T. Hoppen, Review of W.A. Maguire, *The Downshire estates in Ireland, 1801–45: the management of Irish landed estates in the nineteenth century* (Oxford, 1972) in *Irish Historical Studies*, 18:72 (Sept. 1973), pp 637–9.   9 Terence Dooley, *The big houses and landed estates of Ireland: a research guide* (Dublin, 2007), p. 28.   10 These include Maguire, *The Downshire estates in Ireland*; J.S. Donnelly Jr, *The land and the people of nineteenth-century Cork: the rural economy and the land question* (London, 1975); Robert McCarthy, *The Trinity College estates, 1800–1923: corporate management in an age of reform* (Dundalk, 1992); Crawford, *The management of a major Ulster estate* and Lyne, *The Lansdowne estate in Kerry*.   11 S.M. Hussey, *Reminiscences of an Irish land agent* (London, 1904), preface.   12 Maguire, *The Downshire estates*, p. 183. See also Dooley, *A research guide*, p. 222.   13 Both Cormac Ó Gráda and L.M. Cullen have asserted this. See Cormac Ó Gráda, 'Irish agricultural history: recent research', *Agricultural Historical Review*, 38:2 (1990), p. 164.   14 Quoted in Anne L. Casement, 'The management of landed estates in Ulster in the mid nineteenth century with special reference to the career of John Andrews as agent to the third and fourth marquesses of Londonderry from 1828 to 1863' (PhD, Queen's University, Belfast, 2002), p. i.

unflattering to his wife, Dufferin also stated that apart from his bride, the agent was the most important choice in life that a landlord had to make.[15]

Thus, the primary aim of this book is to address this lacuna in Irish historiography by providing a comprehensive and systematic examination of land agents and their role in estate management during the period 1830 to 1860, with particular emphasis on the Famine period. By examining the social world, background, profession, religion etc. of the land agent it is possible to provide a picture of the men who administered landed estates in Ireland. This book also introduces into the historical debate of the Great Famine the role of the land agent during that period. Assessing how qualified such men were for their positions, and indeed the hardships and trials they faced, is central to understanding the Famine. Were agents prepared for this great calamity? In the immediate pre-Famine decades agents were certainly aware of some of the potential social problems that lay ahead – but the question remains, were they equipped or prepared to face these challenges? This book adopts a case study approach of an Irish county, King's County (Offaly), in order to examine the world of the land agent.

* * *

Historians (and others) have long surmised that the basic activity of the agent was simply to secure the payment of rents. In 1802, for example, John Dubourdieu claimed that 'the management of estates is very simple; it consists of letting the different farms, receiving the rents and regulating turf plots'.[16] Maguire's eminent study of the Downshire estates in Ireland reiterated such sentiments and concluded that the basic duties of the agent was to present rentals and accounts, which were clear and up to date, and to secure the full and partial payment of rent.[17] However, among the other numerous duties performed by him (and occasionally her, as in the case of Barbara Verschoyle who acted as agent on the Fitzwilliam estates in Co. Dublin in the early nineteenth century) were the collection of tithes up to c.1838 (and in some cases beyond), making leases, surveying land, corresponding with the landlord, keeping accounts and allotting work on the demesne.[18] Others were also charged with the task of representing the landlord on special committees and as magistrates, organizing agricultural shows and instructing tenants on new farming methods. This study, among other things, examines these duties in terms of the overall management of the estate and how the agent's policies impacted upon landlord–tenant relations. Focusing on the period 1830 to 1860 it is intended to

15 Ibid., p. 48.   16 John Dubourdieu, *Statistical survey of the county of Down* (Dublin, 1802), p. 29.   17 Maguire, *The Downshire estates*, p. 173.   18 See, for example, Eve McAulay, 'Some problems in building on the Fitzwilliam estate during the agency of Barbara Verschoyle', *Irish Architectural and Decorative Studies*, 2 (1999), pp 98–116.

highlight the function and activities of land agents during a time when their
skills and knowledge were severely tested. It also aims to test the historical
validity of their representation in social memory, which, it appears, was more
often than not influenced by works of fiction. By examining the careers of land
agents it is hoped to provide a greater understanding of Irish rural, social and
agrarian history.

Over 100 land agents in King's County have been identified as being involved
in the management of an estate or estates either for the entire, or part of the, span
of this study.[19] These include, among others, individuals such as Francis Berry,
agent on the Charleville estate at Tullamore; Thomas Murray on the Downshire
estate at Edenderry; the Manifold brothers – Thomas, Daniel, John and William
Ross – agents to several landowners in the south of the county; George Heenan
on the Rosse estate at Parsonstown (now Birr) and George Garvey who managed
seven estates in total. These agents in particular will figure prominently
throughout, while others outside of King's County are also examined for
comparative purposes. First, this study analyses the social background of agents;
how they were educated/trained, if at all, to work as agents; how their role
differed from estate to estate, depending on whether their employer was resident
or absentee, and whether it was a large or small estate. Part of the methodolog-
ical approach is the use of specific case studies of individual agents, such as those
named above, in order to understand their day-to-day functions and roles,
especially at the height of the Famine. In many cases, and at certain times, it was
a thankless job being an agent. This is most clearly evident in the fact that seven
land agents were assassinated in King's County during the period 1830 to 1860,
while a further twenty were shot or otherwise injured. In fact, only Tipperary
had a higher rate of murder or attempted murder of land agents during this
period. One of the main case studies deals with the murder of Lord Norbury in
1839, arguably in consequence of the management activity of his agent, George
Garvey. This particular incident provides an insight into the socio–economic and
political context in which murders and attacks on landlords and their agents took
place.

Poetry, fiction, drama and folklore all provide stereotypes of the nineteenth-
century agent. Claire Connolly has noted that in Irish fiction and drama one of
the most popular stereotypes has been that of the villainous land agent.[20] But
just how accurate were such representations? To a large extent this negative
depiction of land agents in works of fiction had begun even before the Great
Famine. Pre-Famine novels such as Charles Lever's *Jack Hinton, the guardsman*

---

19 The 100 men identified were described as 'agent' in a variety of contemporary sources
ranging from estate papers to newspapers. Some land stewards also carried out the role and
function of an agent and in some cases are referred to throughout the course of this work.
20 Quoted in Joe Cleary and Claire Connolly (eds), *The Cambridge companion to modern Irish
culture* (Cambridge, 2005), p. 323.

(1843) and *Tom Burke of Ours* (1844) depict the eviction of impoverished tenants and the distraining of crops and animals for rent.[21] Attacks perpetrated on land agents are features of the novels of William Hamilton Maxwell, including *The fortunes of Hector O'Halloran* (1843) and the earlier *The wild sports of the west, with legendary tales and local sketches* (1838).[22] Likewise, in H.G. Curran's novel *Confessions of a whitefoot* (1844), Hynes, the leader of the peasantry, believed that the agents use of the hanging gale was a means to keep the tenants in continued subjection.[23] The aforementioned Edward Wakefield argued that the hanging gale was 'one of the greatest oppressors ... the lower classes are kept in perpetual bondage ... this debt hangs over their heads ... and keeps them in a continued state of anxiety and terror'.[24] The immoral actions of the land agent are also depicted in Lever's *St Patrick's Eve* (1845), where the agent is portrayed as ruthless and impersonal. According to Lever 'the agents get a guinea for every man, woman and child they turn out of a houldin [sic]'.[25] What is particularly interesting for this study is that Lever's brother, John, was a rector in King's County from 1823 to 1862 where he served in Tullamore, Ardnurcher and more importantly at Durrow, part of the aforementioned Norbury estate. It was here that the agent Garvey was accused of many wrongdoings and where the second earl was murdered in 1839. It has been suggested that Charles Lever wrote some of his books while visiting his brother in the county.[26] Indeed, one of his later novels, *Lord Kilgobbin* (1872), is partly based in the Tullamore district.

Similarly, the novelist Anthony Trollope spent much of the 1840s in the Irish midlands at Banagher, King's County. In his novel *The Kelly's and the O'Kellys* (1848), Trollope claimed that an agent managed property 'in that manner most conducive to the prosperity of the person he loved best in the world and that was himself'.[27] Possibly Trollope's agent was based on the real-life Arthur Baker who managed the nearby Armstrong estate; his work, as in the case of Carleton, may have fed into later recollections of land agents. Perhaps of most interest is the writing of Canon John Guinan; born in Millbrook House, Cloghan, King's County, in 1864, he included real-life characters such as Toler Garvey, son of George Garvey, in his works of fiction. In Guinan's work agents were generally depicted as cruel and oppressive or weak and inferior characters, and the Famine acted as the backdrop to many of his stories. Overtly pro-Catholic in tone, Guinan's novels depict Protestant agents as being the root cause of the people's

---

21 Quoted in Padraig G. Lane, 'The boys was up: Connacht agrarian unrest in fiction, *c.*1800–1850', *Journal of the Galway Archaeological and Historical Society*, 58 (2006), p. 43. 22 Ibid., pp 44–5. 23 Ibid., p. 47. In some cases the hanging gale suited tenants, especially where the agent was lax in collecting the rent. 24 Quoted in Cecil Woodham Smith, *The Great Hunger: Ireland, 1845–1849* (London, 1962), p. 17. The hanging gale was also known as the 'trail term', 'dead half year' or 'running half year'. 25 Lane, 'The boys was up', pp 48–9. 26 I am grateful to Michael Byrne for drawing my attention to this. 27 Anthony Trollope, *The Kelly's and the O'Kelly's: a tale of Irish life* (London, 1848), p. 20.

woes. Indeed, in the novel *The priest and people of Doon* (1907), Guinan writes that Mooney, a Catholic agent, who after thirty years' service to the estate was considered 'a true friend to the tenantry, beloved by all and universally respected'.[28] By contrast, when a new Protestant agent, Toler Garvey, was put in place 'his will was law and his power despotic'.[29] His other works *The Moore's of Glynn* (1907); *The island parish* (1908), *The Famine years* (1908) and *Annamore* (1928) also depict the agents and landlords as weak and inferior characters.[30]

Perhaps most influential with regard to the memory and representation of agents was the work of William Carleton who created a number of memorable characters such as 'Greasy Pockets' and 'Yellow Sam', both of whom typified the stereotypical representation of agents. It is very likely that such characters were based on real-life agents. In Carleton's novels these agents were seen as being a source of ridicule, greed and tyranny, highlighting the many wrongdoings that were perpetrated against the Irish peasantry. 'Yellow Sam', who appears in the novel *The poor scholar* (1833), was metaphorically born without a heart and carried 'black wool' in his ears to keep out the cry of widows and orphans 'who are now long rotten in their graves through his dark villainy'.[31] He takes advantage not only of the tenants but also his employer, the absentee Colonel B, a 'good hearted and principled man' whom he has been cheating for many years. Carleton believed that 'needy men' made for bad agents. While agreeing that they were necessary in the day-to-day management of an estate, Carleton urged that agents should be respectable men and never left in complete control.[32] Of course much of Carleton's writing had an agenda that often reflected the politics of the time. In the introduction to *Valentine McClutchey* (1845), for example, Carleton stated that he hoped that the novel would 'startle many a half-hearted landlord and flagitious agent into a perception of their duty'.[33] According to Eileen Sullivan it was the Young Irelander, Thomas Davis, who encouraged the writing of *Valentine McClutchey* as a means of propaganda for the nationalist cause.[34]

It is arguable that fictional representations of this type influenced later perceptions of land agents. Certainly successive generations of Young Irelanders, and later Fenian separatists, including John Mitchel, John Devoy and Jeremiah O'Donovan Rossa, were particularly hostile towards land agents. O'Donovan Rossa, for example, compared William Steuart Trench to Oliver

28 Revd Joseph Canon Guinan, *Priest and people in Doon* (6th ed., Dublin, 1925), p. 95. Toler Garvey was the son of George Garvey. The Garveys remained as agents of the Rosse estate until the 1940s. 29 Ibid., p. 100. See also Patrick Maume, 'A pastoral vision: the novels of Canon Joseph Guinan', *New Hibernia Review/ Iris Eireannach Nua*, 9:4 (Winter, 2005), p. 83. 30 Ibid., p. 89. 31 Marie Chestnutt, *Studies in the short stories of William Carleton* (Gothenburg, 1976), p. 112. 32 Ibid., p. 111. 33 William Carleton, *Valentine McClutchey: the Irish agent or chronicles of the Castle Cumber property* (3 vols, London, 1845), i, preface. 34 Eileen A. Sullivan, 'William Carleton (1794–1869)', *Éire-Ireland: A Journal of Irish Studies*, 24:2 (Summer, 1989), p. 6.

Cromwell, who had assumed mythical status as a cruel oppressor among Irish nationalists.[35] Significantly, O'Donovan Rossa's vitriolic reminiscences of the Famine in his native Co. Cork do not depict the local agent as despotic or having added to his family's woes. The reason for this may have been because, as he notes, the local agent was his cousin.[36] However, it was not only nationalists who portrayed agents as a source of ridicule, and even members of the landed class highlighted their alleged 'base behaviour'. In her 1812 classic, *Castle Rackrent*, Maria Edgeworth depicts 'Jason Quirk' as an evil middleman/agent who exploited his position to secure the estate for himself. Also, in Edgeworth's *The absentee* (1817), the villain of the story is the land agent – 'a perfect picture of an insolent petty tyrant'.[37] Moreover, as W.E. Vaughan argues, the fictional works of Trollope and others may have been as influential on estate management as those of de Moleyns or Brown.[38]

From Fenian rhetoric to Land League platforms, land agents, as well as landlords, were blamed for all the social ills of Irish society. By the early 1880s the speeches of Land League leaders very often harked back to the great clearances of the Famine. For example, at Edenderry in King's County, Land League activists and polemicists, the Revd John Wyer and the Revd John Kinsella, frequently castigated the record of local landlords and their agents during the Famine.[39] These sentiments mirrored McManamon's findings for post-Famine Co. Mayo, where survivors interviewed in the 1880s 'speak of famine but not of the "Famine" in that they do not mention the potato blight at all'.[40] Where a particular agenda was being pursued, landlords and their agents were presented as being the greatest threat to the people during the Famine and not potato blight or disease. It was little wonder then that this perception of the land agent became enshrined in folklore and social memory.[41] Cathal Póirtéir, who has examined the

---

35 See John Mitchel, *History of Ireland from the Treaty of Limerick to the present time* (Dublin, 1869); Jeremiah O'Donovan Rossa, *Rossa's recollections, 1838 to 1898: childhood, boyhood, manhood. Customs, habits and manners of the Irish plunder. Social life and prison life. The Fenian movement. Travels in Ireland, England, Scotland and America* (New York, 1898) and John Devoy, *Recollections of an Irish rebel: the Fenian movement. Its origin and progress. Methods of work in Ireland and in the British army. Why it failed to achieve its main object, but exercised great influence on Ireland's future. Personalities of the organization. The Clan-na-Gael and the rising of Easter week, 1916. A personal narrative* (New York, 1929). **36** O'Donovan Rossa, *Rossa's recollections*, pp 130, 140–2. **37** Tom Dunne, 'A gentleman's estate should be a moral school: Edgeworthstown in fact and fiction, 1760–1840' in Raymond Gillespie and Gerard Moran (eds), *Longford: essays in county history* (Dublin, 1991), p. 111. **38** W.E. Vaughan, *Landlords and tenants in mid-Victorian Ireland* (Dublin, 1994), p. 106. In the mid-nineteenth century the standard works on estate management were those of Thomas de Moleyns, *The landowners and agents practical guide* (Dublin, 1860) and Robert E. Brown, *The book of the landed estate* (London & Edinburgh, 1869). **39** On one occasion Revd Wyer told those assembled that 'the day will come when the landlord will be driven bag and baggage out of Ireland'. See Ciarán J. Reilly, *Edenderry, 1820–1920: popular politics and Downshire rule* (Dublin, 2007), p. 58. **40** Sean P. McManamon, 'Irish National Land League, county Mayo: evidence as to clearances, evictions and rack renting etc., 1850–1880', *Cathair na Mairt*, 24 (2004–5), p. 86.

files of the Irish Folklore Commission that were gathered in the 1930s and
1940s, found that agents were remembered as 'mischief makers and always out
to make the most out of every situation to feather their own nests'.[42] Tales
regarding notorious figures such as Marcus Keane, agent of the Westby and
Conyngham estates in Co. Clare, are numerous. Indeed, one such account notes
how Keane's body was dug up and his coffin thrown outside the walls of the
cemetery.[43] In more recent times the avaricious, cruel and oppressive land agent
has been portrayed in television and drama.[44] Even Irish children's stories and
legends are also critical of the agent and landlord.[45]

Equally importantly, Irish traditional music and ballads also depict the agent
as being rapacious and evil. According to Robin Haines, songs relating to the
Famine period suggest resentment to landlords, agents, grabbers, grain dealers
and large farmers rather than the British government.[46] In King's County, social
memory has been particularly unkind to land agents and their employees. Music
and poetry kept alive in rural localities pour scorn on estate officials for their
conduct towards the people. For example, in the poem 'The Boys of Gurteen'
agents and their 'hirelings' are singled out: 'we cried down with coercion, rack
rents and evictions, the bailiff, the sheriff and crowbar brigade, and the landlords
must fly out of Holy Ireland, unless they work for us with the shovel and
spade'.[47] Other King's County poetry is even less kind, directing particular ire
towards the bailiffs and drivers (those who gathered seized crops and animals),
introducing matters of a personal nature. In the poem 'Ballyboy', by Tom Ryan,
two local bailiffs are cursed for their behaviour towards the local population:
'The devil take you long Tom, likewise auld cripple Joe, ye brought disgrace
unto this isle, bad luck attend ye both, but what can we expect from ye, when
your father cut his throat'.[48] More tellingly, the memory of the Famine was
used as a pretext for acts of violence and vandalism during the Irish revolution
of the twentieth century. For example, evictions of forty-three families at
Kinnitty in 1852, carried out by 'Black' Thomas Bernard, were recalled in
December 1922 (some four months after the destruction of the Bernard family
home) when it was claimed that 'the children and grandchildren of the evicted
tenants are awaiting for their own parliament to restore them to their
birthright'.[49] As Tim O'Neill argues, because of the level of evictions in
nineteenth-century Ireland, folk memory has been unkind to landlords and their
agents, resulting in a negative portrait of both of these groupings in verse,

41 See Peter Somerville Large, *The Irish country house: a social history* (London, 1995), p. 226.
42 Cathal Póirtéir, *Famine echoes* (Dublin, 1995), p. 216.   43 Ibid., pp 222–3.   44 See, for
example, Robert Cooper and James Mitchell (Producers), 'The Hanging Gale' (BBC & Irish
Film Board, 1995), produced as part of the sesquicentenary commemoration of the Great
Famine.   45 See, for example, Felicity Trotman, *Irish folk tales* (Dublin, 2008), p. 14.
46 Robin F. Haines, *Charles Trevelyan and the Great Irish Famine* (Dublin, 2004), p. 22.
47 'The Boys of Gurteen' (Manuscript material, ORC).   48 'Ballyboy' (Manuscript material,
ORC).   49 *FJ*, 28 Dec. 1922.

painting and illustration.[50] However, the social memory of the Famine appears selective and it is interesting what was remembered or more importantly forgotten about eviction, clearance and agents in general. For example, by 1867, social memory at Parsonstown did not reflect what had occurred in the town twenty years previously. At the raising of the monument to William Parsons, third earl of Rosse, who had died that year, the Roman Catholic priest, the Revd Egan, stated that he had never heard of a tenant of the Rosse estate being ejected except for non-payment of rent.[51] However, as will be shown in chapter seven, Rosse carried out some of the largest evictions in King's County during the Famine period, some of a selective nature.

A pervasive aspect of Irish history, and importantly fiction, is the charge that landlords and their agents acted in a predatory manner, particularly towards the wives and daughters of tenants. Such charges were levelled at William Steuart Trench and, more infamously, William Sydney Clements, third earl of Leitrim.[52] Similarly, the Co. Monaghan land agent, Sandy Mitchell, regarded as 'the most iniquitous and tyrannical estate agent ever', was accused of arranging marriages and taking advantage of female tenants.[53] Were the same charges levelled at King's County agents? Brendan Ryan argues that many evictions in King's County took place because a 'pretty face' did not see eye to eye with the landlord or the agent.[54] In his erudite analysis of the origins of *Ius primae noctis* or *droit de seigneur*, the right of landlord to sleep with brides on the first night of their marriage, MacPhilib notes that such practice may have existed in Ireland as early as the coming of the Vikings. He questions, however, the validity of claims that all landlords, and by extension agents, engaged in such practices and argues that only forty-four references to such are to be found in the records of the Irish Folklore Commission.[55] It is interesting to note that of this number, the Catholicism of some was seen as no barrier to vice.[56] One instance of *Ius primae noctis* in King's County somewhat sarcastically recalls how a tenant who had just married put an old, ugly woman in the bride's bed and sent the landlord in: 'when the landlord saw her he was disgusted ... going out the door he said "bad luck to your taste! You can have her!".'[57] Again, writers such as Carleton may have been responsible for these charges as characters such as 'Yellow Sam' were accused of having illegitimate children, adding to stereotypical perceptions of agents.[58]

Until recently, much of this stereotypical representation was carried through

50 Tim P. O'Neill, 'Famine evictions' in Carla King (ed.), *Famine, land and culture in Ireland* (Dublin, 2000), p. 30.   51 *Times*, 24 Mar. 1868.   52 Quoted in Lorcain O'Mearain, 'Estate agents in Farney: Trench and Mitchell', *Clogher Record*, 10:3 (1979–81), pp 405–13.   53 Peter Collins, *County Monaghan sources in the Public Records Office of Northern Ireland* (Belfast, 1998), p. xix.   54 Brendan Ryan, *A land by the river of God: a history of Ferbane parish from the earliest times to c.1900* (Ferbane, 1994), p. 105.   55 Seamus MacPhilib, '*Ius primae noctis* and the sexual image of Irish landlords in folk tradition and in contemporary accounts', *Bealoideas*, 56 (1988), pp 101–2.   56 Ibid., p. 105.   57 Ibid., p. 112.   58 See Chestnutt, *Studies in the short stories of William Carleton*, p. 113.

1   Statue of the third earl of Rosse, erected in 1867 in Parsonstown
(courtesy of Offaly Historical Society)

into Irish historiography. Writing in 1956, Roger McHugh in his contribution, *The Great Famine*, edited by Edwards and Williams, asserted that in the Irish oral tradition agents are remembered as having been 'merciless and harsh, grinding for arrears of rent, evicting, levying fees for improvements or without cause'.[59] In the early 1970s, Maguire's *The Downshire estates in Ireland* became one of the few studies that illuminated on the world of the nineteenth-century agent. Thereafter, aspects of the lives and role of land agents were examined in studies of landlords and tenants in a handful of works by historians such as Donnelly, Vaughan, Crawford and Norton.[60] In his study of *Landlords and tenants in mid-*

59 Roger McHugh, 'The Famine in Irish oral tradition' in R.D. Edwards & T. Desmond Williams (eds), *The Great Famine: studies in Irish history, 1845–52* (Dublin, 1956), p. 429.   60 See Donnelly Jr, *The land and the people of nineteenth century Cork;* W.E. Vaughan, *Landlords and*

Victorian Ireland (1994), Vaughan concluded that stereotypical perceptions of agents were impossible to avoid as 'it was widely believed that they were the cause of the trouble for both the landlords and tenants'.[61] One of the more recent studies of a land agent concludes that it was 'unsurprising that some might conspire to murder him' given the harshness of life and ill feelings generated by evictions.[62] Another study makes the legitimate point that 'land agents in Ireland have not had very good press but then the story of landlord–tenant relations has been told very much from the tenants' point of view'.[63] By building on the more recent historiography of land agents this book aims to provide a comprehensive study of their world in one Irish county during the period 1830 to 1860 and therefore to test the historical validity of their representation in social memory.

tenants in mid-Victorian Ireland (Oxford, 1994); Crawford, *The management of a major Ulster estate* and Desmond Norton, *Landlords, tenants, famine: the business of an Irish land agency in the 1840s* (Dublin, 2005). **61** Vaughan, *Landlords and tenants*, p. 111. **62** Michael McMahon, *The murder of Thomas Douglas Bateson, county Monaghan, 1851* (Dublin, 2005), p. 35. **63** Dennis Marnane, 'Such a treacherous country: a land agent in Cappawhite, 1847–52', *Tipperary Historical Journal* (2004), p. 233.

1 King's County: landscape and people

> We saw no symptoms of improvement in the state of the people, no inhabitants being visible but the worn and ragged tenants of filthy cabins.[1]

Situated in the centre of Ireland, King's County is bordered by seven counties; to the east, Kildare and Queen's County (now Laois), to the west, Galway and Roscommon, to the south Tipperary and to the north by Westmeath and Meath. In the mid-nineteenth century the county was divided by five Catholic dioceses, namely – Clonfert, Kildare & Leighlin, Killaloe, Meath and Ossory, while the Church of Ireland diocese of Meath and Killaloe included King's County within their boundaries. At 445 miles long and 39 miles wide the county comprised almost 500,000 acres, divided into 1,000 townlands, 51 civil parishes and 12 baronies.[2] In their report of 1836 the Commissioners of Public Works found that there was 341,310 acres of cultivated land in the county; 80,900 acres of land uncultivated and capable of improvement, while there were 34,954 acres deemed unprofitable.[3] That a high percentage of the land needed improvement or was unprofitable was suggested as early as 1801, when Sir Charles Coote noted that the soil 'is not very fertile and only rendered so by manures of bog stuff and various composts' and that on the whole the county was 'a dreary and comparatively sterile tract, the general character is barren and melancholy'.[4]

Mirroring the national trend, the population of King's County increased from 113,000 in 1813 to just over 131,000 in 1821.[5] By the eve of the Famine it had increased again to just over 144,000. Thus in less than three decades the population had risen by twenty-seven per cent. This increase was concentrated primarily 'on the land' as it remained essentially a rural county. Its rural nature was emphasized by the 1841 census returns, which showed that 63 per cent of the county's population was employed in agriculture, with only 16 per cent in manufacturing and 9.4 per cent as domestic servants.[6] Manufacturing and industry were primarily centred on the towns of Tullamore, Parsonstown,

---

1 Baptist Wriothesley Noel, *Notes on a short tour through the midland counties of Ireland in the summer of 1836 with observations on the condition of the peasantry* (London, 1836), p. 230. 2 Grainne Breen, 'Landlordism in King's County in the mid-nineteenth century' in Nolan & O'Neill (eds), *Offaly history and society: interdisciplinary essays on the history of an Irish county* (Dublin, 1998), p. 629. 3 *Select committee on amount of advances by Commissioners of Public Works in Ireland, first and second reports, minutes of evidence, appendix, index 1836*, HC 1836 [573], xx, 169, p. 107. 4 Sir Charles Coote, *Statistical survey of the King's County* (Dublin, 1801), p. 56 & 158. 5 Arnold Horner, *Mapping Offaly in the early 19th century with an atlas of William Larkin's map of King's County, 1809* (Bray, 2006), p. 7. 6 The remaining occupations included 2.26 per cent in industry; 1.9 per cent in trade; 0.71 per cent in mining; 1.9 per cent in building; 0.28 per cent in transport while 1.53 per cent were deemed paupers.

Banagher, Philipstown, Edenderry, Clara and Shinrone – each with a population of over 1,000. Opportunities were limited and only 30 per cent of the population was recorded as being literate, while 26 per cent lived in fourth-class housing. Many of these houses were centered on the county's largest town, Tullamore, which had a population of 5,517 while the smallest village was Cadamstown with a population of just 90 people.[7]

In the late eighteenth century the completion of the Grand Canal, which entered the county at Edenderry and proceeded towards the River Shannon in the west, advanced the prosperity of the region by providing new and wider markets for agricultural produce. For example, in 1801 some 110,855 tons were shipped from Tullamore to Dublin along the Grand Canal; by 1845 the figure had increased to 280,000 tons.[8] The Grand Canal significantly changed the fortunes of Tullamore, which by the 1830s was the established county town and among the most prosperous in the midlands.[9] The entrepreneurial Berry family of Eglish, near Parsonstown, who had stores in Tullamore, Shannon Harbour and Dublin, were instrumental in its development. According to Coote, Tullamore was 'certainly the best town in the county and bids fair to be little inferior to any town in Ireland; the houses are all slated built mostly in two stories in height and ornamented with window stools and top corners of fine hewn stone'.[10] While the Berrys made a significant contribution, so too did the landlord, Charles William Bury, who had succeeded to the Charleville estates in 1785. That year part of the town was destroyed by fire when a hot air balloon crashed and burned a number of houses. A major building programme commenced driven by favourable leases that were granted to an entrepreneurial middle class comprised of professionals and merchants.[11] Landlord and merchant class were linked by two of the Berry brothers, William and Francis, who served as land agents to the earls of Charleville.[12] Other entrepreneurs who played a major role in the development of Tullamore included Acres, Slator and Crowe. When Thomas Acres died in 1836 he owned 140 houses in Tullamore or about 4 per cent of the total number in the town.[13] Landlord influence was also evident in the development of Edenderry, even though the marquis of Downshire was an absentee proprietor. In 1831 Edenderry was described as 'very clean, and several of the poor people's houses have been washed with lime' and in general 'the town is free from fever'.[14]

In the countryside, the quality of land varied greatly from the fertile baronies

7 Horner, *Mapping Offaly*, p. 10.   8 Michael Byrne, 'Tullamore: the growth process, 1785–1841' in Nolan & O'Neill (eds), *Offaly history and society*, p. 579.   9 Michael Byrne, *Legal Offaly: the county courthouse at Tullamore and the legal profession in county Offaly from the 1820s to the present* (Tullamore, 2008), p. 13.   10 Coote, *Statistical survey of King's County*, p. 176. 11 Byrne, 'Tullamore: the growth process', p. 592.   12 Ruth Delany, *The Grand Canal of Ireland* (Newtown Abbot, 1973), p. 76.   13 The leases are part of the Acres estates collection belonging to Hoey & Denning Solicitors, Tullamore, Co. Offaly.   14 See Binns, *Miseries and beauties of Ireland* (2 vols, London, 1837), ii, pp 57–60.

of Clonlisk and Ballybritt in the south of the county, to the boggy and uncultivated baronies of Coolestown to the east and Garrycastle to the west. In the long
term these variations influenced how landlords and agents developed estate
policies in terms of leasing, subdivision and agriculture. By 1830 there were
approximately about 170 estates, of which, 25 were over 2,000 acres.[15] The five
largest landowners in King's County between them owned 109,071 acres, or
twenty-two per cent of the total acreage of the county; namely the aforementioned Digby, Lord Rosse (25,167 acres), Lord Charleville (23,370 acres),
Colonel Bernard (15,979 acres) and Lord Downshire (13,928 acres).[16] Two of
these landlords were absentees: Digby who resided at Sherborne Castle, Dorset,
and the marquis of Downshire who resided at Hillsborough, Co. Down. Other
absentees included Charles William Baldwin who lived in London (where he
practised as a solicitor),[17] as did Henry Kemmis and Charles Molloy, while Sir
William Cox lived in Co. Wexford. It was these absentees who received particular criticism when the Famine struck. At the time Arthur Fitzmaurice, himself
a land agent in King's County, was critical of absentees, believing that they 'only
care to get the money' as opposed to resident proprietors who 'always manage
better'.[18]

Although Arnold Horner has suggested that King's County landlords were in
general absentee (and thus their commitment to their estates questionable), on
closer examination it appears that more than half of the largest landowners in
the county were resident on their estates during this period.[19] Indeed, in the
decades prior to the Famine some of these had consolidated their residency by
building substantial mansions, discussed below. Moreover, in terms of residency,
the county was also noted for the number of minor gentry, described as 'the
guardians of everything which makes the county respectable'.[20] Many of these
landed families could trace their ancestors to the colonists of the sixteenth and
seventeenth centuries including the Biddulphs of Rathrobin, the Wakelys of
Ballyburley and the Dames of Greenhills. Below this minor gentry was a
burgeoning class of farmers, labourers and cottiers. Not surprisingly then, the
size of agricultural holdings also varied throughout the county and it was also
clear that there was a growing pressure for land among the inhabitants; by 1841
there were more than 13,000 holdings of one acre or more.[21] In the main, as
Coote recorded, 'the cottages of the peasants are miserably poor and wretched,

---

15 For a sample of the estates of over 2,000 acres see appendix one.   16 There were other types
of estate owners in King's County including those owned, for example, by Trinity College
Dublin (3,885 acres); Dr Steeven's Hospital (2,237 acres) and Erasmus Smith Schools (1,315
acres).   17 Baldwin papers (NLI, PC 313).   18 *Report from Her Majesty's commission of inquiry
into the state of law and practice to the occupation of land in Ireland*, HC 1845 [605] [606] xix.1, 57,
p. 574. [Hereafter cited as *Devon Commission*].   19 Horner, *Mapping Offaly*, p. 8.   20 Coote,
Statistical survey, pp 17–18.   21 *Dublin directory*, 1848, p. 202. Approximately one-third of the
county's population consisted of holdings less than five acres, while on the other hand, only two
per cent of the holdings were over 200 acres. See also Breen, 'Landlordism in King's County', p.

in few instances weather proof; yet fondly clung to by the natives, who are attached to them by custom, and perhaps also from the warmth occasioned by their smoke and lowness', while labourers were described as a 'wretched class and not better treated than slaves'.[22] Indeed, even the more wealthy farmers were said to 'live well but are dirty' and 'they all refuse to live in slated houses, many of which have been erected by the gentry and are very ornamental to their demesnes, but are of no farther use, as they prefer clay huts'.[23] It was little wonder then that Elizabeth Smith exclaimed about the inhabitants of King's County that:

> they are the strangest people! … what has made them so it would be hard to tell; maybe misgovernment and certainly want of education and most undoubtedly the priesthood; but here they are, neither honest nor truthful nor industrious and full of wild fearful passions that won't be rooted our for many generations.[24]

For the majority of the population, poverty and destitution were endemic. Famine had occurred periodically in the previous half century, but, in the main, it was localized and sporadic. In 1782, for example, John Lloyd at Gloster, Shinrone, despaired that 'the present alarming aspect of the season gives but too much cause for the most serious apprehensions for the spring corn and the potatoes. I am really filled with terrors at the prospect of a scarcity approaching to famine the next year'.[25] Likewise, at Edenderry the agent of the Blundell estate, John Hatch, frequently reported Famine conditions throughout the late eighteenth-century.[26] Frequent failure of the potato crop, particularly during the years 1815–17, 1821–2, 1830–1 and 1839–40, led to continued localized Famine and perhaps, as William Carleton claimed, no year in Irish history was without Famine.[27] In addition, in the early decades of the nineteenth century there were several outbreaks of cholera and typhus – 1817 and 1832 were among the worst – and this added to the plight of the lower orders.[28]

Part of the reason for the destitution in the pre-Famine period lay in the collapse of the cottage industries after the ending of the Napoleonic War. In 1760 the linen output of King's County had been estimated at £50,000 but by 1816 had fallen to just over £20,000. By the 1830s in the country as a whole the manufacture of linen was in irreversible decline.[29] The smallholders of King's

---

654. **22** *Royal com. on condition of poorer classes in Ireland*, HC 1836, [35] [36] [37] [38] [39] [40] [41] [42] xxx.35, 221, xxxi.1, xxxii.1, xxxiii.1, xxxiv.1, 427, 643, 657 [hereafter cited as *Poor Law Inquiry*]. **23** Quoted in Wakefield, *An account of Ireland*, ii, p. 686. **24** 'Diary of Elizabeth Smith, 30 Nov. 1840' (in private possession). **25** John Lloyd to John Foster, 13 May 1782 (PRONI, D562/1404). **26** See Reilly, *Edenderry, county Offaly and the Downshire estate*. **27** William Carleton, *The black prophet: a tale of the Irish famine* (London and Belfast, 1847), p. 175. **28** See Tim P. O'Neill, 'Cholera in Offaly in the 1830s', *Offaly Heritage*, 1 (2003), pp 96–107. **29** Helen Sheil, *Falling into wretchedness: Ferbane in the 1830s* (Dublin, 1998), p. 29.

1 Major towns and villages of King's County, *c.*1845

County who had supplemented their income through the linen industry witnessed a dramatic decline in their fortunes.[30] By 1839 there were only two mills in King's County, employing fifty-six people.[31] In an effort to reinvigorate these cottage industries landlords such as Lord Ponsonby provided flax spinning machines to tenants, but these efforts to create employment and prosperity ultimately failed, while as a means of reviving the manufacture of flax in the 1820s the King's County and Westmeath Flax Spinning Association was formed, but achieved little success.[32] A similar decline in the woollen industry had also occurred, most notably at Edenderry.[33] As a result of this economic collapse almost three per cent of the county's families were living purely on 'vested means' (charity) and only counties Dublin and Wicklow had a higher proportion

30 George O'Brien, *The economic history of Ireland from the Union to the Famine* (London, 1921), p. 317. 31 Ibid., p. 307. 32 'Introduction to the Molesworth papers' (PRONI, Molesworth papers, D/1567/E/13/1). See also A.G. Richardson to Colonel Westenra, 23 Mar. 1824 (Rossmore papers, D207/28/80). 33 'Petition of the worsted weavers of Edenderry to the Marquis of Downshire, Oct. 1810' (DP, D/671/C/254/12).

of their population in this situation.[34] In addition, quite a high proportion of the county's population also depended on the dreaded loan fund system operated either by the landlord, his agent or the 'gombeen man'.[35] Loan funds operated by advancing money to tenants, usually charging exorbitant interest rates.[36] Although the system was widely criticized, it did have its supporters.[37] In general, the odium towards the loan fund was due to its allowing landowners to dictate how tenants were to spend loan fund money; in some cases even forbidding the purchase of alcohol. Of course, in many cases tenants borrowed money from the loan fund to pay their rent, meaning that they were in continual debt to their landlord.[38] However, an act of parliament reducing the interest that could be charged, meant that by 1845 many funds had ceased operating.[39]

With the collapse of cottage industries also came an increase in competition for land. By the mid-1830s the hunger for land in King's County was said to be so great that people were willing to pay well above market value for even the smallest patches of ground.[40] In Garrycastle, described as 'the most extensive but inconsiderable' barony in the county, competition for land characterized the violence and lawlessness of the area.[41] Adding to the problem the value of land had risen in the early nineteenth century as a result of the Bank Restriction Act of 1797, but more importantly, the rise in agricultural prices during the Napoleonic War.[42] Added to this there was considerable unrest about the measurement and valuation of land. In measuring land, agents had to contend with the various measurements in practice, particularly among Scottish agriculturalists, which inevitably led to increased tensions around access to land.[43] Reflecting this fact, by 1843 the landlords of the baronies of Upper and Lower Philipstown, Geashill, Warrenstown and Kilcoursey unanimously deplored the 'unexampled competition for land' that had led to so many social and economic problems in the county.[44]

Naturally, this competition led to problems of subdivision, overcrowding, the

---

34 Tim P. O'Neill, 'The Famine in Offaly' in Nolan & O'Neill (eds), *Offaly history and society*, p. 684.   35 Gombeen – from the Irish *gaimbin* ('usury'), a derisive term reserved in rural Ireland for those who lent money at exorbitant rates of interest. See D.J. Hickey & J.E. Doherty, *A new history of Irish history from 1800* (Dublin, 2003), p. 171.   36 *Devon Commission*, p. 605. 37 Ibid., p. 308.   38 'Notices regarding the Strokestown Loan Fund' (Strokestown Park House Archive). I am grateful to the board of Westward Holdings and the staff of the OPW/NUI Maynooth Archive & Research Centre at Castletown for permission to quote from these papers. 39 *Devon Commission*, p. 605.   40 *Times*, 7 July 1837.   41 Coote, *Statistical survey of King's County*, p. 103. For an in-depth analysis of the barony of Garrycastle in the 1830s see On his majesty's orders: social relations in west Offaly – The barony of Garrycastle, 1801–1851' (MLitt, NUI Maynooth, 2009).   42 *Devon Commission*, p. 644.   43 The 'Irish' acre was most commonly used by agents, but in counties Antrim, Derry, Donegal, Down and Tyrone the 'Cunningham acre' (a Scottish measurement) was the favoured measurement. Elsewhere, in some southern counties, including Cork and Waterford, agents used the British or statute acre of measurement. See Tom Yager, 'What was rundale and where did it come from?', *Bealoideas*, 70 (2002), pp 153–86.   44 *Devon Commission*, pp 639–40.

decline in viability of holdings and the inevitable rise in agrarian disorder. As a land agent, Daniel Manifold found it difficult to comprehend how the small holders could improve their lot given the dramatic increase in population that could only further compound social problems.[45] Unfortunately many land agents and their employers left it to the so-called middlemen to deal with these social problems.[46] Middlemen had emerged in the eighteenth century as something of a Catholic 'semi-gentry' despite the existence of the penal laws.[47] Some had been granted extended leases; for example, on the Dowdall estate at Clara and Ballycumber one middleman held a lease for 999 years, while on the Lloyd estate at Shinrone several middlemen held leases for 500 and 1,000 years.[48] Initially, the system was attractive to landlords because it essentially facilitated the easy collection of rents and meant that landlords and agents did not have to mix with the lower orders. However, during periods of economic growth it became frustrating for those whose ancestors had granted extended leases and who were unable to raise their rents to exploit market forces. Maria Edgeworth was particularly hostile towards middlemen who 'relet lands and live upon the produce, not only in idleness, but in insolent idleness'.[49] Moreover, she believed that they were 'men without education, experience or hereditary respectability' and in some cases 'over leaped the bounds of law'.[50] These sentiments were reflected in social memory and, as Maura Cronin contends, the middlemen, or tiarnaí beaga ('little lords') as they were known, were denounced in their attempts to lord it over their social inferiors.[51] By the 1840s it was a system very much despised and agents in King's County were convinced that middlemen were 'ruinous'. Arthur Fitzmaurice suggested that the number of middlemen were declining in the county because landlords were refusing to renew their leases as they fell in. This he considered to be a good thing as 'they [middlemen] take no interest to encourage improvements. They take all they can of the land knowing that they will have done with it shortly'.[52] The generality of his claim may be questionable, but it did suggest that in the future, middlemen would come under increased scrutiny and pressure from agents.

The holdings of middlemen were, more often than not, overpopulated with cottiers living in mud walled cabins on tiny patches of land.[53] For example, in

---

45 Ibid., p. 567. See also Charles Vallency, *A report on the Grand Canal or southern line* (Dublin, 1771), p. 29.   46 For example, in the barony of Ballybritt in 1821 seventy-four farmers held as much land as the remaining 1,008 holders. Quoted in Cormac Ó Gráda, 'Poverty, population and agriculture, 1801–45' in W.E. Vaughan (ed.), *A new history of Ireland*, vol. v: *Ireland under the Union, I, 1801–70* (Oxford, 1989), p. 114.   47 A.W. Hutton (ed.), *Arthur Young, a tour through Ireland, 1776–1779* (Shannon, 1970), p. 26.   48 Dowdall papers (NLI, Ainsworth papers, Report on Private Collections no. 99). See also Lloyd papers (NLI, MS 44,810 (5)).   49 Quoted in Tom Dunne, 'Edgeworthstown in fact and fiction, 1760–1840' in Gillespie and Moran (eds), *Longford: essays in county history* (Dublin, 1991), p. 103.   50 Maria Edgeworth to Mrs Ruxton, 20 Apr. 1795 (NLI, Edgeworth papers, MS 126).   51 Maura Cronin, *Agrarian protest in Ireland, 1750–1960* (Dundalk, 2012), p. 61.   52 *Devon Commission*, p. 573.

the barony of Warrenstown there were 21,462 people crowded onto 4,213 acres, an average of 5.1 persons per acre, while the situation was somewhat similar in the barony of Coolestown. The latter had experienced an increase in population of almost 8 per cent from 1831 to 1841.[54] In these conditions families were prepared to crowd onto bog lands where they constructed hovels. Maunsell Dames, a landlord in the barony of Warrenstown, believed that the people 'fancy the bogs to be free property for all, and that often a man may find a house upon his bog in the morning where there was not a sign of such a thing the previous evening'.[55] Some of these may have been turf cutters about whom the Halls, during their travels through King's County in 1840, wrote that 'it is hardly possible to imagine more wretched hovels than those which the turf cutters live in'.[56] Clamouring together on tiny patches of land these inhabitants pinned their annual agricultural hopes on the rundale system. Landlords condemned the practice of rundale believing that it was generally the cause of disputes and the reason why so many were reluctant to adopt new agricultural practice. As a result agents were determined to 'affect a permanent improvement of the lands by abolishing the pernicious farming called rundale'.[57] The system was also responsible for the endless quarrels and litigation which afflicted rural Ireland.[58] It was hardly surprising then that the Co. Donegal landowner Lord George Hill would boast that abolishing the system of rundale was his greatest achievement.[59]

The problems that stemmed from the system of landholding in King's County during the years 1830 to 1860 will be dealt with in more detail below. Suffice to say for the moment, that by 1845 the problem of overcrowding on the land exacerbated the plight of the tenantry who had endured several failures of the potato crop. For example, in 1838 Robert Nugent, agent at the King estate at Ferbane, lamented that the potatoes were so wet 'that the poor people hardly eat them, and find they disagree with their health'.[60] Moreover, the trend in the post-Napoleonic era to shift from pasture to tillage had increased the pressure on the land giving rise to the growth of at least ten different secret societies (but perhaps one and the same) that operated in King's County, including Caravats, Shanavests and Rockites, and whose agendas were driven by the need to control the agrarian economy.[61] In 1836 George Cornewall Lewis was informed that in

53 See Caoimhin O' Danachair, 'Cottier and tenant in pre-Famine Ireland', *Béaloideas*, 48–9 (1980–1), pp 154–65. 54 *Census of Ireland, 1841*, p. 70. 55 Quoted in Oliver P. Dunne, 'Population and land changes in Croghan District Electoral Division, 1841–1911' (BA thesis, NUI Maynooth, 2002), p. 30. 56 M. Scott (ed.), *Mr and Mrs Hall's tour of Ireland* (London, 1840), pp 186–9. 57 Bell & Watson, *A history of Irish farming*, p. 28. 58 See Feehan, *Farming in Ireland*, p. 119. 59 Bell & Watson, *A history of Irish farming*, p. 30. 60 Sheil, *Ferbane*, p. 18. 61 For works on agrarian secret societies see, for example, Michael Beames, 'Rural conflict in pre-Famine Ireland: peasant assassinations in Tipperary, 1837–47', *Past and Present*, 96 (Nov. 1981), pp 75–91; Samuel Clark & J.S. Donnelly Jr (eds), *Irish peasants: violence and political unrest, 1780–1914* (Dublin, 1983), p. 87. See also J.S. Donnelly Jr, *Captain Rock: Irish agrarian*

King's County 'the character [of agrarianism] appeared ... to be resulting from a conspiracy to prevent any person from taking land, or from possessing land, from which the previous tenant had been ejected for rent, and threatening strangers of every description from coming into the country'.[62] Disturbances of this nature pitted cottiers and labourers against strong farmers as well as against agents and landlords. In some cases disturbances led to a degree of paranoia among sections of the ascendancy class especially when agrarianism became associated with sectarianism. This paranoia was evident when disturbances in King's County in the early 1820s led to the formation of a Protestant Association, which included among its members many land agents and landlords.[63] Also in 1820, the wife of John Legg, who was employed by the second earl of Rosse in the management of his estates, caused considerable panic among the inhabitants of Parsonstown when she allegedly posted notices claiming that the Protestants of the town were to be massacred in their sleep, thereby giving rise to the so-called 'Birr rebellion'.[64] Legg was not alone in her thinking and in 1822 Lord Rosse discovered that the writings of 'Pastorini' had been in circulation among the lowest orders for over three years. While these incidents did not escalate and were largely isolated, they illustrate the hysteria and fear that prevailed as agrarianism continued to characterize the life of King's County over the next two decades. As chapter seven will show, at the height of the Famine the county had the third-highest level of agrarian outrage and only counties Longford and Tipperary had higher.[65]

The plight of the poorer classes was partially alleviated by seasonal labour or emigration. Long before the Famine struck many had chosen emigration (seasonal in some cases) as a means of survival. These emigrants included a surprisingly large number of people from the parish of Clonsast in the north-east of King's County who had settled in areas such as Oneida County, New York, in the early 1820s.[66] In the pre-Famine decades over 800 people took part in the seasonal expedition from the parish of Durrow to England, while from Tullamore the number was almost double.[67] Extensive emigration, both voluntary and landlord assisted, on the Digby estate at Geashill also helped alleviate the pressure for land.[68] Similarly, Lord Ponsonby organized assisted emigration schemes at Philipstown, as did Lord Ashtown on his Clonsast estate in order to further facilitate the consolidation of small holdings into more viable farms.[69]

rebellion of 1821–1824 (London, 2009), p. 124.   62 Quoted in George Cornewall Lewis, *On local disturbances in Ireland 1836 and the Irish church question* (Cork, 1977), p. 91.   63 'Disturbances in King's County, c.1820' (BCA, E/35/41).   64 'John Legg to earl of Rosse, 1812–14; 1823 various correspondence' (NLI, Rosse papers, Special List 319).   65 O'Neill, 'Famine evictions', p. 36.   66 I am grateful to Michael Lennon for bringing this to my attention. See also Peter Gray, *The making of the Irish poor law, 1815–43* (Manchester, 2009), p. 61.   67 *Poor Law Inquiry*, appendix A, pp 83–4.   68 *Devon Commission*, p. 638.   69 'Rent ledger of an estate at Clonsast, Edenderry, 1840–1850' (NLI, MS 4,337). This author has identified that the rent ledger belongs to Lord Ashtown's estate located in the barony of Coolestown at Clonsast and

However, emigration, at least on a seasonal basis, was not always socially accept-able. This was aptly portrayed in Canon Guinan's novel, *The priest and people in Doon* (1903), set in King's County where the central character Bryan Coghlan, a small tenant farmer, goes annually to Lancashire, England, for seasonal work to supplement his agricultural income. This seasonal migration remains a family secret because, as Guinan suggests, it would have been beneath a farmer to have to resort to such measures.[70] On the other hand remittances sent home by emigrants not only allowed families to retain possession of holdings, but literally helped them survive. For example, in the late 1830s there was a constant flow of money from America sent to tenants on the King estate at Ferbane. Robert Nugent, the land steward/agent, was regularly in receipt of 'American notes' which in turn were lodged to the Revd King's account at Parsonstown.[71]

King's County was no different than anywhere else in that there was a huge dichotomy between rich and poor, landless and landlord. Many landlords, for a variety of reasons, were on the verge of bankruptcy even before the Famine and some estates suffered from the spendthrift nature of their owners or heirs. For some, continued absenteeism placed considerable strains on estate finances. At Franckford the Magawley estate was in the possession of Francis, third Count Magawley, who was appointed the ambassador for Pope Pius VII to Napoleon I and in 1814 prime minister to the duchess of Parma and thus spent much of his time on the Continent.[72] Expensive election campaigns by Charles Bury, the second earl of Charleville, in his attempts to remain a member of parliament in the 1830s added to the financial woes of his estate. In addition, the Bury family were particularly fond of undertaking grand tours of the Continent and lived lavish lifestyles. From one such tour in Italy in 1821 the agent, Francis Berry was bluntly reminded not to disappoint Lord Tullamore (Bury) by furnishing him with money as 'you probably have more than sufficient in your hands at this time of year'. This of course coincided with times of severe want at Tullamore when Berry laboured to help tenants in the midst of famine and disease.[73] Despite an annual rental of almost £16,000, the estate was in serious financial difficulties by 1844 when Lord Charleville auctioned crops, stock and farm implements and moved abroad.[74]

While there were those like William O'Connor Morris who believed that he had been left 'an embarrassed heritage in a season of dire distress' when his father died in 1846, there were others who devoted their wealth and energy

Bracknagh. See also *Documents on which baronies of King's County were declared to be in state of disturbance* [1834] (241) p. 395. **70** Canon Joseph Guinan, *Priest and people in Doon* (6th ed., Dublin, 1925), p. 103. **71** 'Account book of Rev Henry King, 1835–50' (NLI, MS 41,210). **72** See *Dublin Evening Post*, 22 Mar. 1856. **73** Francis Berry to Lord Charleville, 28 Mar. 1822 (Charleville papers T/3069/B/16). See also earl of Charleville to Francis Berry, 6 May 1821 (Charleville papers, T3069/B/18). **74** 'Statement of the value and location of the Charleville estates in Ireland, *c.*1830' (PRONI, Charleville papers, T/3069/B/19) and *LE,* 7 Sept. 1844.

2 Painting of Charleville Castle (south east angle), 1843
(courtesy of Offaly Historical Society)

elsewhere.[75] William Parsons, Lord Oxmantown (1807–41) and later third earl of Rosse (1841–67), was preoccupied with astronomy and the building of the telescope, known as the 'Leviathan', which was at the time the largest in the world. Such research and building naturally reduced the financial resources of the estate. Philipstown, in the main owned by Lord Ponsonby, was also in decline owing to the spendthrift nature of its owner.[76] John Hussey Walsh (1791–1853), a neighbouring proprietor, was particularly critical of the management of the Ponsonby estate.[77] In 1837 Jonathon Binns highlighted that at Philipstown 'trade has disappeared, many of its houses are in ruins, its shops falling into decay', while the tenants were poor and wretched.[78] Another in serious financial diffi-

---

75 O'Connor Morris, *Memories*, p. 129. As early as 1823 Andrew Gamble was experiencing financial difficulties and looked to sell his interest in the house and demesne at Derrinboy, near Frankford, which had a rent of £981 15s. annually. See *FJ*, 25 Jan. 1823.   76 In 1793 Richard, fourth Viscount Molesworth, died and the family estates passed into the hands of his brother-in-law and successor William Brabazon Ponsonby of Imokilly, Co. Cork. At Philipstown the Ponsonby and Molesworth property was divided between three heirs, thus causing major problems where improvements and management were concerned. See 'Lease of the Molesworth estate, 1790–1801' (PRONI, Molesworth papers, D/1567/A/9A).   77 *Devon Commission*, p. 632. As an absentee landlord, Ponsonby left the management of the estate to various agents which included in the nineteenth century Robert Kennedy, Mr Hopkins and Edward Shawe.   78 Binns, *The miseries and beauties*, 2, pp 31–40.

culties was Denis Bowes Daly who borrowed more than £57,000 during the Napoleonic War to maintain and enhance his estates, the rental of which was little over £3,500 per annum. Such borrowing eventually bankrupted Daly who was forced to sell the estate.[79]

Family charges were ubiquitous and another significant drain on landlord incomes.[80] At the Rolleston estate at Shinrone as many as nineteen family members were entitled to an income from the property.[81] The family were also heavily indebted to several neighbouring landowners as a result of loans drawn down over successive generations.[82] Similarly, the King estate at Ballylin was heavily mortgaged to meet family charges.[83] Others had been placed in a precarious position by their lavish expenditure and/or their building of great houses. For example, Cangort was built for William Trench in 1807; Gloster House, designed by Edward Lovett Pearce, was extensively remodelled in the early nineteenth century when Hardress Lloyd was elected MP for the county, while Woodfield was designed and built by Richard Morrison for the dowager Lady Rosse.[84] What is also significant in this respect is Andrés Eiríksson's remark about the number of landlords who had accumulated debts by the mid-1840s, highlighting the availability of capital in pre-Famine Ireland.[85] Naturally, when a decline in the economy came such men were reluctant to discontinue their spendthrift lifestyles. On the eve of the Famine there were numerous inherent problems on many landed estates that contributed to their demise. The difference in circumstances of the county's population could not have been more contrasting. At the top landlords spent lavishly and borrowed heavily to maintain their opulent lifestyles and add to their country retreats. At the opposite end of the spectrum there was an increasing number of cottiers and labourers who vied for access to land. As will be shown in the coming chapters, land agents in King's County in the pre-Famine period were aware of the potential social problems that lay ahead. The question is, were they equipped to deal with these challenges and if so how did they strive to meet or avert the crisis? First, let us examine the social profile and function of the land agent.

79 Francis Hely-Hutchinson, Oldtown, Naas, Co. Kildare to Lord Donoughmore, 13 June 1814 (PRONI, Donoughmore papers, T3459/D/48/69). **80** For an example see 'Account book of Rev Henry King, 1835–50' (NLI, MS 41,210). **81** Rolleston papers (NLI, MS 13,794 (10), **82** Ibid. (NLI, MS 13,794 (1)). In the late eighteenth century Rolleston had his estate surveyed in the hope of having it mortgaged for £4,000 or more. **83** 'Rents received on the lands of Ferbane belonging to Rev Henry King, 1845–51' (NLI, MS 41,210). Another protracted case from 1838–63 involved the Tyrrell & Gifford estates near Edenderry (Gifford estate papers, in private possession). **84** Vaughan papers (NLI, MS 29,806 (209)). **85** Andres Eriksson, 'Irish landlords and the Great Irish Famine' in *Working Papers Series, 1996* (Centre for Economic Research, Dept. of Economics, UCD), p. 8.

2 The social profile and function of the land agent

> The post of the land agent itself confessed that kind of status i.e. of the gentry, and any Irish land agent moved virtually as a matter of course into the magistrate class; he lived, entertained and hunted like a gentleman and he took his part like a gentleman in displaying the authority of the established regime. In effect Irish land agents were members of the landed class.[1]

Land agents were central to Irish rural history, even more so than landlords. This is understandable in the sense that it was agents who dealt with tenants on a daily basis, and who, one would expect, should have been acutely aware of the problems that existed in the Irish countryside. But were they? Who were these men that administered landed estates during the mid-nineteenth century? What was the social background and training, if any, of King's County land agents and what was their function and role in estate management? The point has been made in the introduction that while there are studies of landed estates in the nineteenth century, few of them offer any significant insight into the men who ran them.[2] Writing in the late 1940s, Constantia Maxwell highlighted the importance of the land agent in the eighteenth century and contended that he was 'more than a glorified bailiff; he was a much more responsible officer, the landlord's man of business'.[3] Providing a brief description of their origins J.S. Donnelly Jr argues that Irish land agents were of the class 'of the small Irish gentry'.[4] Thus he was suggesting that the sons of lesser landlords found a niche for themselves in Irish rural society by becoming land agents. His study of Sir John Benn Walsh begins in 1823 five years after J.C. Curwen noted that 'latterly the agency business of landed property has been undertaken by men of talent and character'.[5] To what extent are these claims true: did land agents come predominantly from the small Irish gentry and were they men of talent and character?

To a large degree, Irish land agents were often measured against their contemporaries in England and Scotland, something which was both unfair and pointless given the differences that existed between the countries.[6] It also added

---

1 G.E. Mingay (ed.), *The Victorian countryside* (London, 1981), p. 453. 2 See, for example, Joseph P. McDermott, 'An examination of the accounts of James Moore Esq., land agent and collector of port fees at Newport Pratt, county Mayo, 1742–65' (MA, St Patrick's College, Maynooth 1994), p. 1. 3 Constantia Maxwell, *Town and country under the Georges* (Dundalk, 1949), p. 115. For the role of the eighteenth-century land agent see Toby Barnard, *A new anatomy of Ireland: the Irish Protestants, 1649–1770* (London, 2003), pp 208–38. 4 James S. Donnelly Jnr, 'The journals of Sir John Benn Walsh relating to the management of his Irish estates 1823–64 [Part I]', *Journal of the Cork Historical and Archaeological Society* (1974), p. 91. 5 Maguire, *The Downshire estates*, p. 154. 6 Mingay, *The Victorian countryside*, p. 439. In England the agent was often referred to as the 'Commissioner' while in Scotland they were

to the profession being greatly misunderstood. In England the agent was respected, knowledgeable and impartial, while in Ireland he was depicted as the symbol of landlord neglect and exploitation. Another contrast was the hands–on approach of English land agents who were engaged in every aspect of estate management including haymaking, timber cutting, cattle grazing and the erection of hedges and fences.[7] They were also said to have mastered the details of electoral organization – selecting agents, canvassing tenants and publishing broadsides.[8] In contrast, it was argued, coercion and threats were the preferred tactics adopted by the Irish land agent at election time. While in England agents were essential proponents of the landed estate over several hundred years, in Ireland the evolution of the agency in some respects is difficult to trace. The position of land agent had originated in medieval times when landowners left their estates for business or on extended leave. Significantly, in many instances the position of land agent had fallen into disrepute because landowners had permitted agents to abuse the wide discretionary powers that were entrusted to them.[9] As early as 1727 Edward Laurence had warned landowners and those 'who have already suffered the knavery and unfaithfulness of their stewards' of the dangers of absenteeism.[10]

Land agents operated on landed estates in Ireland from the end of the Cromwellian wars of the mid-seventeenth century in many different guises. A century later the terms of an agent's employment remained simple, and at best he was only expected to visit the estate yearly, perhaps sending prior word of the date of his arrival. In many cases these men were referred to as 'attorney', the term agent was not widely used until at least the 1750s.[11] By the end of the century the term agent was the preferred choice, perhaps because many disliked being referred to as the landlords 'acting man' or as the duties became more defined. It is also likely that the term 'steward' came to refer to the 'subordinate estates officials', who although competent and experienced, were not educated gentlemen.[12] Perhaps, more tellingly, the willingness or availability to pay an agent's salary, regularly five per cent of the rental of the estate, may also have dictated the title that was assigned to the manager of an estate.

Regardless of the title, for many eighteenth-century agents the position brought the opportunity for their accession to the highest social echelons. Henry

known as the 'Factor'. 7 Leland J. Bellot, 'Wild hares and red herrings': a case study of estate management in the eighteenth-century English countryside', *The Huntington Quarterly*, 56:1 (Winter, 1993), p. 19. 8 David Spring, 'A great agricultural estate: Netherby under Sir James Graham, 1820–1845', *Agricultural History*, 29:2 (Apr. 1955), p. 75. 9 Donnelly Jr, *The land and the people*, p. 173. 10 Edward Laurence, *The duty of a steward to his Lord* (London, 1727), preface. 11 See, for example, Francis Blundell to Nathaniel Taylor, 11 May 1705 (PRONI, Blundell papers, MIC/ 317). 12 G.E. Mingay, 'The management of landed estates' in Mingay (ed.), *English landed society in the nineteenth century* (London, 1963), p. 157. Others have argued that the term or definition of agent was not stable and was often substituted with 'steward' depending on the estate . See Webster, 'Estate management', pp 47–69.

Hatch's (1680–1762) qualifications for the position of Lord Blundell's agent in King's County were merely that he was 'a man of fortune and character' and one who would not allow sympathy delay ejectment of a tenant who was in arrears.[13] Despite this, many eighteenth-century land agents and middlemen were described by their counterparts as 'half gentry and half commonality', indicating a degree of snobbery towards the position from the upper echelons.[14] As land agency was not deemed an exclusive or full-time calling, agents revelled in their freedom to explore their own pursuits and most happily did so.[15] For example, Andrew Armstrong was left in charge of the family estates at Clara and Ballycumber, only receiving advice intermittingly from his father, Warneford, in England, on how best to proceed with the estate management.[16] Others of course took a more active interest in estate matters and were atypical in their approach. Samuel Cooper, agent at the Erasmus Smith Schools estates, noted in his diary for 1785 that he had travelled some 2,540 miles that year, remarkable for a land agent who could not be considered resident on any property he administered.[17] Despite remaining aloof, by the end of the eighteenth century the agent, probably owing to increased powers, had become a target of agrarian outrage and dislike in general. During the 1798 rebellion, agents were frequently the target of agrarian outrage. Often perceived to have been committed by United Irishmen, these attacks were probably more closely associated with local grievances and disputes over employment, access to land and religion. For example, at Rathangan, Co. Kildare, the duke of Leinster's agent, James Spenser, was piked to death by rebels in July 1798, while Lord Downshire's agent at Edenderry, John Hatch, was repeatedly targeted by Defenders.[18]

Having examined the careers of over 100 agents in King's County it appears that the majority came from a landed background, but many were trained in a wide variety of different professions or were businessmen who acted simultaneously as agents for different estates. It is probable that the position of land agent attracted the younger sons of landlords largely because, as one historian remarked, 'there seemed nothing else in Ireland for them to do'.[19] Take the example of one of the most prominent land agents of the nineteenth-century, William Steuart Trench (1808–1872), who during the Famine managed the Lansdowne estate in Co. Kerry and who came to King's County in 1857 to

13 Toby Barnard, *A new anatomy of Ireland: the Irish Protestants, 1649–1770* (London, 2004), p. 235. See also W.J. McCormack, *The silence of Barbara Synge* (Manchester, 2003), p. 32. Hatch was involved in the establishment of English Protestant Schools in Ireland in 1755. 14 McDermott, 'An examination of the accounts of James Moore', p. 42   15 Barnard, *A new anatomy of Ireland*, p. 209.   16 Warneford Armstrong to Andrew Armstrong, 22 Aug. 1752 (Cornwall Record Office, Armstrong papers, X/819/1).   17 Marnane, 'Samuel Cooper of Killenure', p. 119.   18 For more on this incident see Ciarán Reilly, *Edenderry, county Offaly and the Downshire estate, 1790–1800* (Dublin, 2007), p. 33.   19 Quoted in Vaughan, *Landlords and tenants*, p. 134.

manage the Digby estate at Geashill. He also resided for a period at Cangort Park, near Shinrone, 'the residence of my much loved and valued uncle, from whose vast experience and knowledge of country life I derived many and lasting advantage'.[20] In addition, Trench also served as secretary of Parsonstown Agricultural Society.[21] Born in 1808 at Bellegrove, near Portarlington, Queen's County, he was the fourth son of Thomas Trench (1761–1834), dean of Kildare and a nephew of Frederic Trench, first Lord Ashtown. Trench had also landed connections on his mother's side who was the eldest daughter of Walter Weldon MP. According to his own account his father was a 'highly educated and polished gentleman'.[22] From an early stage it was clear that Trench's education was in training for his future career as a land agent. He was educated at the Royal School in Armagh and was later admitted to Trinity College, Dublin, in 1826 where he studied Classics and Science but left without taking a degree.[23] In his memoirs he recalled that both classical and scientific courses stood him well in his later profession.[24] More significantly he stated that he had 'long set my heart upon the profession of an agent, as being the most suitable, in its higher branches to my capacities' and 'lost no time in acquiring information which might qualify for such an office'.[25] It is likely that he was also influenced by the lifestyle led by his uncle, Francis Trench, sometime agent for the duke of Leinster, whom he acknowledged as his mentor.[26]

The employment of family members, including sons and younger brothers, was favoured by many King's County landowners. Henry Warburton was employed by his father and his two uncles to manage their estates at Killeigh, while Edward Briscoe at Ballycowan, near Tullamore, and John Drought at Lettybrook employed their sons and younger brothers to manage their affairs. Henry Lovett acquired the agency of the Rolleston estate at Shinrone following his marriage into the family, while Christopher Hamilton, a Dublin solicitor, married Elizabeth Tyrrell in 1838 and subsequently took on the management of the Castlejordan estate on behalf of his wife and the co-heiresses.[27] Michael Commins, agent for Major Barry Fox of Annaghmore, was also chosen (and retained) because of such relations, although at times he appears to have been inept in his dealings with the tenantry.[28] Family connections were often not

20 Trench, *Realities*, p. 45. **21** *The substance of a speech of the earl of Rosse on 14 October (1840) at the dinner of the Parsonstown Union Farming Society corrected and reprinted for distribution among his tenants* (BCA, J/ 7/1–26). **22** Trench, *Realities*, p. 38. **23** See C.L. Falkiner, 'Trench (Richard) William Steuart (1808–1872)', 'Revd Anne Pimlott Baker', *Oxford dictionary of national biography* (Oxford University Press, 2004) (http://www.oxforddnb.com/view/article/27704) [accessed 10 July 2010]. **24** Trench, *Realites*, p. 45. **25** Ibid., p. 38. **26** Ibid., p. 45. **27** Rolleston papers (NLI, MS 13,797) & Ballinderry papers (in private possession). Thomas Murray's appointment as agent of the Downshire estate at Edenderry may have been influenced by family connections. In fact three Murray brothers who were employed at the vast Downshire estates were married to three Bradshaw sisters from the village of Hillsborough, Co. Down, where the marquis had his principal residence. **28** See, for example, Maire Smith, *The Killoughy*

enough to avoid issues of fraud or irregularity on the part of the agent. Robert Johnston Stoney was particularly slovenly in his collection of the rent and was said to have only been in the habit of paying his aunt every fifteen or sixteen years.[29] Others acquired their position by friendship with the landlord's family, which in some cases extended over successive generations. Thomas Taylor, for example, agent of the Blundell estate at Edenderry was proud that his great-grandfather and grandfather had acted as agents and 'had come from their native place with Sir George Blundell' and had 'continued with great satisfaction from father to son for more than four score years and the land much improved'.[30]

King's County land agents also included those who were trained in the legal profession; about ten per cent of agents were men who had acquired legal training either as an attorney, solicitor or as a judge. The benefits of employing men from these professions probably was that they were at least perceived to understand land law, ejectments and proceedings of the court, while also being aware of the inherent problems with jointures and family settlements already alluded to. It was also possibly the intentions of their fathers to educate their sons in legal matters so that estate business would be kept within the family circle. Francis Berry, agent at the Charleville estate, George Greeson at the Holmes estate at Shinrone and Richard Gamble, who administered his father's estate at Killooly, were all members of the legal profession; a number of agents had been educated at Banagher Royal Classical School before entering King's Inns.[31] Curiously, despite the number of legal men, George Heenan, Lord Rosse's agent, a doctor by profession, noted that it was unusual for an agent to be a solicitor or an attorney in his part of the county, which was around Parsonstown.[32] Knowledge of business and knowledge in commerce were also seen as essential prerequisites for the agency, more so than the management of land.[33] Not every agent though possessed the same literacy skills. Examination of the communication between John Long, agent at the Holmes estate at Ballycumberm, and the agent George Greeson reveals the former to have had little formal education and a poor level of literacy.[34] Long's social inadequacies mirrored those of Sir John Benn Walsh's bailiff, John Sheehan, whose 'Irish accent, want of teeth and his peculiar voice, or rather his two voices one a high treble, the other a deep guttered bass, rendered him almost unintelligible to me'. Benn Walsh it seems disliked his bailiff whose 'small twinkling cunning eye' and

barracks affair (Tullamore, 2007). **29** *Devon Commission*, p. 583. **30** Thomas Taylor, Drumcooley, Edenderry to Miss Blundell, 16 June 1758 (PRONI, Blundell papers MIC 317). **31** Edward Keane, P. Beryl Phair & Thomas U. Sadlier (eds), *Kings Inn admission papers, 1607–1867* (Dublin, 1982), p. 202. See also 'Rental of the estate of Andrew Gamble Esq., 1843–47' (NAI, Gamble papers, M 3521). **32** *Devon Commission*, p. 576. **33** Thomas Taylor Killyleagh, Co. Down to Lord Dufferin, 11 Apr. 1853 (PRONI, Dufferin papers, D1071/H/B/T/73). **34** Long's correspondence forms a large part of the collection known as the Greeson papers (in private possession).

3 Francis Berry, agent of the
Charleville estate (1820–64)
(courtesy of Offaly Historical
Society)

'his hard crab apple face' made him untrustworthy.[35] Nonetheless, despite his
lack of education, Long appears to have been a successful agent at Ballycumber.

Perhaps the most astute land agent in King's County at the time was the
aforementioned Berry (1779–1864), a noted entrepreneur who took full advantage of the progression of the Grand Canal through the county in the early
nineteenth century and controlled the canal trade from Shannon Harbour and
Tullamore to Dublin. By 1812 Berry claimed that the family had consolidated
the trade on the canal 'in a more spirited and extensive manner than any other
trader'.[36] His career emphasized the importance of landed and commercial
connections. Berry was employed as agent on the Charleville estate for over forty
years from *c.*1820 to 1864.

While astuteness was an admirable trait, many landlords looked to the agent
to be authoritative and effective in disciplining his tenants. Some agents, in fact,

35 J.S. Donnelly Jr, 'The journals of Sir John Benn Walsh relating to the management of his
Irish estate 1823–64', *Journal of the Cork Historical and Archaeological Society*, 80 (1975), p. 18.
36 Thomas Sterling Berry also secured the agency for Guinness brewery in Ballinasloe, Co.
Galway, which had become an important distribution centre for the west; about 2,500 tons of
porter were carried to the town each year. See Ruth Delany, *The Grand Canal of Ireland*
(Newtown Abbot, 1973), p. 71.

had a military background. However, having such an authoritarian approach was not always successful, as tenants were repulsed at the idea of being coerced by the agent. Although he did not have a military training, William Steuart Trench remarked that from his education he had learned authority, respect and discipline, principles that landlords demanded from their tenants and by extension their agents.[37] George Garvey was perhaps the best known (if somewhat infamous) of the 'military' agents in King's County. Throughout his career he managed the Bennett, Bloomfield, Drought, Holmes, Mooney and Norbury estates, often at the same time, while in the early 1850s when Lord Rosse sought the massive overhaul of his estate by bringing recalcitrant tenants into line, it was Garvey he sought out to carry out his plan. Garvey was a retired officer, having joined the Royal Navy in 1807, and after a distinguished career which included British victories at the surrender of Helgoland in 1807, at Cadiz in 1811 and at Genoa in 1814, he settled close to Laughton, Moneygall, the residence of his uncle-in-law, Lord Bloomfield, who provided him with his first job as an agent.[38] Other agents with military backgrounds in King's County included Capt Charles Cox, agent of the St George estates, and the Repealer, Capt. Alfred Richardson, Lord Rossmore's agent.

The background of other King's County agents included merchants, coroners, clergymen, farmers, millers and a bank manager. Paul Fawcett, a Tullamore merchant and large farmer, was agent for the Revd Ralph Coote's estate at Rahan and sometimes sub-agent at Edenderry for the marquis of Downshire. The Revd Henry King employed several men in the administration of his estate at Ferbane, including the Revd Henry Fitzgerald, a Church of Ireland rector and Abraham Bagnall, a notable businessman who later had sufficient capital to buy significant lands in the Incumbered Estates Court after 1850. Quite frequently Church of Ireland clergymen were deemed suitable and agreeable agents because of their social standing in a community. However, their success after emancipation in 1829 waned, when the Roman Catholic clergy began to become more powerful and dictate to tenants what should and could be done. There were more still who had apprenticed in other professions. Henry Sheane's qualifications before commencing the agency of the Revd Bell's estate at Banagher are unclear but he may have had some experience in matters of drainage and inland navigation.[39] Thomas Richard Murray, who replaced his father as agent of the Downshire estate at Edenderry in 1850, was a railway engineer, sometimes employed by the noted William Dargan, whose projects

37 Trench, *Realities*, p. 2.   38 John Wright, *The King's County directory* (Parsonstown, 1890), pp 308–9. Garvey's father was also an officer in the British army and was killed at the British capture of St Lucia in the West Indies in 1796. His son, Toler, was later to become agent of the Rosse estate, but unlike his father and grandfather before him, he did not undertake a military career, but looked instead to full-time land agency. In fact the Garvey's were to continue as agents for the Rosse estate until the 1930s. See also A.P.W. Malcomson, *Calendar of the Rosse papers* (Dublin, 2008), pp 139–40.   39 *KCC*, 2 Feb. 1848.

included the development of Kingstown pier and railway.[40] William White, a bank manager, was briefly agent on the Rosse estate in the early 1850s, while George Walpole, a wealthy shopkeeper from Dundalk, Co. Louth, was Thomas Bergin's agent at Ettagh. Six millers doubled as agents, but the reason for this was that it provided, the opportunity to control the supply of grain and other cereals locally.[41] These included Henry Odlum and the four Manifold brothers, Thomas, Daniel, John and William Ross.[42] The management of the county's largest estate, that of the absentee earl of Digby, was left to the charge of Robert Tarleton, a miller and large farmer. Tarleton's competing interests invariably led to tension with local tenants, and at the height of the Famine it was little wonder that the estate was drifting into ruin. Indeed, when William Steuart Trench commenced the management of the estate in 1857 he noted the wilful neglect of his predecessor.[43]

There were also a few examples of men who rose through the estate employment ranks having served something of an apprenticeship at different levels. For example, Robert Pyke, agent for Robert Cassidy at Killyon, near Parsonstown, was originally brought to the estate as a drainage instructor, but later replaced John Corcoran as agent. Frederick Ponsonby believed that James Deverys 'judicious' management was enhanced by his being 'born on the estate and I have known him intimately since his childhood'.[44] Moreover, by the 1840s Irish landlords increasingly understood that their children would derive some lasting knowledge of the management of land by attending in the company of a land agent. And so, when the obvious monetary value in 'teaching' the son of a landlord, agents also relished the social company in their day-to-day activity. Here visiting tenantry, superintending works or representing the owner of the estate, the land agent was accompanied by what he perceived to be his social equal. The sons of Valentine Bennett of Thomastown were apprenticed to George Garvey, who trained them in all matters of estate management until such time as they were ready to manage their father's estate themselves.[45] Professional land agencies such as Guinness and Mahon and their Dublin counterparts Stewart and Kincaid also apprenticed the sons of landlords, where they learned the necessary skills of land management.[46] However, while all of the above mentioned agents brought individual and varied experience to the management of an estate, it is doubtful, as we shall see below, that they possessed the qualifications that the celebrated English agent, James Caird, believed were necessary:

40 See Revd E. O'Leary, 'Notes on the collection of Irish antiquities lately at Edenderry', *Journal of the Kildare Archaeological Society*, 3 (1899–1902), p. 325.   41 William E. Hogg, *The millers and mills of Ireland about 1850* (Dublin, 1998), p. 77.   42 P. Frazer Simons, *Tenants no more: voices from an Irish townland, 1811–1901 & the great migration to Australia & America* (Victoria, 1996), p. 83.   43 Trench, *Realites*, p. 257.   44 'Cloghan report'.   45 *KCC*, 5 Jan. 1853.   46 Norton, *Landlords, tenants, famine*, p. 22. See also Dermot James, *John Hamilton of Donegal, 1800–1884: 'this recklessly generous landlord'* (Dublin, 1998), p. ix.

Honesty and uprightness are indispensible, capacity and personal activity, with an inquiring and unprejudiced mind, sound judgment, and decision of character, are all necessary ... The presence of such an agent is visible at once in the general air of comfort, activity, and progress which animates all classes connected with the estate which he superintends.[47]

If there was a degree of homogeneity with regard to Irish land agents it was in relation to their religion. The vast majority were Protestant, therefore sharing the religion of their landlord employers. This is perhaps best explained in the context of the much wider 'Big House' culture, which determined that those employees in administrative positions should share the religion of their employers, as was the case with higher order of servants.[48] On the wider demesne the trend in relation to those in positions of authority was usually the same.[49] In 1840, for example, Thomas Murray's preferred choice to replace his bailiff at Edenderry was for Protestant 'as the Roman Catholics all pull together and will go through any oath for each other ... [and] a stranger for they all too soon get accompanied with the people and have favourites to accommodate'.[50] Whether Catholic or Protestant the appointment of a bailiff was something to which the agent gave considerable thought, particularly since the position was open to abuse. In general, bailiffs were distrusted as they 'exercise a private influence over the tenants that I consider very prejudicial to any property'.[51] They were equally unpopular among the tenantry, largely because they were expected to be confrontational and unafraid to serve writs, level huts, demand rent and distrain animals and crops. Murray further required that his bailiff would be:

steady, resolute, able to go out at all hours thro the estate either to distrain or detain persons found committing trespass or cutting trees and in fact he must be on his port at all times he is wanted, he should not be above drawing a beast to town or doing many little things of that nature.[52]

The most obvious reason for these religious trends is that the backgrounds from which agents were drawn, such as the landed class or the legal and military professions, were all Protestant-dominated well into the nineteenth-century. However, there were always exceptions: for example, Laurence Parsons, second earl of Rosse, employed a Catholic agent in the early 1820s. Although Rosse

---

47 James Caird, *English agriculture in 1850 and 1851* (London, 1852), p. 493.   **48** See Dooley, *The decline of the big house in Ireland: a study of Irish landed families, 1860–1960* (Dublin, 2001), chapter seven.   **49** Ibid.   **50** Thomas Murray to Lord Downshire, 2 Mar. 1840 (DP, D/ 671/ C/ 9/ 627).   **51** *Devon Commission*, p. 777.   **52** Thomas Murray to Lord Downshire, 7 Mar. 1840 (DP, D/671/C/9/630).

described him as a man of 'ordinary capacity' who 'had but a poor education', what appealed to him most was that he 'never knew an honester [sic] man or of more strict veracity and he continued in my service till his death'. An added incentive was that 'no one would have known the middle and lower order of Catholics better'.[53] There were other Catholic agents including Michael and Joseph Grogan on the Ponsonby estate at Philipstown and Michael Moylan at the Haughton estate at Banagher, but in the main these were isolated examples. Although members of the Society of Friends or Quaker community were warned against the dangers of becoming land agents (and on occasion expressly forbidden), in King's County some were enticed into doing so, probably because of the financial reward such posts offered.[54] These included Robert Goodbody, who was sometime agent for the earl of Mornington at Clara, and John Pim, agent at the Sabatier estate near Portarlington.[55] A more prominent Quaker land agent was John Gatchell who was murdered in 1843 while carrying out estate duties at Clonbullogue, near Edenderry.

Invariably, especially during periods of crisis, land agents were accused of sectarian bias, particularly with regard to the issuing of leases. This was largely because, given the overwhelming Catholic majority on estates, agents had to accommodate a majority of Catholic tenants. In the early 1840s George Garvey was one such agent who provoked the wrath of the local Catholic clergy who believed that he had carried out ejections for religious reasons. In this instance the Revd John Dalton of Newport, Co. Tipperary, condemned Garvey's management policies at the Bloomfield estate at nearby Moneygall, claiming that there was a 'disposition to encourage Protestant tenants in preference to Catholic tenants'.[56] He was joined in this assessment by Edward Meares Kelly, a Parsonstown barrister, who claimed that landlords in the county were determined to keep leases from Catholics and to eject those who had leases, further evidence of the motive for clearing estates.[57] In particular, Kelly noted how Roman Catholic tenants on the Rosse estate 'who live in and near Parsonstown are allowed to register their families; those at a distance remained unregistered'. It was also claimed that it was necessary for the agent, George Heenan to do the same, as he would have little influence on these people when placed against the priests.[58] Similarly, Thomas Murray was accused of religious bias when he refused fourteen applications for leases in 1841, all from Catholics.[59] Charges of bias were frequent and agents took every opportunity to deny such

53 Lord Rosse to Lord Redesdale, 3 May 1822 (BCA, D/ 20/ 3). **54** Quoted in David Dickson, *Old world colony: Cork and South Munster, 1630–1830* (Cork, 2006), p. 596. **55** Michael Goodbody, 'The Goodbodys of Tullamore: a story of tea, tobacco and trade', *Offaly Heritage*, 5 (2007–8), p. 173. **56** Thomas McGrath, 'Interdenominational relations in pre-Famine Tipperary' in Thomas McGrath & William Nolan (eds), *Tipperary history and society* (Dublin, 1985), p. 277. **57** Edward Meares Kelly, Parsonstown to Lord Downshire, London, 14 Aug. 1837 (DP, D/671/C/12/690). **58** Colonel Hardress Lloyd to Lord Downshire, 2 May 1841 (DP, D/671/C/12/783). **59** Reilly, *Edenderry, 1820–1920*, p. 31.

allegations, mainly in an effort to preserve the peace. Some agents like Francis Berry were adamant that issues of religion would not interfere with their professional duties; when elected chairman of the Tullamore Board of Guardians during the Famine, for example, he declared that if matters of a 'religious or political nature' were introduced into the boardroom he would at once vacate the chair.[60] It should also be borne in mind that religious bias was often directed from the top and agents were merely asked to follow orders. For example, during the eighteenth century the trustees of the Blundell estate at Edenderry informed the agent, Henry Hatch, that 'it would be always more agreeable to us to have, if we could, Protestant tenants, and we would be glad if you note in your next rent roll which of our tenants are Papists'.[61]

The aloofness of agents from the lower orders resulted in the creation of a widely held perception among contemporaries and later commentators that these men cared little for the tenantry. The perception was aptly summed up by Maurice Collis on the eve of the Famine when he noted 'the general class called agents are nothing but receivers. The majority of them care nothing for the estates they profess to represent'.[62] There were a variety of other reasons for such perceptions. First of all, many agents may have been employed for the wrong reasons: for example, family connections as noted above may have overrode consideration of competence for the job. One of the weaknesses of Irish landed estates seems to have been that there were agents who were employed simply because they facilitated the easy acquisition of income for their employers. Writing in 1848, the Quaker Jonathon Pim noted that the ability of the agent to advance the landlord ready capital when required was the 'chief qualification for the position'.[63] It was certainly the case with the dowager Lady Rosse who, when interviewing for an agent in 1820, was even more candid about the situation and claimed that a Colonel Moffett would make a good choice 'as he had made his fortune in India' and therefore would have personal security.[64]

Equally problematic was the system of payment to agents. Evidently, the position was a lucrative one and it brought to the holder a life of relative comfort and social respectability. The salary of the nineteenth-century land agent varied from estate to estate, depending on the value of the rental received and, in some cases, the status of the agent. When the agent experienced a bad year in collecting rents his salary was thus affected, thereby providing a reason why many chose to exert pressure on tenants to pay their rent and arrears. At larger estates the wages were sufficient to put the agent firmly in the middle class, and

60 Michael Murphy, *Tullamore workhouse: the first decade, 1842–1852* (Tullamore, 2007), p. 81. 61 A.M. Blundell, M. Raymond, W. Trumbull to Henry Hatch, 1 Mar. 1758 (PRONI, Blundell papers MIC/317). 62 *Devon Commission*, p. 247. See also McCarthy, *The Trinity College estates*. 63 Jonathon Pim, *The conditions and prospects of Ireland and the evils arising from the present distribution of land: with suggestions for a remedy* (Dublin, 1848), p. 48. 64 Earl of Rosse to Lady Rosse, 2 Feb. 1820 (PRONI, Rosse papers, T/3498/ D/ 7/109).

to enjoy a lifestyle that afforded him the opportunity to mix with those in local high society. Anxious to attract the best of agents, the third earl of Rosse frequently enquired about the management of the largest landowners of his day. In this regard he noted that the duke of Leinster had a rental of £50,000 and that his agent had no house but that his office and expenses were paid by his employer. Earl Fitzwilliam, with a rental of £30,000, provided a salary of £1,000 with house and office, while the marquis of Drogheda had a rental of £15,000 and paid his agent an annual salary of £700 with house and offices.[65] With a salary of £500 per annum Francis Berry was the best-paid land agent in King's County. For some, like Thomas Murray, it seems the salary was not enough to sustain his lifestyle. Responding to claims in 1828 that his management of the Edenderry estate was somewhat 'dilatory', Murray claimed that as he had quite a large family to provide for and no other income he was as anxious as anyone to get his percentage from the rental.[66]

Although paling in significance to the Leinster, Fitzwilliam and Drogheda agents, the salaries of Berry and Murray dwarfed those of even the best paid 'Big House' employees such as the butler who could hope to earn only around £100 per annum at this time.[67] The agents' social status meant that they could mix with the landed gentry, at least on the hunting fields – for example, Thomas Manifold, agent on the Bernard estate, was treasurer of the King's County and Ormond Hunt[68] – and at 'Big House' functions, and there were cases such as that of George Heenan whose sons were educated together with those of Lord Rosse by a private tutor.[69] A further reflection of the agents' social status were the houses they built or purchased. Thomas Murray's home, Blundell House at Edenderry, built in 1813 by the then agent of the estate James Brownrigg, was valued at £35, a sum greater than the town's impressive market house.[70] George Garvey's house at Thornvale, Parsonstown, was described as being 'situated in the most picturesque part of the country. It was a plain roomy cottage but overtime it became a very picturesque and comfortable dwelling'.[71] However, following the murder of Lord Norbury in 1839, for whom he was agent, and the subsequent threats to his life, Garvey resided at Rathmines Road, Dublin.[72] A retired doctor, George Heenan, agent of the Rosse estate, lived at the neo-classical mansion at Tullynisk Park (sometimes Woodfield) at Parsonstown, built in 1815 by Sir Richard Morrison as a dower house for the Rosse family.[73]

65 'Correspondence and letters of the third earl of Rosse' (BCA, J/3). 66 Maguire, *The Downshire estates*, p. 171. 67 For an insight into the life of a butler see, for example, the memoirs of Thomas Kilgallon, butler at Lissadell House, Co. Sligo (PRONI, Lissadell papers, D/4131). 68 Thomas Manifold to Lord Rosse, 3 Dec. 1832 (BCA, E/25/11). See also 'Diary of hunts made by the King's County Fox Hounds' (NLI, MS 16,193). 69 Information supplied by Tim Insley, a descendant of the agent, George Heenan, 4 Feb. 2009. 70 'Valuation of the town of Edenderry, parish of Monasteroris, barony of Coolestown, King's County 1854'(NAI). 71 Wright, *King's County directory*, pp 308–9. 72 *Dublin directory 1841*, p. 456. See also Pey (ed.), *Eglish*, p. 254. 73 Pey (ed.), *Eglish*, p. 306.

Naturally, many agents preferred the social climes of Dublin and other larger centres where they could mix with the landed class. Directories of Dublin's most popular streets and addresses in the 1840s and 1850s reveal a considerable number of land agents among its inhabitants. For example, Richard Wilson Gamble resided at 51 Fitzwilliam Square, and George Greeson at 10 South Frederick Street, probably to facilitate their professional occupations as solicitors.[74] Others resided further afield. Agents of the Trinity College estates at Tubrid, near Ferbane, were long-term absentees: the Revd J.H. Sheppard residing in Doncaster, England, and Francis Hastings Toone in Rome, Italy.[75] For a select few, like Lord Blundell's agent, John Hatch, parliamentary business ensured that they spent long spells away from the estate.[76]

However, not all agents were drawn from the upper echelons of society or lived in comfortable surroundings, nor indeed was it necessary for them to do so. Some agents were little more than sturdy farmers of two or three hundred acres. Importantly for their employers they gained respect locally and their manners and appearance were far superior to that of their tenants.[77] More prudent landowners insisted that the agent would be a married man – obviously equating marriage with respectability and reliability.[78] But regretfully many landlords also appointed men who were far from desirable candidates for an agency. An English travel writer, the Revd J. Burrows, was particularly critical of the character of one such man, Charles Mayne, the father of ten children:

> I cannot pretend to judge of agents when I see them in company with their Lords. It is very odd to see a man ride out with a footman and keep two carriages, one of them a post chaise, and then to see the door of his house, in a market town, always open, and his dirty, ragged children playing about it with the neighbouring cottagers, with hardly any clothes upon them.[79]

In his analysis of the eighteenth-century land agent, David Dickson questions whether the potential for fraud resulted in many agents being dishonest.[80] Once appointed to the agency one could expect to be paid a percentage of rents collected, which naturally led to allegations of corruption, bribery and fraudulence. The issue of remuneration was, as we have seen, one which occupied the

---

74 *Thom's directory*, 1850, p. 386.   **75** McCarthy, *The Trinity College estates*, p. 4.   **76** See Hatch papers (NLI, MS 10,212). See also Reilly, *Edenderry, county Offaly and the Downshire estate*, p. 12.   **77** When supporting an application for the position of agent on a Co. Down estate during the Great Famine, a referee remarked that the applicant, William Hunter, was 'a farmer of great experience and skill; he knows the character of the country people'. See George Dawson, Londonderry to Revd John Moore, n.d. (PRONI, D/1854/6/6).   **78** See, for example, Revd John Moore to Dominick McCausland, 31 Oct. 1846 (PRONI, D/1854/6/3).   **79** 'Diary of a journey through England and Wales by Revd J. Burrows, 3 June 1773–12 Aug. 1773' (PRONI, T3551/1).   **80** Dickson, *Old world colony*, p. 596.

mind of most agents, who were anxious to get their return from the rental, particularly in light of the daily threats they faced. In addition, it was widely believed that land agents accepted 'glove money' from tenants to purchase their good will.[81] Some tenants it was claimed 'by means of a compliment' would pay the agent a guinea for the granting of a lease.[82] In some instances the taking of bribes by agents extended to receiving presents for their wives or families.[83] Captain Sandes, who managed Charles Coote's estates in King's County, believed that it was only agents of a 'secondary class' who were in the habit of taking gratuities.[84] Perhaps as a result of such improper conduct landlord and agent often enjoyed strained relations. This was most obvious in the case of Lord Downshire and Thomas Murray at Edenderry in the 1830s, examined in further detail below. Embezzlement was a frequent abuse and one that landlords had to be very careful to counteract. The fraudulent character of agents is evident in the obituary of one eighteenth-century practitioner, which went to great lengths to state that he had an 'unblemished character'.[85] Robert Nugent, the land agent/steward at the King estate at Ferbane, was the subject of numerous allegations and threatening letters throughout his tenure there. In 1837 King's attention was drawn to the alleged fraud that was perpetrated by his agent. It was claimed that Nugent had accumulated vast and unaccountable wealth, which was not from remittances from his son in America, as the agent had claimed.[86] It was inevitable that because of these malpractices agents became unpopular and their lives were threatened. In 1844 Roger North, a King's County landlord and magistrate, argued that among agents there is 'scarcely any of the breed left that is affectionate as well as faithful and diligent for love rather than self interest'.[87] North's claim may be somewhat exaggerated; on the other hand, there is probably also some truth in Helen Sheils' contention that landlords retained dubious and fraudulent agents because they did not want to be seen to bend to the demands of secret societies and disgruntled tenants.[88] This is not to say that all estates in King's County were mismanaged or that agents were universally corrupt and capricious or that relations with their employers were always strained. As Gerard Lyne points out, the relationship between landlord and agent was sometimes personal rather than professional.[89] Moreover, one of the most prominent land agents of the nineteenth century, Samuel Hussey, declared in his memoir that in his experiences the relationship between landlord and agent 'has in most cases been intimate and cordial'.[90]

---

81 *State of Ireland. Minutes of evidence taken before the select committee appointed to inquire into the disturbances in Ireland, in the last session of Parliament; 13 May–18 June, 1824*, HC 1825 [20], vii.1, p. 844. 82 *Devon Commission*, p. 574. 83 Maguire, *The Downshire estates*, p. 194. 84 *Devon Commission*, p. 615. 85 *General Advertiser*, 25 Aug. 1746. 86 'Anonymous letter to Rev Henry King, Ballylin, Ferbane' (NAI, Outrage papers King's County, 1837) [hereafter cited as OPKC]. 87 Sheil, *Ferbane*, p. 43. 88 Ibid. 89 Lyne, *Trench*, p. 19. 90 Hussey, *Reminiscences*, p. 43.

Notwithstanding this, some relationships often ended in bitterness because of the 'imprecise responsibilities of agents and their unclear codes of conduct'.[91] This was almost certainly the case with Thomas Misset, who was relieved of his duties in the mid-eighteenth century from the Blundell estate at Edenderry and who made the role extremely difficult for the incoming agent by taking with him the administrative papers of the estate.[92] It was a frequent occurrence in Ireland in the eighteenth and nineteenth century, and a landlord had to be careful when removing an agent deemed to be dishonest or incompetent. This may suggest why some agents were never removed from their position despite being guilty of malpractice, and seems to have been the case with John Hatch, who offered his resignation as agent of the Downshire estate in the 1790s when a large debt was uncovered; the marquis replied that the agent was irreplaceable and that 'we all think that you are incapable of any misconduct towards us'.[93] Naturally, many landlords did not tolerate such behaviour. In 1851, a Co. Limerick agent was sentenced to fourteen years transportation when he was found to have embezzled his employer.[94] A year later when Lord Mountcashel caught an agent 'red handed' he declared somewhat cheerfully that 'at last I have caught the bird, and he is at present in the care of the officials. He was a most slippery fish'.[95]

By the mid-nineteenth century there was a growing realization among landlords that they needed to oversee proper estate management. This was certainly the case for large absentee landlords such as Lord Downshire who instructed his agents that all of his properties were to be under the 'same regular and proper management'. In his opinion it was the duty of the agent to be 'active' and have 'constantly the improvement of the estate in view'.[96] The problem was that on an estate as vast as that of Downshire's, the agents' duties were so varied that unless he was a good delegator it was impossible to maintain control over all aspects of its management. It was a similar scenario on the Charleville estates where Francis Berry's duties ranged from inspecting the earls Limerick properties and reporting to his employer on the number of the trees on the estate to purchasing items of clothing and household materials for the earl.[97] However, some agents, such as Daniel Manifold, believed their duties were much less cumbersome; he informed the Devon Commission that his duties mainly concerned levying for rent.[98] The Co. Wicklow land agent Robert Chaloner was equally modest, noting that the primary duty of an agent was 'to view farms, know the value of them and the ins and out of every tenant, and to regulate all disputes among them'.[99]

91 Ibid., p. 596. 92 See William Trumbull to Henry Hatch, 8 Mar. 1760 (PRONI, Blundell papers, MIC/ 317). 93 Hatch papers (NLI, MS 10,212). 94 'Case of James Maloney 9 Jan. 1851' (NAI Transportation records, 10, p. 155). 95 Quoted in Donnelly Jr, *The land and the people of county Cork*, p. 175. 96 Lord Downshire to Trevor Corry, 22 Feb. 1811 (DP, D/671/C/17/4). 97 Francis Berry to earl of Charleville, n.d. (Charleville papers, T/ 3069/ B/ 24). See also miscellaneous Charleville papers at the Offaly Research Centre. 98 *Devon Commission*, p. 567.

4 'Before the agent on rent day' (*The Graphic*, 4 June 1870)

The duties of an agent, as already noted, were administrative, legal, social and quite often political. In most cases the agent was required to deal with the legal matters of grand jury business, the magistracy and policing the estate. Undertaking the duties of magistrate, the agent was also associated with the imposition of law and order emanating from a widening state control that was often resented by the lower orders. This was particularly the case after the establishment of the police force in 1822. By the mid-1880s it was notable that some 448 magistrates in Ireland were also employed as land agents.[1] It was little wonder then that contemporary commentators such as Alexander de Tocqueville believed that for the majority of the people the magistrates were their oppressors.[2] Even King's County landlords such as Robert Cassidy were critical of his fellow magistrates, labelling them a 'very stupid party and not over civil', while Christopher Banon believed that his fellow magistrates were 'ignorant and prejudicial'.[3] These opinions, however, may say more about the

99 Quoted in Nolan, 'Land and landscape', p. 670. However, the letter books kept by Chaloner during the Great Famine would indicate that his responsibilities and duties consisted of far more than regulating disputes and letting farms. 1 Richard Barry O'Brien, *Dublin Castle and the Irish people* (London, 1909), p. 102. 2 Quoted in M.A.G. O'Tuathaigh, *Thomas Drummond and the government of Ireland, 1835–41* (Dublin, 1977), p. 11. 3 'Personal diary of Robert Cassidy, 10

political differences of these men, as in both cases they were members of the
Repeal party. Nonetheless, for the lower orders magistrates/land agents were the
epitome of everything they hated.

Where a landlord was an absentee the agent assumed the public duties for the
estate and was 'de facto Lord and master'.[4] Thus, as Maguire has argued, agents
needed to possess 'manners and habits' that 'permitted easy social intercourse
between employer and agent'.[5] When representing the landlord, agents were
expected to act with the social grace of their employer and were warned not to
resort to the manners of the people they were dealing with. By doing so they were
further alienating themselves from the local population, and often such course of
action backfired. In 1846 a Co. Down landowner complained that his agent was
'hated by the tenants; he does nothing but abuse them and one of the largest
farmers on the property told me the other day he is in the habit of even cursing at
them'.[6] In most cases the management of a landed estate was carried out through
the regular correspondence of an agent with his employer, allowing the landlord
to enjoy long absences away from the estate. Frequent and informative correspondence with the agent ensured that an absentee proprietor was kept up to
speed with the management of his affairs. Where an agent was diligent and
respected, both landlord and tenant alike benefited. Furthermore, it was desirable
that an agent should have 'sufficient justice and honesty to prevent them from
having recourse to means which may injure or oppress the tenants'.[7] James
Brownrigg was regarded as influential and popular at the Downshire estate
(1800–17) and one whom it seems won favour with both employer and tenant. He
was described as being 'discharged with great judgment, fidelity and advantage
tempered with prudence and conscientiousness, tenderness towards the many
people committed to his charge'.[8] His funeral in 1817 was thus described:

> in this part of the country there never was anything known like the
> universal lamentation through all ranks of people which was evinced by
> every mark of respect and such a funeral as Edenderry never saw. The
> whole town, road and church yard were a solid mass of carriages and
> people, consisting of all respectability of the country and the lower
> classes in thousands![9]

Mar. 1835' (NLI, Cassidy papers); Christopher Bannon, Broughall Castle to Lord Rossmore, 15
Jan. 1836 (PRONI, Rossmore papers, T/2929/4/60). See also *Returns of Courts of Petty Sessions
in Ireland*, 1835, HC [415] xlii, 463, p. 114.   **4** See Collins, *County Monaghan Sources*, p. xvii.
5 Maguire, *The Downshire estates*, p. 191.   **6** Revd John Moore to Colonel Robert Shaw, 6 Nov.
1846 (PRONI, D/1854/6/3).   **7** Wakefield, *An account of Ireland*, i, p. 297. In King's County
there appears to have been several personalities of this nature. In the post-Famine period William
J.H. Tyrrell was deemed a good agent by his employer because of his 'ability to deal with troublesome tenants' and that he had 'a thorough insight into the character of Irish tenants'. See
Ballindoolin papers (in private possession).   **8** Revd Charles Finney, *Records of Castro Petre from
the Representative Church Body* (Dublin, 1978), p. 46.   **9** John Brownrigg to Lord Downshire, 9

A similar feeling of regret was expressed by Lord Charleville's tenants when Francis Berry died in October 1864; he was described as being 'kind and considerate to the tenants and had won the esteem of all who knew him'.[10] While one should guard against the bias of such sources from which these examples are taken there is enough evidence to suggest that not all agents were perceived as the capricious evictors of nationalist tradition. Occasionally, tenants showed their deference to the agent in other guises. In November 1836, for example, Colonel Bernard's tenants at Kinnitty blocked bailiffs who were distraining crops and animals belonging to Daniel Manifold. When the bailiffs arrived at Cadamstown they were met by over thirty tenants armed with pitchforks, spades and stones. Only the arrival of William Ross Manifold, who negotiated a settlement, prevented bloodshed.[11] However, such instances may have been the exception to the rule, as in most cases the death or ill-treatment of a land agent was met by universal celebration among the tenantry. When Sandy Mitchell, Lord Shirley's agent in Co. Monaghan, died in 1843 the news was greeted by the lighting of bonfires in Magheracloone.[12] A century previous the dismissal of Thomas Misset as agent of the Blundell estate was greeted by similar scenes.[13]

Land agents in King's County during this period were not a homogenous group. They came from a variety of social backgrounds (although predominantly from a landed background) and had various educational experiences. In fact, according to W.E. Vaughan, some land agents were men who failed to get beyond 'compound fractions and copper plate' and their social skills were the result of local balls 'to which everyone is admitted'.[14] The central question remains, did they have the relevant experience to manage a landed estate, which by the mid-nineteenth century was a complex task and required a high level of competence and organization in matters such as the collection of rents, the keeping of accounts, the making and granting of leases and other legal matters, dealing with tenant difficulties, while also sometimes having to act as a justice of the peace, poor law guardian and occasionally grand juror? Many land agents faced the unenviable task of administering estates that were heavily embarrassed owing to the decline of the economy, the extravagant spending of landlords and the building and enhancing of demesnes and country seats. It is arguable that it was difficult for one man to have had all the required capabilities to manage such a wide range of affairs and it seems that some agents were employed for what might now be deemed the wrong reasons; for example, a former army officer

July 1817 (DP, D/671/C/232/168). Likewise, the funeral of John Corcoran, Robert Cassidy's agent, who died at an advanced age in 1909, was described as being 'immense proportions'. See *KCC*, 25 Mar. 1909. **10** *KCC*, 2 Nov. 1864. **11** Bernard Cummins, Kinnitty to Dublin Castle, 10 Nov. 1836 (OPKC, 1836). **12** P.J. Duffy, 'Assisted emigration from the Shirley estate, 1843–54', *Clogher Record*, 14:2 (1992), p. 13. **13** See, for example, Henry Hatch to William Trumbull, 29 Oct. 1757 (PRONI, Blundell papers, MIC/ 317). **14** Quoted in Vaughan, *Landlords and tenants*, p. 110. See also Anon., *Remarks on Ireland as it is; as it ought to be; and as it might be … by a native* (London, 1849), p. 13.

might have been employed because a landlord saw him as a means to disciplining his tenants. Others might have been employed because they had a legal background but, importantly, this did not mean they had a sound knowledge of good agricultural practice. Patrick Lacey, a large farmer in the barony of Warrenstown, contended that the 'attorney' agent in particular did little to improve the estate. According to Lacey, the general case was that a local landlord appointed

> some Dublin attorney as his agent; this man, however responsible in his profession, is of all others the worst selection that could be made for the duty of land agent. He drives down to some neighbouring town twice or thrice a year. He there screws out all the money he can by threats of law, seizure and 'John Thrustouts'.[15]

His sentiments were reiterated by John McNamara, a farmer at the nearby Lansdowne estate at Ballyboggan, who argued that agents were sometimes angry men and often 'worse than that and they will get all that they can'.[16] For many people it was hard to escape such conclusions.

---

15 *Devon Commission*, pp 663–7. In 1837 a bill was passed in the House of Commons regulating the profession of attorney and solicitor perhaps indicating that the occupation attracted men of varying character. See *Attorneys and Solicitors (Ireland). A bill for the better regulation of the profession of attorney and solicitor in Ireland and the several offices connected therewith*, HC 1837–8 [256] i, 35.   16 *Devon Commission*, p. 668.

3 Challenges and problems affecting estate management

The management of a landed estate in Ireland by the mid-nineteenth century was a complex task. Indeed, G.E. Mingay, writing about the situation in Great Britain, argued that the management of estates was much more difficult than running a factory, railway or house of commerce.[1] The various social issues and land-related problems resulting from the economic collapse after 1815 were compounded by a demographic explosion. Agents and their employers attempted to address these issues, but in many cases their efforts were opposed by tenants who revolted against modernization. The growth of secret societies during the 1820s and 1830s reflected the increased pressure for land, as it remained the only occupational outlet for the vast majority of people in rural Ireland. Something as simple as the destruction of ploughs, a regular occurrence in King's County, suggested that the employment of men was deemed more important than modernization. In this atmosphere of opposition, and the need to reform agricultural practice, agents and landlords welcomed the introduction of the 1838 Irish Poor Law Act. This act, as will be discussed in the next chapter, provided the stimulus for the clearance of estates by moving impoverished tenants into the workhouse or assisting in their emigration, allowing for the consolidation of small holdings into more viable farms. Thus the period after 1838 was arguably one characterized by the clearing of estates and the filling of the workhouses, and this in itself brought further problems.

Upon coming of age in 1809 Arthur Hills, third marquis of Downshire, inherited the family properties amounting to over 115,000 acres. This included almost 14,000 acres in King's County, centred on the town of Edenderry. Prior to this, the second marquis had only visited his Edenderry estate once, which ultimately led to various estate management problems.[2] The third marquis assumed a more rigorous management policy of the family estates and promoted the greater involvement of agents, who in turn assumed a professional role within a professional estate administration. Among the agents appointed at Edenderry during his tenure was Thomas Murray who had been one of the partners of Brownrigg, Longfield and Murray, land surveyors.[3] In 1804 Murray became chief surveyor of the Downshire estates, having parted ways with Brownrigg and Longfield. While he effectively remained chief surveyor from then until 1850, he was also appointed agent on Downshire's estate at Blessington, Co. Wicklow, in 1809 and then at Edenderry in 1821. Obviously, his

---

1 Mingay, *The Victorian countryside*, p. 439. 2 For an insight into the management of the estate see Reilly, *Edenderry, county Offaly and the Downshire estate*. 3 John and James Brownrigg, father and son, were also agents of the Downshire's Edenderry estate from 1799 to 1819.

remaining chief surveyor when he took on the role of land agent made his estate management duties more onerous. It possibly made it difficult for him to put into practice Downshire's estate management philosophy that agents should familiarize themselves with the tenants by 'constantly going over the estate'.[4] Inheriting massive debts from previous generations the third marquis' main priority was to reverse the family's financial decline, to check needless expenditure and to increase the revenue that could be generated from rents. To do this agents were expected to keep 'a tight ship' in the running of the estate.[5] It was within this context that the then chief agent, George Matthews, suggested to Downshire that it would make better business sense to employ Murray as agent at Blessington where a position had become available (he had been earning £150 as chief surveyor).

Thomas Murray's tenure as agent at Edenderry lasted for three decades, from 1821 to 1850, when he was replaced by his son, Thomas Richard. Arriving to Edenderry he faced problems that were common to many new agents, primarily tenants who were in arrears and who were reluctant to negotiate with the estate management, coupled with the problems of subdivision and subletting. Indeed, Edenderry was, in his opinion, 'the most miserable town in Ireland'.[6] Murray's correspondence with Downshire suggests that he adopted a hands-on approach to the management of the estate and his letters indicate that he at least wanted to portray to his employer that he was fulfilling his obligation to familiarize himself with the tenants – on one occasion, for example, informing Downshire that he had helped tenants bring in their oats and crops.[7] But during this period Murray continuously ran into difficulties with regard to the collection of rents, which at times, he blamed on the influence of the local Roman Catholic priest, the Revd James Colgan, about whom he lamented 'there is a great leaning'.[8] His denunciation of the priest was based on his belief that 'tenants on this estate if left to themselves would be quite happy but they will not be allowed'.[9] He also believed that, because of Colgan's influence, tenants were more likely to pay their religious dues than their rent. In fact, in 1837 Murray warned recalcitrant tenants that if they could find money for the priest's schoolhouse (which had been built in 1835), then they could find money for the rent.[10] Certainly Murray's pressing of the tenants for the rents did not endear him to either Catholic clergy or tenantry; another of the Catholic priests, the Revd Richard Cullen, referred to him as a 'jackal' who was intent on intimidating the tenantry.[11] But he was not alone in his clash with the local clergy; indeed most agents wrestled for the control of the tenantry, particularly in the wake of the granting of Catholic Emancipation in 1829.

4 Maguire, *The Downshire estates*, p. 198. 5 Ibid., p. 7. 6 Reilly, *Edenderry, 1820–1920*, p. 30.
7 Thomas Murray to Lord Downshire, 18 Mar. 1842 (DP, D/671/C/9/712). 8 Ibid., 22 May 1839 (DP, D/671/ C/9/599). 9 Ibid., 24 Jan. 1839 (DP, D/671/C/9/590). 10 Ibid., 7 June 1837 (DP, D/671/C/9/502). 11 Revd Richard Cullen to Robert Cassidy, 24 Mar. 1832 (NLI, Cassidy papers).

As a result of such clashes, Murray often found himself the target of abuse and intimidation. In 1835 the feeling against the collection of rent at Edenderry was so great that he feared that there would be 'more Rathcormick work' – a reference to a serious tithe affray in Co. Cork the previous year. He also seemed to be living in genuine fear for his safety, noting that 'there is hardly a day I don't get a coffin or deaths head sent to me'.[12] Moreover, rather craftily the tenantry devised a system of lighting signal fires announcing Murray's imminent arrival to an area; such was the extent of this activity that in 1843 Lord Downshire was forced to address the matter, warning tenants not to make or allow signal fires on their farms and were they found to be found guilty of such he would 'consider them disloyal subjects and dangerous persons'.[13] As a result of such intimidation, there were times when it was impossible for Murray to collect the full rental. Indeed, on one occasion he lamented that the rent in Edenderry was 'coming like drops of blood'.[14] With increased social disorder in the 1830s, he looked to the forces of law and order. To help in the maintenance of social stability, Murray recruited those who had 'subdued the late rebellion' [1798], including the 'shuffling' Pilkington Homan. In 1798 Homan was one of a number of informers on the estate who provided information on the Defender and United Irishmen conspiracy at Edenderry, but who by the 1830s was among the largest defaulters at the estate.[15] Murray frequently complained that his task was made difficult by the shortage of resident magistrates to keep the tenants in check. Appealing in 1836 for a resident magistrate to deal with the petty sessions, Murray stated that 'there was only old Brownrigg, eighty-seven years old, and old Grattan who was seldom present. The petty sessions court had become kind of a sport since Brownrigg was deaf'.[16] He did have intermittent periods of success – for example, in the late 1830s when he actually managed to increase the annual rental – but, by 1843, large arrears had once again accumulated. On this occasion he informed tenants that 'his Lordship having been displeased at my rental and accounts for the estate not having been closed as ordered at the end of the half year … I request that you will attend to my regulations in order to meet his Lordships most reasonable and proper wishes'.[17] This was not the first time that Downshire was displeased with Murray's accounts. In his comprehensive study of the Downshire estate, Maguire contends that the basic duty of the agent was to secure the full or partial payment of rent and to present rentals.[18] The latter task, if, for example, an estate clerk was not available, which seems was often the case at Edenderry, added to the workload of an overburdened agent. In addition, Murray was required to keep several books and records on a daily basis. A minute book was used for recording day-to-day management activities; a rent ledger to keep an account of each tenant; a rent book

12 Thomas Murray to Thomas Parry, 25 Jan. 1835 (DP, D/671/C/9/ 410). 13 *The Times*, 4 Dec. 1843. 14 Thomas Murray to Lord Downshire, 2 June 1839 (DP, D/671/C/9/603). 15 Ibid., 24 Jan. 1839 (DP, D/671/C/9/590). 16 Ibid. 17 Maguire, *The Downshire estates*, p. 172. 18 Ibid., p. 173.

for entering rent received; a cash book outlining expenses incurred; a registry book for the leases and the annual rental and account to be made up and returned each half year. The point has been made in chapter one that the system of rent collection and payment was fraught with difficulty and sometimes led to embezzlement or fraud. In 1836 Murray came under suspicion for dishonest practice. That year the dowager marchioness, Mary Sandys, died and the third marquis began an audit of the Edenderry estate from which his mother had been receiving two-thirds of the rental as part of her jointure. Major discrepancies (up to £1,500) were discovered between the amount of rent received and that forwarded to the dowager. Irately, Downshire informed Murray that his 'conduct is inexplicable. You must be a very unhappy man – ask yourself if you are an honest man?' He also reprimanded the agent for sending his son among the tenants to collect the rent.[19] A grovelling Murray replied to Downshire, insisting that there 'must be some mistake for want of vouchers' and that 'your Lordship may be assured that if it was the last penny I had on earth that I would pay it to clear off any sum I owe'. Murray was willing to sell a farm and a house in Hillsborough, Co. Down, to clear his debts.[20] Although showing some mercy on this occasion, Downshire insisted that in the future he wanted to know 'every month every farthing that has been received in the preceding month and every farthing which has been spent'.[21]

There are a number of interesting aspects connected to this incident that reveal something of landlord–agent relations and the management of estates in general. First, it was not to be the last time that Murray was to be reprimanded for irregularities. In 1838, as a follow up to the audit two years previous, Murray was removed from the agency of Downshire's Co. Kilkenny property at Tullaroan.[22] Later, in 1841, Murray's brother John, who had been agent at Downshire's Blessington estate, died and discrepancies were found in his accounts. To avoid further embarrassment and sanctions, he undertook to act as security until his brother's debt was paid.[23] Indeed, even his professional skills as a surveyor were frequently questioned. When the first Ordnance Survey of Ireland was carried out in the 1830s it provided another example of Murray's inefficiency as numerous maps and surveys posed problems for those carrying out the new scheme.[24] Yet Downshire did not remove him from his position. Why was he prepared to tolerate such inadequacies and failings? The simple answer may be that to find a suitable alternative, or someone who knew the tenantry and estate in such detail, would have been extremely difficult. Also, by the late 1830s, as will be discussed below, Downshire had effectively decided to retrain his agent.

19 Maguire, *Letters of a great Irish landlord*, p. 45. This son was probably Thomas Richard Murray who was agent of the estate from 1850 to 1893. 20 Thomas Murray to Lord Downshire, 18 Jan. 1838 (DP, D/671/C/9/541). 21 Maguire, *The Downshire estates*, p. 182. 22 Ibid., p. 196. 23 Thomas Murray to W.E. Reilly, 25 Apr. 1842 (DP, D/671/C/9/714). 24 Maguire, *The Downshire estates*, pp 179–80.

Second, the fact that it took fifteen years from Murray's appointment to the death of the marchioness to discover the discrepancies that caused Downshire so much distress suggests that the latter did not keep a close eye on how his agents operated, particularly on his outlying estates. If Murray was not dishonest, then he was certainly slovenly in his bookkeeping. Third, Murray, it appears, found great difficulty in managing the social problems and the agrarian issues of overpopulation, subdivision and increased arrears. In the early 1830s Francis Farrah was sent from the estate head office at Hillsborough to advise on how to manage those in arrears; he suggested that the 'defaulters must be well watched and hard pressed for without sticking to them they will not do what they ought, being unquestionably disposed to take every advantage they can'.[25] In addition, Farrah also advised Murray not to replace tenants with those evicted from neighbouring estates. He was also opposed to accepting rent in instalments and was surprised by the number of tenants who were disputing their levels of arrears, again indicating slovenly record keeping.[26] Finally, the correspondence between agent and landlord indicates that Downshire was largely disappointed with the return from his southern estates because he promoted the same management on them as he did on the more prosperous and efficient estates in Co. Down. However, it might be instructive to note that these estates were located in close proximity to the prosperous urban areas of Newry, Lisburn and Belfast.[27] The benefits of urbanization and industrialization were not as readily available to the tenants on the Edenderry estates to the same extent.

By 1838 Downshire had decided to retrain Murray in the art of estate management. Twenty years before, a decade after taking control of the estate, Downshire had realized that the proposed reform of his estate management policies was proving slow and frustrating, so much so that he lamented 'the frequent and nearly futile directions which have from time to time been given for a series of years to those employed upon my estates'.[28] After an increased period of extended economic downturn landlords and agents alike had come to realize they had lost control of the situation because there were simply too many tenants, and too many small holdings that were unviable.[29] Little had changed by the time Downshire sent Murray to Belgium and Holland in 1838 to acquire knowledge of the European methods of farming. Reporting back on his trip Murray noted that he had 'got some useful lessons in the management of lands and other things that may be useful over here'.[30] It is not exactly clear why Murray was sent to Belgium and Holland but the trip coincided with the claims that Murray had mishandled or misappropriated funds. On his European tour Murray may have realized the benefit of larger-scale farming because it was around this time that he began clearances in order to consolidate holdings; he

25 Ibid., p. 82. 26 Ibid., pp 83–4. 27 Ibid., p. 212. 28 Ibid., p. 7. 29 W.H. Crawford, 'Landlord tenant relations in Ulster, 1609–1820', *Irish Economic and Social History*, 2 (1975), pp 5–21. 30 Thomas Murray to Thomas Parry, 3 Oct. 1838 (DP, D/671/C/ 9/ 576).

would then re-let these to more progressive tenants. Of course his priority here would have been to increase the annual rent and to bring him back into favour with Downshire.

Equally significant here is the fact that these clearances took place in the same year that the Irish Poor Law Act was introduced. The terms of this act facilitated the clearance of impoverished tenants and cottiers and their removal to the county's workhouses. Indeed, Murray was one of the agents who openly supported the building of workhouses throughout the country. In 1838 he cleared twenty-nine families on the very site where the Edenderry workhouse was later built.[31] Two years later he wrote with optimism to Downshire of the possibility of further clearing the estate of paupers, beggars and 'bad' tenants, believing that the construction of the workhouse would facilitate this. He had, it seems, been waiting for some years to rid himself of some of these tenants who he once described to Downshire as a 'cunning and knavish population', and insisted that 'the persons I wish to get rid of are the poorer class of farmers or rather land holders who cannot get work for their families and eat up all that the land produces so that they never have a shilling in money to meet the rent day'.[32] The 1838 clearances included a widow O'Brien, who had been continually in arrears since the early 1830s, and her 'host of under tenants'.[33] It should also be noted that Mrs O'Brien had built a substantial Georgian farmhouse, Killane House, which following the clearances became the residence of the bailiff, Robert McComb.[34] It was little wonder that as a result of Murray's policies an alleged plot was foiled when a man was overheard at Edenderry to say that he would 'blow Downshire's brains out'.[35] Obviously aware that there was a threat posed by the building of the workhouse, the tenantry actively combined to stop its progress.[36] To negate tenant opposition, Murray informed the townspeople that if they conducted themselves with honesty and sobriety they would be employed in the construction of the workhouse.[37] He insisted that those ejected were 'men of loose character' and that it was just as well 'to banish them'.[38] He also warned that he would have 'no unpleasant feelings about clearing the estate' and would have little sympathy for those who would be forced unto the edges of the bog as they were 'the ones that never part a shilling for their holdings'.[39]

Murray's actions were fairly typical of how agents used the 1838 Poor Law

31 Maguire, *The Downshire estates*, p. 59.   32 Thomas Murray to Lord Downshire, 22 June 1834 (DP, D/671/C/9/455).   33 Ibid., 21 Feb. 1840 (DP, D/ 671/ C/ 9/ 625); 5 Mar. 1840 (DP/D/671/C/9/628) and 12 Mar. 1840 (DP, D/ 671/ C/ 9/ 633). Ibid., 12 Mar. 1840 (DP, D/671/C/9/633). In total sixty families were cleared and the incident caused such controversy that Murray warned Downshire that the widow O'Brien intended to go directly to Hillsborough to see him in person.   34 Ibid., 29 Apr. 1840 (DP, D/671/C/9/638).   35 *FJ*, 24 July 1840. 36 Thomas Murray to Lord Downshire, 10 Mar. 1840 (DP, D/671/C/9/632).   37 Ibid. 38 Ibid., 6 Mar. 1840 (DP, D/ 671/C/9/629).   39 Thomas Murray to Thomas Parry, 1 Feb. 1840 (DP, D/671/C/9/623).

Act to facilitate the clearance of their estates. His policy created increased tensions in the area, and made him a subject of popular odium. This was compounded by his clearing of a number of tenants in the cottages beside the Roman Catholic chapel at Edenderry, something that may have been as a result of his ongoing feud with the Revd James Colgan.[40] Complaining that 'the priests rule the land', he sought to establish Protestant freeholders at Edenderry.[41] The proposed introduction of these men to the area could only have heightened local tensions and may be the reason why he gave up his practice of riding over the estate, as he had done in the past.[42] Despite his involvement in the establishment of the Edenderry Poor Law Union, Murray subsequently played a limited role throughout the 1840s. During the course of the Famine his wife and two children in its affairs died, which may largely explain his limited involvement in local affairs after 1845.[43] His tenure as agent on the Downshire estate encapsulates some of the issues that agents had to face in the lead up to the Famine and indicates how they used the Poor Law Act of 1838 to address problems associated with increased impoverishment. What they did not expect was that within a decade of the passing of the act workhouses would be unable to cope with the dramatic influx of people suffering from the effects of Famine.

By the 1830s other land agents found themselves in similar circumstances with regard to the management of estates. Chronic subdivision had produced an uneconomic and impoverished tenantry, a problem exacerbated by middlemen. Although several attempts were made by government to forbid the practice, including the introduction of the 1826 Subletting Act, agents looked to their employers to put an end to subdivision. In 1832 Earl Fitzwilliam's agent in Co. Wicklow, Robert Chaloner, sought to ban the subdivision of land 'except in the most urgent necessity as the larger class of farms is at present too small'.[44] In many instances the problem of subdivision was more prevalent on estates where there was a negligent system of management.[45] As early as 1816 James Brownrigg, Murray's predecessor on the Downshire estate, predicted a bleak future for the country as a whole were claiming that the system of middlemen and the subdivision of land was the greatest evil facing Ireland.[46] Brownrigg also made the interesting point that 'landlords in general don't understand' the management of an estate and 'their agents think they are bound to let the land to the highest bidder' and by doing so 'they are ruining their estates'.[47] As Brownrigg suggested some agents had actively encouraged subdivision,

40 Thomas Murray to Lord Downshire, 7 Mar. 1840 (DP, D/671/C/9/630). **41** Ibid., 17 Aug. 1837 (DP, D/671/C/9/507). **42** Thomas Murray to Thomas Parry, 1 Feb. 1840 (DP, D/671/C/9/623). **43** Edenderry Historical Society, *Carved in stone: a survey of graveyards and burial grounds, Edenderry & environs* (Naas, 2010), pp 131–2. **44** 'Memoranda dealing with tenancies, 1796–1841' (NLI, Fitzwilliam papers, MS 4948). **45** Bell & Watson, *A history of Irish farming*, p. 24. **46** James Brownrigg to Lord Downshire, 1 Jan. 1816 (DP). **47** Ibid., 31 Aug. 1815 (DP).

particularly prior to the abolition of the 40s. freeholders in 1829 when it was 'advantageous' to their interests.[48]

Be this as it may, much of the cause of these problems of estate management lay with middlemen who were widely condemned. However, not every landlord or agent advocated the ending of the system of middlemen: some preferred to retain them, believing that there was a better chance of collecting rents from them than from impoverished tenant farmers. For example, Richard Gamble, agent for his father's estate near Frankford, was aware of the problem of subletting but conceded that middlemen were inevitable.[49] Indeed, even Ireland's premier peer, the third duke of Leinster, facilitated the presence of middlemen on his vast estates in Co. Kildare.[50] Notwithstanding this, it was evident to all that change was needed. Writing in 1822, in something of a variant on the same theme, Lord Rosse was particularly critical of subdivision in Ireland, highlighting that 'forty years ago, the lands of Ireland were let in farms of 500, 1,000 or 1,500 acres. Now landlords, finding that they can get higher rents and have more voters, let them to Catholics in portions of 20, 30 or 40 acres, and these, as they multiply fast, again sub-divide them among their sons and daughters as they marry'.[51] This was the situation, for example, on the Downshire estate at Edenderry where subdivision caused such confusion for the agent that it was impossible to know which tenant held what land. Indeed, in 1839 Murray noted that 'there are some cases where the people hold in common and have no regular divisions but lump together as say, two cows grass, three cows and two calves'.[52]

Increasingly, the middleman system, particularly the way it squeezed the smallholders below them, led to increased agrarian tensions. As a result, agrarian disputes were more often than not played out between smallholder and middleman rather than tenant and landlord. Much of the agent's time was given over to trying to prevent or solve such disputes, and in many ways he was a mediator of the peace. Part of the difficulty for agents was that the middleman often had more freedom to exert pressure on his under tenants and frequently took the law into his own hands. For example, in April 1835 a widow named Hamilton had her cabin burned by the son of a middleman at Carrick, near Edenderry; the likely cause was that his father wanted her evicted because she could not pay her rent to him.[53] A similar incident occurred in April 1838 at

---

48 In 1793 the electoroal franchise in Ireland was extended to those who owned property worth forty shillings or more. The introduction of Catholic Emancipation in 1829 raised the qualification to ten pounds, thereby disinfranchising many voters. *Devon Commission*, p. 574 & p. 638. 49 Gamble papers (NAI, M 3493). 50 See Ciarán Reilly, 'A middleman in the 1840s: Charles Carey and the Leinster estate' in Terence Dooley, Patrick Cosgrove and Karol Mullaney Dignam (eds), *Aspects of an Irish aristocratic life: essays on the FitzGerald's of Kildare and Carton* (Dublin, 2014). 51 Lord Rosse to Lord Redesdale, 30 Mar. 1822 (PRONI, Rosse papers, T3030/13/1). 52 That year it took Murray and his newly appointed clerk, James Stafford, ten days to organize the necessary paper work prior to an audit of the estate. See Thomas Murray to Lord Downshire, 20 May 1839 (DP, D/671/C/9/598). 53 Constable Baily to under secretary, Dublin Castle, 7

Clonlion, near Clonmacnois, when a family called Mitchell were put out of their holding and the walls pulled down by the middleman Charles Claffey.[54] In other areas the middleman system led to the wholesale breakdown of law and order where local communities were said to be 'at war everyday' with each other.[55] Thus it was little wonder that the Revd William Minchin at Moneygall commented that there was no sympathy felt on the ejectment of a middleman and that in many instances they were 'hunted out'.[56] His sentiments mirrored those of Lord Dufferin who queried:

> How comes it about that the middleman, the respectable farmer, is so badly off in Ireland at present. One can understand the cottier, the man who lives upon his potatoes and has nothing else now finding himself in a starving condition. But the man who grew the corn that has been exported and sold it for a good price in the English market, why had he not money?[57]

One of the main social changes brought about by the Famine was the ending of the middleman system. While this was largely inevitable because of the socio-economic impact of the Famine it is arguable that it was also somewhat deliberate on the part of land agents who wanted to end what was perceived as a pernicious system. While the attempts to get rid of middlemen had been ongoing for some time, the Famine acted as a catalyst. As the calamity progressed and eviction became commonplace, landlords and their agents shifted their attention to the host of middlemen and large farmers who thwarted the advancement of the estate. Describing these efforts, Margaret Power notes that 'it took patience, vigilance, careful management and the catastrophe of the Famine to effectively get rid of the system of middlemen'.[58]

A study of estate records for King's County would suggest that there were considerably more middlemen holding long-term leases prior to the Famine than

Apr. 1835 (OPKC 1835). In December of the same year at Kilclonfert, near Philipstown, William and Catherine Gerathy had their cabin burned after failing to pay the middlemen the rent. See William Henderson, Ballycumber to under secretary, Dublin Castle, 28 Dec. 1835 (OPKC, 1835). **54** D.C. Jennings, Banagher to under secretary, Dublin Castle, 25 Apr. 1838 (OPKC, 1838, 114/15) **55** See Ciarán Reilly, 'Agents, eviction and assisted emigration during the Great Famine on the Strokestown estate' in Enda Delaney and Brendan MacSuibhne (eds), *Power and hunger: popular politics in Ireland's Great Famine, 1845–1852* (New York, forthcoming). **56** *Devon Commission*, p. 600. Not all middlemen exploited the situation. At Parsonstown the judicious management of land and tenants by Michael Kearney won the praise of Lord Rosse. See 'Survey of an estate in Ballybritt [King's County]' (NLI, MS 2025). **57** Lord Dufferin to John Howe, 8 Jan. 1847 (PRONI, D/1071/A/K/1/A/1). **58** Margaret M.C. Power, 'Sir Richard Bourke and his tenants, 1815–55', *North Munster Antiquarian Journal*, 41 (2001), p. 76. **59** For example, on the Charleville estate there were 762 leaseholders in 1845; on the Downshire estate there were over 300 leaseholders, while on the Gamble estate, which comprised three small townlands, the majority of holders held long-term leases.

might have been previously assumed.[59] Significantly, there were substantially more people crowded onto these estates than agents realized. An underbelly of sub-tenants lay beneath these middlemen or lease holders, so-called tenants at will, which meant that considerable time was spent by agents in the consideration of leases, their terms and so on. Leases varied from one estate to another but generally agents believed that medium-term leases were the best option as they encouraged improvement among tenants. With short-term leases there was no incentive for improvement as the tenant had no security in his holding. On the other hand long-term leases increased the likelihood of the subdivision of the land. John Dunne, the aforementioned Frankford grazier, believed that the 'casual passerby can observe where there is a lease or not or whether the lease is newly out for in cases where the lease is nearly out the parties not only neglect the land and let it go on into a state of dilapidation, it is disfigured'.[60] The granting of a lease for the term of a named person such as the duke of Wellington, the Prince of Wales or a local person had its inherent problems from the scattered nature of some estates and by the more recent developments of increasing emigration. Where the named local person emigrated it was often difficult to ascertain if he was still living, thus causing trouble for the agent. Verbal leasing arrangements were made with landlords but often these were merely a farce, such as the case of a man named Molloy, a tenant on the Bloomfield estate at Moneygall, illustrated. Here, when George Garvey, Bloomfield's agent, increased the rent Molloy refused to pay it, claiming a binding agreement had been made with the landlord. His protestations came to nothing and he was imprisoned in Nenagh jail for non-payment of rent.[61] The Revd William Minchin noted that he generally found it hard to find tenants who would take out a lease; perhaps this was a result of such incidents.[62] Indeed, his case was not helped by some agents, like Arthur Fitzmaurice, arguing that tenants would be better off not taking a lease.[63] Overall, the issue of leasing was one that appears to have bedevilled pre-Famine estates and rural Ireland in general. In many cases of agrarian unrest it was the terms of a lease which were found to be the root cause of the problem. This was confirmed by a House of Commons report of 1832, which noted that small farmers believed that agrarian outrages were necessary to prevent them losing their lands on the expiration of their leases.[64]

Agents argued that the benefit of leases lay in the power it gave landlords to exert pressure on tenants to improve their holdings. However, in the pre-Famine period, as the problem of subdivision escalated, it became more profitable for middlemen to sublet at an unprecedented and dangerous scale. In turn it became

60 *Devon Commission*, p. 640.   **61** Breen, 'Landlordism in King's County', p. 658.   **62** *Devon Commission*, p. 600.   **63** Ibid., p. 574.   **64** Questioning their use in the first place, the earl of Glengall of Cahir, Co. Tipperary, queried whether 'any tenant in Ireland perform the covenants in his lease towards a landlord?'. See earl of Glengall to Lord Charleville, n.d. (1838–9) (Charleville papers, T/3069/D/22).

impossible for agents in King's County to monitor exactly what was happening on their estates. By the 1840s many of the pre-existing long-term leases had either 'fallen in' (expired) or were due to do so. This resulted in a disincentive to improve holdings at a time when it was arguably most imperative to do so. It also coincided with a period when agents were being pressed at an unprecedented level by their employers to collect rent. Although venturing into hostile territory to collect rent was fraught with danger it was a job which had to be carried out, lest they displease their employer. For the more caustic contemporaries this was to ensure the continuity of landlords' lavish lifestyles. During his tour of Ireland in 1844, James Johnston quoted Lord Byron who contended that with regard to landlords: 'their good, ill, health, wealth, joy, or discontent, being, end, aim, religion, rent – rent – rent!'.[65] Frustratingly for agents, efforts to collect rent were regularly thwarted by tenants. For example, Lady Milltown's agent near Shinrone, who met with continued opposition, declared in exasperation that:

> the tenants will pay a small proportion, fall on their knees, declare they cannot pay another penny, a thousand excuses from different pieces of ill fortune. When he [the agent] calls in the driver and orders him to proceed immediately to distrain their goods and then from out of some secret pocket comes the whole rent to a fraction.[66]

It was when agents could not collect their rents and so looked to methods of enforcement that tensions naturally increased.

An agent had several methods of forcing payment from defaulting tenants, but in the main opted for seizing the tenant's property or threatening ejectment.[67] Before 1816, ejectments could only be obtained in a superior court and at a cost of £15, which proved costly, but new legislation made it possible to bring ejectments for as little as £2.[68] No period of notice or court order was required for the seizure of crops or animals, thus this became the preferred method of the agent and his bailiff. There were, however, disadvantages to such a method, as quite often tenants combined to rescue crops and animals, or boycott the sale of seized goods. The seizing of crops by distress was said to have been one of the biggest grievances in the pre-Famine Irish countryside. Crops and animals were removed by the bailiff and his team, and tenants were given eight days to pay the rent/arrears. If they failed to do so the landlord reserved the right to sell the crops and animals by public auction. There can be little doubt but that many bailiffs acted callously in carrying out their duties and may, on occasion, have done so beyond the limits of the law. As de Moleyns noted in his

---

65 Quoted in James Johnston, *A tour in Ireland: with meditation and reflections* (London, 1844), p. 211.   66 'Diary of Elizabeth Smith, 1 Mar. 1855' (in private possession).   67 See Vaughan, *Landlords and tenants*, pp 21–5.   68 Patrick Dardis, *The occupation of land in Ireland in the first half of the nineteenth century* (Dublin, 1920), pp 32–7.

estate management compendium 'a chronic warfare appears to have raged
between Irish landlords and their tenants on the subject of distress'.[69] After 1832
the law required that seizures were to be carried out by the sheriff, prompting
many agents to change their tactics.[70] Hereafter, as Francis Longworth Dames
argued, in King's County ejectment was the most common method in preference
to driving or distraining in the recovery of rents.[71] It was a practice particularly
favoured by Thomas Murray at Edenderry where a number of watchers were
put in place under the superintendence of the bailiff, Robert McComb, to keep
an eye on tenants who had been served with an ejectment.

The distraining of crops and animals in lieu of rent and arrears was naturally
dangerous to the lives of both agents and bailiffs. For example, in July 1838,
Edward Bracken, a receiver appointed by the Court of Chancery to an estate
at Lumpcloon, near Cadamstown, was physically prevented from carrying out
his work by a combination of tenants. In the same year John Kinna, a bailiff,
was severely beaten when he went to distrain crops and animals, the property of
Denis Egan, near Kinnitty. These are just two examples of attacks of a type that
characterized the 1830s and 1840s – a period of assassination attempts,
threatening letters, beatings, burning of crops and the mutilation of animals.
Most attacks were linked with attempts to raise rents or to change estate management policy, the eviction of tenants or distraining animals and crops. In June
1836 Thomas Molloy, land steward on the Trench estate at Shinrone, was
severely beaten because of his management policies, while in May of the same
year the home of William Lusk, a small landowner at Bloomhill, near Frankford,
was burned on the day that his bailiff had served notice on four of his tenants to
quit. In 1842 Michael Roberts, under agent at Lord Bloomfield's Moneygall
estate, was murdered by 'those people who for their own interests stir up the
peasantry' and wish to 'break up land and to cut in potato ground'.[72] According
to Lord Rosse, the 'very barbarous murder' of Roberts was indicative of the
extent to which the 'great crimes of the previous five years' had gone unsolved
and unpunished in King's County.[73] It could be argued that these outrages
were symptomatic of a general rise in agrarian and secret society crime that
characterized King's County and other areas around this time. Indeed, it was
suggested that it was 'next impossible' to live in King's County without being
sworn into a secret society,[74] the main object of which was to prevent 'any

69 Quoted in L. Perry Curtis, *The depiction of eviction in Ireland, 1845–1910* (Dublin, 2011), p.
17. **70** Samuel Clark, *Social origins of the Irish land war* (Princeton, 1979), p. 30. **71** *Devon
Commission*, pp 604–5. However, distraining did take place even though agents, such as William
Steuart Trench, believed it to be grossly intrusive on the tenants' rights. Quoted in Maguire,
Letters of a great Irish landlord, p. 87. **72** See Sub Inspector Crawford, Tullamore to under
secretary, Dublin Castle, 19 June 1836 (OPKC, 1836); William Henderson, Ferbane to under
secretary, Dublin Castle, 4 May 1836 (OPKC, 1836) and Charles Lucas to Earl de Grey, 11 May
1842 (Bedfordshire & Lutton Archives, earl de Grey papers, L29/700/21/35). **73** Earl of
Rosse to Earl de Grey, 22 Apr. 1842 (B. & LA, earl de Grey papers, L29/700/21/19). **74** Sheil,
Ferbane, p. 38. These societies included the Rockites, Steelboys, Starlights, Terryalts, Blackfeet,

landlord under any circumstances whatever from depriving a tenant of his land'.[75]

Invariably agrarianism and sectarianism became entwined in different places at different times. For example, at Clara in the 1820s 'Cathelicks' (sic) attempting to buy anything from a Protestant were threatened with murder.[76] At Ferbane and Edenderry 'twelfth day' riots frequently broke out and notices were posted reminding Protestants that the Papists were assembling to massacre them.[77] Such rivalries were carefully orchestrated and used to the advantage of agrarian secret societies. Lord Charleville was said to have been 'reliably informed' that the Ribbon society in King's County was comprised of county masters, parish delegates and committee men.[78] However, Ribbonism was quite often a label attached by the police to crimes that they could not detect or even prevent, and so its affects and popularity may have been greatly exaggerated.[79] Perhaps more worryingly for agents was the connection between the Chartist movement in Britain and the King's County Ribbonmen, with many of the seasonal labourers going to Manchester and other industrial cities carrying communications between the two groups.[80] In January 1841, a Scottish delegate from the Chartist movement spoke at Shannon Harbour to workmen about the commencement of the public works at Banagher. Later, a Chartist society was formed at Lusmagh to prevent outside labour from being employed on work schemes.[81]

Agrarian crime and agitation in the 1830s, of course, had much to do with the issue of tithes, with which many land agents found themselves embroiled. The tithe system underwent important changes in the years preceding the Famine and the collection of the tax was a hotly contested issue.[82] Both tenant farmers and cottiers considered it unjust that, in addition to paying their rent, they should be forced to pay an annual tax on the produce of their land, known as the tithe, towards the upkeep of the Established Church. The tithe varied from district to district and was paid in kind, in corn mostly and potatoes. Opposition to tithes in the 1830s proved universal, and one contemporary commentator believed that neither Catholics nor Protestants were to be trusted.[83] In King's

Shanavests, Caravats and Ribbonmen among others.   **75** Trench, *Realities*, p. 48. This was also a popular interpretation of the cause of agrarian crime espoused by George Bennett and others. See Cornewall Lewis, *On local disturbances in Ireland*, p. 91.   **76** Stephen Gibbons, *Captain Rock, night errant: the threatening letters of pre-Famine Ireland* (Dublin, 2004), p. 177.   **77** Such was the sectarian divide in the county that a poem, written in 1843, appealed for unity and peace among all sections of society. See 'Song for the 12 July 1843 by John D. Frazer' (ORC).   **78** 'Information on the Ribbon Society in King's County, c.1835–Feb. 1836' (Charleville papers, T//3069/D/5).   **79** See Michael McMahon, *The murder of Thomas Douglas Bateson, county Monaghan, 1851* (Dublin, 2006), p. 31.   **80** *Select committee of the House of Lords on the state of Ireland, 1839*, p. 160.   **81** John Kelly to Dublin Castle, 16 Jan. 1841 (OPKC, 1841).   **82** See 'Notice posted at Edenderry, July 1838' (OPKC, 1838/18521).   **83** Quoted in Michael O'Hanrahan, 'The tithe war in county Kilkenny, 1830–1834' in William Nolan & Kevin Whelan (eds), *Kilkenny history and society: interdisciplinary essays in the history of an Irish county* (Dublin,

County, as elsewhere, the tithes dispute led to mass demonstration and agitation.[84] The most celebrated incident was the death of Thomas Tiquin, known as the 'Last Tithe Martyr' of Ireland. In November 1835, Mr Smith, agent for the Revd William Brownlow Savage of Shinrone, filed two bills for tithes against Tiquin, a miller at Rusheen, near Kilcommon. Tiquin refused to pay the tithes and a court case ensued. Although defended by Charles Rolleston QC, the son of a King's County landlord, Tiquin lost his case, was arrested and confined in the barracks at Shinrone, before being transferred to Newgate prison where he died shortly afterwards.[85] His funeral procession from Dublin was a huge display of public indignation to the collection of tithes.[86] Commenting on the situation, the *Leinster Express* noted that 'the manifestation of public opinion exhibited in the King's County almost exceeds credibility'.[87] The case of Tiquin did not end the disturbances, but unrest towards the collection of tithes eased somewhat after the Tithe Commutation Act of 1838, which converted the tithe into a rent charge payable by the head landlord.[88]

Perhaps of more significance here is that in King's County the areas where agrarianism and opposition to tithes was most pronounced coincided with those where secret society activity had been prevalent since the late eighteenth century.[89] Considerable Defender activity in the years preceding the 1798 rebellion had threatened the Downshire, Dames and Gifford estates near Edenderry and the Molesworth (later Ponsonby) estate at Philipstown. However, many of those who stood accused of Defender or United Irish conspiracy were acquitted and allowed to remain as tenants on these estates.[90] This, however, was not the case in the southern baronies of Clonlisk and Eglish where Defender and United Irish conspirators were ruthlessly suppressed and transported. This was particularly the case at Shinrone where many were transported for life for their part in the rebellion. A lasting bitterness for the transportations remained in the locality, which resurfaced in the agrarian tensions of the 1820s and 1830s.[91] So prevalent were secret societies that by 1834 it was deemed necessary to have the baronies of Clonlisk, Eglish, Ballybritt and Garrycastle proclaimed. Crime was committed not just on land agents and their employees but on all who were seen to interfere with land and the rights of tenants. In 1835, for example, Daniel

1990), p. 483.   **84** See, for example, *Select committee on disturbed state of Ireland* [1831–2] (677), p. 39 & *FJ*, 24 Oct. 1838.   **85** Valentine Trodd, *Midlanders: chronicle of a midland parish* (Banagher, 1994), pp 13–14.   **86** *LE*, 10 June 1837.   **87** Ibid., 10 June 1837. See also *Tipperary Free Press*, 10 June 1837.   **88** O'Hanrahan, 'The tithe war in county Kilkenny, 1830–1834', p. 481.   **89** Michael Beames, 'The Ribbon societies: lower-class nationalism in pre-famine Ireland', *Past and Present*, 97 (Nov. 1982), pp 128–9. For a further examination of Ribbonism see Jennifer Kelly, 'A study of Ribbonism in Leitrim in 1841' in Joost Augusteijn & Mary Ann Lyons (eds), *Irish history: a research yearbook 2* (Dublin, 2003), pp 42–52.   **90** For more on the Defender movement in King's County see Reilly, *Edenderry, county Offaly and the Downshire estate, 1790–1800*, pp 21–31.   **91** See Ruán O'Donnell, 'Kings County in 1798' in Nolan & O'Neill (eds), *Offaly history and society*, pp 485–514.

Ryan, a schoolteacher at Liss, near Ballycumber, was attacked by fourteen men and cut with a razor over the 'taking' of an acre of land.[92] It was one of several hundred reported attacks in King's County, but remarkably, as Lord Oxmantown, the son of the second earl of Rosse, commented, 'as large as the number [outrages] appears to have been from the official returns it falls far short of the reality'.[93] Many outrages went unrecorded simply because 'the peasant who has been injured prefers to submit quietly rather than to expose himself to another attack by complaining to the proper authorities' who, protested Oxmantown, 'have no power to protect them'.[94] On the eve of the Famine such was the wholesale terror imposed by secret societies that it was claimed that in King's County 'not a night passes without an outrage being committed in the county which bids fair to out rival – in deeds of blood and savage barbarity, neighbouring Tipperary'.[95]

So how did such terror and outrage impinge on estate management? Both Lyne and Vaughan have questioned the extent to which such violence was directed towards agents and landlords and the effects that it had on frightening them or slowing the progress of estate management.[96] Lyne notes that 'contrary to certain schools of nationalist mythology Irish tenants generally spent much more of their time doffing their hats to landlords and agents than shooting at them'.[97] In general this was true, but there were many agents in King's County who took the threats seriously enough to consider their position. For example, George Garvey resided in Dublin throughout much of the 1840s after surviving as many as seven attempts on his life (one for each estate he managed). Others succumbed to threats by offering abatements of rent to tenants. Few agents, it seems, showed the bravado of Samuel Hussey who claimed that threatening letters counted for nothing and that he had 'more than one hundred in my time and I shall die in my bed for all that'.[98] Although it is difficult to quantify, given the dearth of estate records, it was probably the case that much of the agrarian crime on King's County estates prior to 1845 was a result of poor management policies. As already noted, this had given rise to a proliferation of subdivision and overcrowding, leading to impoverishment and a variety of other social problems that affected the lower classes.[99]

Years of carelessness and neglect had also taken its toll by the early 1840s. On one King's County estate a tenant who had not paid rent for twenty-one years was declared as the owner in fee having challenged an ejectment decree.[1] At

---

92 William Henderson, Ballycumber to Dublin Castle, 3 Feb. 1835 (OPKC, 1835).   93 Beames, *Peasants and power*, p. 51.   94 See A.P.W. Malcomson, 'A variety of perspectives on Laurence Parsons' in Nolan & O'Neill (eds), *Offaly history and society*, pp 460–1.   95 *Times*, 25 Dec. 1844.   96 Lyne, *The Lansdowne estates*, p. 718. See also Vaughan, *Landlords and tenants*, p. 157.   97 Ibid.   98 Hussey, *Reminiscences*, p. 61.   99 See, for example, Law Walker to Stewart & Kincaid, 22 Dec. 1842 & Arthur Guinness, Rutland Square to Stewart & Kincaid, 31 Mar. 1843 (S & KA).   1 'Rental of the earl of Rosse's estates and cash account for one year beginning 1 Jan.

Tullamore inaccurate leases and accounts hindered Francis Berry's management, and even Lord Charleville was unsure about the value of the estate.[2]
Moreover, in 1839 Berry complained that the estate maps that he was using had
been made over fifty years previously and did not include some 5,147 acres of
bog which had been reclaimed in the intervening period.[3] The employment of
an agent who held multiple agencies was another major problem with regard to
effective estate management, the reason being that it was not possible for agents
like George Garvey to cater for the needs of the tenants on all of the estates for
which he was agent, at least not in any consistent way. Employed by at least seven
landlords during this period, Garvey's management was at best distracted.
Agents such as George Greeson, Arthur Fitzmaurice or Thomas Hughes
Graydon (who by his own admission held eighteen to twenty agencies), who
resided outside the county and knew little of tenants daily activity, had an even
more difficult task.[4]

Conversely, there were agents who actively strove to improve the lot of their
tenantry, as will be discussed in more detail in chapter five.[5] For example,
advances in farming methods in the decades preceding the Famine were due
mainly to the efforts of individual agents.[6] However, just as with the Luddites in
England there was opposition to modernization.[7] Indeed, local secret societies
used the same tactics as Luddites: in 1836 the breaking of a 'Scotch plough' at
Capagolan was proof that some of the King's County tenantry were reluctant to
see change introduced in agriculture.[8] In the 1830s, Connaught men working in
the barony of Clonlisk had their barrows broken to pieces to prevent them
continuing work, which could be viewed as either oppition to modernisation or
opposition to bringing in outside workers.[9] It was widely believed that the rural
population were scared of change and saw the increased use of the plough as
detrimental to their livelihoods.[10] There were numerous other problems that
hindered estate management in the decades prior to the Famine. Attempts by
agents to address many of these problems were neither consistent or concerted,
or organized through any effective coordinating body or organization. Even
attempts at the promotion of agricultural societies, as we shall see below,
foundered because of the unevenness of support for the same. There were those
who feared that a calamity might be on the horizon, particularly in relation to the
potato crop, and that there was no plan to avert such a disaster. For example, in

to 31 Dec. 1854' (BCA, Q/106/B).   2 'Statement of the value and location of the Charleville
estates in Ireland, *c.*1830' (Charleville papers, T/3069/B/19).   3 James Perceval Graves to
Lord Tullamore, 6 Mar. 1839 (Charleville papers, T/3069/B/95).   4 *Devon Commission*, p. 501.
5 George Lewis Smyth, *Ireland: historical and statistical* (London, 1849), p. 87   6 Feehan,
Farming in Ireland, p. 102.   7 D. George Boyce, *Nineteenth-century Ireland: the search for
stability* (Dublin, 1990), p. 99   8 Bernard Cummins, Kinnitty to Lord Lieutenant, Dublin
Castle, 19 Feb. 1836 (OPKC, 1836). Similarly, in 1838 a plough was broken in Walsh Island in an
attempt to promote employment among local labourers.   9 *Poor Law Inquiry*, appendix D, p.
23.   10 Ibid.

1835 George Greeson cautioned that in King's County there was 'no plan having ever been practiced here to preserve the surplus of an abundant crop to meet the possible failure of the crops of succeeding years'.[11] Moreover, successive crop failures from 1838 to 1841, resulting from dramatic climatic conditions, contributed to a severe agricultural downturn. At Moneygall Lord Bloomfield's tenants were said to be greatly affected during this period by the severe wet weather, which completely destroyed the potato crop, while at Philipstown the situation was similar.[12]

In the midst of all this and to compound matters further came the 'Night of the Big Wind' on 5 and 6 January 1839, an event which has been surprisingly ignored by historians to date. Describing the damage caused by the storm at Edenderry, Thomas Murray noted that 'the town at this moment looks like a place which had been destroyed by an army'. In particular, Murray highlighted how the calamity affected tenants on the estate: 'your lordship cannot imagine the state of confidence of the labouring class have got to, they will shortly do nothing but what they will themselves; but they will soon become more civil as they will feel the want of labour and the scarcity of provisions'.[13] Charleville demesne, in Tullamore, was said to 'have suffered more perhaps, than any other place in Ireland. It is calculated that upwards of ten thousand pounds of timber has been destroyed'.[14] Despondently, John Hussey Walsh believed that 'the destructive storm of 1839 and the subsequent succession of bad crops have swept away nearly all the previous savings as well as most of the live stock of the farmers'.[15] As a means of relieving the plight of those affected by the storm, land agents, such as Mr Sherrard, who was employed at the de Sales, Robinson and Smith Berry estates, were reported to have visited the tenants and investigated the effect of the storm and where necessary rendered assistance.[16] One can only imagine the devastation caused to the thousands of landless poor who were huddled together in the mud and turf cabins on the great bogs of King's County. Given all these factors, as well as the various barriers to improvement, including opposition to modernization and a continued demographic growth that focused more attention than ever on access to land, from an agent's viewpoint there was an even greater need to make farms more economic in order to secure their own profits. It was little wonder then that King's County agents looked with a great deal of interest towards the 1838 Irish Poor Law Act.

---

11 *Poor inquiry*, appendix E, p. 12. Ironically, the potato was believed to have been planted in Ireland chiefly as a means of preventing Famine. See David Nally, *Human encumbrances: political violence and the Great Famine* (Indiana, 2011), p. 249. 12 William Wray to lord lieutenant, Dublin Castle, May 1841 (OPKC, 1841). 13 Thomas Murray to Lord Downshire, 7 Jan. 1839 (DP, D/ 671/C/9/589A). 14 Peter Carr, *The big wind* (Belfast, 1991), p. 121. 15 *Devon Commission*, p. 627. 16 *The Pilot*, 21 Jan. 1839.

4 The struggle for power: agents and the political world

There was no organized system of poor relief in Ireland until the late 1830s. By then, increasing pressure to relieve poverty on grounds of both natural justice and economic utility prompted government action.[1] In 1833 a royal commission to investigate the causes and extent of poverty in Ireland was established; it was chaired by the archbishop of Dublin, Richard Whately. After Whately reported his findings, the government sent George Nicholls, an English poor law commissioner, to Ireland. Following two short visits Nicholls reported that roughly one per cent of the population were living in poverty and that the English workhouse system should be applied to Ireland.[2] However, Nicholls specifically warned that in the event of a famine the workhouses would not cope.[3] The commission's final report was ignored in favour of a poor law based closely on the English model. The new act created a system of poor relief financed by rates paid mainly by Irish landowners. Given this added burden on them, it was feared by some politicians and commentators that the act would be exploited in order to facilitate the clearance of estates. Land agents in King's County certainly saw the opportunity to solve some of their problems by exploiting various provisions within it.[4]

Throughout the 1830s the clearance of smallholders from Irish estates had generated considerable political debate. Leading figures such as Daniel O'Connell, for example, lent his support for the introduction of a poor law if it ended 'politically motivated clearances' and 'prevented the retaliatory violence they provoked'.[5] O'Connell's assertion was particularly true of King's County where there was certainly evidence of land agents (and it must be added members of the Catholic clergy) agitating the people according to their political persuasion, to the extent that the 1841 election proceedings in King's County were said to have degenerated into 'a perfect riot'.[6] While some clearances were undoubtedly politically motivated – there were also claims that 'politics had induced landlords not to give leases'– other clearances had an economic basis.[7]

---

1 Virginia Crossman, 'Poor relief' in S.J. Connolly (ed.), *The Oxford companion to Irish history* (Oxford, 1998), pp 452–3. See also Helen Burke, *The people and the poor law in nineteenth century Ireland* (England, 1987) and J. O'Connor, *The workhouses of Ireland: the fate of Ireland's poor* (Dublin, 1995). In King's County a petition seeking the introduction of a poor law similar to England was signed by 100 inhabitants of Clara and Tullamore in 1829. See Gray, *The making of the Irish poor law*, p. 61. 2 Christine Kinealy, *A death dealing Famine: the Great Hunger in Ireland* (London, 1997), pp 39–40. 3 Paul Bew, *Ireland: The politics of enmity, 1789–2006* (Oxford, 2007), p. 151. 4 *Poor relief (Ireland). A bill for the more effectual relief of the destitute poor in Ireland*, HC, 1837–8 [38] iii, 451. 5 Gray, *The making of the Irish poor law*, p. 151. 6 'Diary of Elizabeth Smith, 24 Feb. 1841' (in private possession). 7 *Devon Commission*, p. 588.

In 1838 the chief secretary for Ireland, Lord Morpeth, declared in the House of Commons that there was a 'wholesale expulsion of tenants' occurring in Ireland.[8] Thomas Davis, later founder of the Young Ireland movement and editor of the *Nation*, feared that poor law guardians would act as agents for 'clearance projects' and emigration schemes.[9]

Soon after the introduction of the act in 1838, there was evidence in King's County that these fears were being realized. Although legislation enacted in 1840 strove to provide greater protection for tenants issued with ejectment notices, undoubtedly there were some who were cleared who went unrecorded or unknown to the courts.[10] It has already been noted above that Thomas Murray was anxious to remove small holders at Edenderry because the new poor law rates added considerably to the estate's existing financial burden. For agents the introduction of the act relieved their conscience about the fate of the tenants that they evicted because there was a perception that they could be thrown on the workhouse system that would provide them with relief.[11] Evidently, there were a number of reasons for clearances that included difficulties in collecting rents, possibly in particular areas or estates due to tenants' inability to pay the same. For example, in 1838 there were a number of clearances on the Armstrong and Mullock estates that resulted in a large meeting of the tenantry at Lemanaghan, near Ballycumber. The estimated 2,000 people in attendance were told by the local parish priest, the Revd McKeon, that some measure of poor law for Ireland should be introduced and he denounced the fact that a number of tenants had been 'turned out upon the world's wide waste'. Those responsible, including John Ennis, were denounced as 'depopulating landlords'. Many of those affected by the Lemanaghan clearances were particularly aggrieved because they had previously been punctual with their rent.[12] There were also cases whereby landlords wanted to clear unsightly cottiers' cabins from their estates. In 1844 John Hussey Walsh believed that most landlords in the county wanted to remove poverty out of sight, rather than to relieve it. In the barony of Upper Philipstown there was evidence of several tenants having been ejected from unsightly cabins on to the edges of the bog.[13] Clearances often had more sinister motives and for various reasons escaped popular censure. When the Revd Burdett of Banagher died in 1840 his successor, the Revd James Paul Holmes evicted most of the tenants on the Church of Ireland glebe lands at Ballyshale, near the town. The tenants, nine of whom were cleared to make way for two graziers, claimed to have paid the rent to Burdett's son but were still ejected.[14] Holmes later defended his position to remove tenants from the glebe lands on

---

8 Earl of Glengall to earl of Charleville, n.d [1838] (Charleville papers, T3069/D/22). 9 Gray, *The making of Irish poor law*, p. 306. 10 *Ejectment and replevin (Ireland). A bill to amend the laws relating to ejectment and replevin in Ireland*, HC, 1840 [13] ii, 391. 11 Samuel David Clark, 'The Land War in Ireland' (PhD, Harvard, 1973), p. 22. 12 *FJ*, 12 June 1838. 13 *Devon Commission*, p. 631. 14 Ibid., p. 588.

the grounds that he had been ordered to do so by the bishop of Meath upon his appointment. According to the rector, tenants were given a year to remove and every assistance was provided to them. One tenant was given as much potato ground to plant as he needed, while another was given £27 to emigrate to America.[15]

In a number of cases agents believed that the clearance of tenants was necessary in order for agricultural improvement to take place. In effect, smallholdings had to be consolidated to make more viable farms. In 1844 Dawson French, agent of the Johnson estate, near Tullamore, cleared a number of tenants in an effort to 'square the land'.[16] There were also examples of clearances simply for the aesthetic improvement of demesnes. At Mucklagh, the earl of Charleville evicted several tenants from his estate in 1837 and 1838 in order to extend and embellish his demesne.[17] Further clearances took place on the estate when the Tullamore workhouse was built in 1840. The plight of the Tullamore poor, as elsewhere, had been compounded by the above-mentioned economic downturn from 1839. This was aptly captured in Berry's correspondence of June 1840 when he wrote that 'twenty able bodied men are at my door starving as there is no work, the weather being so wet they cannot cut the hay and the potatoes are all sown'.[18] It was his misguided belief that 'if the workhouse was going on nothing could be wanted'.[19] The clearances on this estate were probably also motivated by the earl's financial predicament. By the early 1840s his debts were close to £100,000, a remarkable debt considering that he had only an annual rental of less than £8,000, and rents were increasingly difficult to collect from the late 1830s. By 1844 the earl had fled to Europe, having closed Charleville Castle and sold the farming implements. Charleville subsequently resided throughout the Famine years in Baden Baden in Germany avoiding debtors.[20]

The most controversial clearance of tenants occurred on the Norbury estate at Durrow.[21] In January 1839, Hector John Toler, second earl of Norbury, was murdered as he was walked through his demesne with his Scottish land steward, Adam Saunderson. Hector John Toler had succeeded to the earldom on the death of his father, the notorious 'hanging judge' in 1831, and began to build a mansion at Durrow and enlarge the demesne, wishing to quickly establish himself among the prominent landowners and gentry of King's County.[22] Norbury, it seems, had a solid relationship with his tenantry. He appears to have made efforts to relieve their plight, and even found favour with the Roman

---

15 Ibid., appendix B, p. 58. 16 *KCC*, 4 Mar. 1846. 17 Francis Berry to earl of Charleville, 19 Sept. 1837 (Charleville papers, T/3069/B/32). 18 Francis Berry to John S. Tisdall, 24 June 1840 (Charleville papers, ORC). 19 Ibid. 20 *LE*, 7 Sept. 1844. 21 The Durrow estate consisted of about 3,600 acres. In total Norbury owned 26,700 acres in counties Clare, Mayo, Sligo and Tipperary. 22 See Ronan Keane, 'Toler, John, first earl of Norbury (1745–1831)', *Oxford dictionary of national biography* (Oxford, 2004) (http://www.oxforddnb.com/view/article/27498) [accessed 20 Nov. 2008].

Catholic priest at Durrow, the Revd O' Rafferty, who praised him as 'one of the greatest benedictions that kind and propitious heaven could dispense among a humble and deserving people'. His agent George Garvey would later cite this as proof that the 'improvement and comfort of the tenantry were among the subjects ever uppermost in the thoughts of the late Lord Norbury'.[23]

The intended target of the assassination was, in fact, Garvey, rather than his employer and it was obvious from the charges made in the weeks following the murder that the agent and his management policies were the real root of the crime. Indeed, Alfred Richardson, Lord Rossmore's agent, believed that the murder was 'due to the authoritarianism of his agent'.[24] Several accounts of Garvey's estate management policy refer to his 'exterminating mania'. Furthermore, he was accused of being intent on the destruction of the 'poor industrious classes' by 'calling for the rents at unreasonable times, yes before the corn can be reaped'.[25] One anonymous writer contended that he was 'avaricious, persecuting and unfaithful' and that he had put the axe to many trees on the estate after the 'Night of the Big Wind' for his own use.[26] In his own evidence Garvey denied that clearances had taken place, stating that as proof of how little his lordship was infected with the horrible 'exterminating mania', it was sufficient to highlight that during his many years in residence on his estate, on which there are more than 120 tenants, many of them having very small holdings, only ten had been dispossessed, and those that were evicted were men of 'indifferent character' who all received large gratuities on their removal.[27] However, the eviction of five families in 1838 was enough to motivate somebody to make an attempt on his life. Moreover, it appears that Garvey's evidence was disingenuous, at least if one is to believe contemporary newspapers reports from both sides of the political divide. The newspapers condemned the clearance policy that Garvey had denied undertaking at Durrow. Refuting Garvey's claims, the editor of the *Pilot* newspaper pointed out that the crime had originated out of the policy of extermination that Norbury and his agent had become obsessed with, what it referred to as 'the horrible exterminating mania', and claimed that Garvey had served over 250 notices to quit on the Durrow tenantry.[28] The editor further lamented: 'what a scene of crime [where] cruelty, calamity and human suffering is presented by the ejection of the homeless, houseless and foodless of 250 families' who were left to starvation and

---

23 *Pilot*, 9 Jan. 1839. It is interesting to note that Norbury's son-in-law, Crofton Moore Vandaleur, would later gain notoriety for his ill treatment of tenants on his estate at Kilrush, Co. Clare during the Great Famine.   24 Alfred Richardson to Col Westenra, 11 Jan. 1839 (PRONI, Rossmore papers, T2929/4/68).   25 Anonymous letter to earl of Norbury, 16 Jan. 1839 (Charleville papers, T/3069/D/13).   26 J. Stewart to earl of Charleville, 20 Feb. 1839 (Charleville papers, T/3069/D/17).   27 George Garvey to earl of Charleville, 26 Feb. 1839 (Charleville papers, T/3069/D/19). According to Garvey only fifteen tenants had been evicted in the previous seven years.   28 *Pilot*, 4 Jan. 1839.

death. Similarly, the editorial in the *Freeman's Journal* claimed that Norbury was about to begin a clearance on the estate when he was shot.[29]

The political fallout resulting from the murder was far reaching: debates raged from Tullamore to the House of Commons and included an attack on Lord Melbourne's administration, and, in particular, the under secretary at Dublin Castle, Thomas Drummond. Lord Charleville chose to attack the under secretary because of his by then infamous letter of 1838 to the Tipperary magistrates, reminding them that property had its duties as well as its rights.[30] In Charleville's opinion this correspondence had resulted in numerous murders in the country, including that of Norbury.[31] Subsequently, a resolution passed by a meeting of the King's County magistrates, assembled on 10 January 1839 to discuss the murder of Norbury, noted that 'it appears to this meeting that the answers conveyed to the magistrates of Tipperary from the under secretary, Drummond had the unfortunate effect of increasing the animosities entertained against the owners of the soil by occupants who now constitute themselves as sole arbitrators of the rights as well as the duties of property'. Drummond duly responded, stating that although he could understand and make allowance for 'excited feelings' which had been produced by the murder of Norbury, he could not but 'lament that a body of magistrates called together as such and presided over by the lieutenant of the county, should so far have forgotten the object of the meeting as to consent it into a display of political feeling'.[32] By the end of March the political fallout from the murder had subsided, and, revealingly, in May Garvey undertook a further clearance of tenants at Durrow. According to contemporary accounts of the evictions 'the miserable beings were required to pull down their own houses. After the thatch and timber were torn off, they further required that the walls should be levelled, and they were levelled with the earth'.[33] His reputation in terms of clearances continued. In evidence given to the Devon Commission one witness claimed that by 1844 clearances on the Bloomfield estate were 'becoming worse and worse' with each passing year.[34] Tenants had been ejected 'to bring land into Lord Bloomfield's demesne' and to get rid of some 'unsightly cabins' near Moneygall.[35]

What this case study illustrates is that there were agents such as Garvey who were prepared to evict tenants, possibly on a large scale, in the aftermath of the passing of the 1838 Irish Poor Law Act, in order to improve the profitability of the estate or even to embellish the landlords demesne. When they did so they incurred the wrath of smallholders and labourers who were anxious to retain their lands, or to secure employment during the difficult years of the late 1830s

29 *FJ*, 29 Jan. 1839.   **30** Thomas Drummond to the magistrates of Co. Tipperary, 23 May 1838 (NAI, Chief Secretary's Office papers, 1838/314).   **31** *Pilot*, 12 Jan. 1839.   **32** Thomas Drummond to Lord Oxmantown and the magistrates of King's County, 17 Jan. 1839 (NAI, Chief Secretary's Office papers, 1838/314, Letter books, vol. 160, p. 117). See also *Pilot*, 23 Jan. 1839.   **33** *FJ*, 22 May 1839.   **34** *Devon Commission*, p. 582.   **35** Ibid., p. 600.

and early 1840s. The tenants on the Durrow estate went a step further than most by attempting to assassinate the agent, but murdered the landlord instead, by mistake it seems. There were several agents, or their underlings, who were also targeted. These, of course, included the aforementioned Michael Roberts, Garvey's under-agent who was shot dead at Ballintemple in April 1842.[36] John Gatchell, a land agent at Clonbullogue, was murdered in May 1843 following the eviction of tenants from the Gardiner estate.[37] In this instance Gatchell was shot, having returned from Edenderry where he had secured ejectment notices on several tenants on the estate. Later that month Daniel O'Connell claimed in the House of Commons that Gatchell had been 'employed for some time past in turning out tenants from a property with which the management he was entrusted'. According to O'Connell 'one family in particular had been driven from their home in pitiless manner and had to take refuge under miserable sheeting', adding that the agent had sold all their property and that the tenants had contracted the typhus fever.[38] The attacks on agents and estate personnel would continue unabated. The number of committals to Tullamore gaol rose from 699 in 1835 to 1,044 in 1838, while the barony of Clonlisk was described in 1841 as a 'confederacy to commit crime'.[39] It seems that the ascendancy became so fearful in rural areas of King's County that by October 1841 the *Times* newspaper noted that 'no man feels safe in the midst of horrors' and the gentry lived in dread of 'whose turn will it be next?'[40] Even during times of relative calm there was always the expectation that violence would erupt. As if he needed reminding, Lord Rosse was informed in 1842 that Ireland was 'universally tranquil but is full of inflammable materials'.[41] The people of King's County were said to be 'in the wildest state of excitement, ready for anything. Many families have gone into Dublin for security, and they have had to put a guard at the door of the Protestant church in Philipstown. All the barracks are fortified and provisioned in expectation of an outbreak'.[42]

Faced with the growing threat of agrarian agitation and threats on their lives, many land agents adopted new methods in the management of estates. In what was an era of triumphalism for the Catholic Church following the granting of Emancipation in 1829 and the National School Act of 1831, the Catholic clergy

---

36 *Nenagh Guardian*, 18 Mar. 1843. **37** *Devon Commission*, p. 627. See also *Nation*, 5 May 1843. **38** *Nation*, 20 May 1843. The social memory of the event includes a conversation said to have taken place between Gatchell and the man accused of the murder. The tenant Dunne had informed the agent that he would 'fox him' in the days before the murder. Such bravado was added to the story in the years that passed celebrating the tenant's victory over landlordism. See 'Statement of Colonel Eamon Broy, 12 Oaklands Drive, Highfield Road, Rathgar, Dublin' (NAI, Bureau of Military History Statement, WS 1280). I am grateful to Declan O'Connor for bringing this source to my attention. **39** Byrne, *Legal Offaly*, p. 211. Also quoted in Seamus O'Rian, *Dunkerrin: a parish in Ely O'Carroll* (Dublin, 1988), p. 107. **40** *Times*, 1 Oct. 1841. **41** Charles Lucas to earl de Grey, 23 Apr. 1842 (B & LA, earl de Grey papers, L/29/700/21/19). **42** 'Diary of Elizabeth Smith, 19 Dec. 1843' (in private possession).

5 Birr Castle, 1826 (courtesy of Offaly Historical Society)

were determined to assert control in local communities. The stumbling block to most of their attempts at control was, of course, the land agent. This new era of Catholic influence on local communities was evident in the building of churches and national schools throughout King's County. In 1829 the Roman Catholic Church of Philipstown was 'greatly extended', that of Kilclonfert 'improved', while a new church was built in Ballycommon in 1841.[43] New national schools were also built in the early 1840s at Tullamore (two), Rahan, Killina, Kilbride, Kilcoleman and Monasteroris.[44] Of course these projects along with others were to be financed by an already impoverished population. Where the agent did not share the same faith, he came into direct opposition with both the local clergy and the tenantry over such projects, which impacted on his ability to collect rent.

The agent also found ready opponents in members of the Loyal National Repeal Association (more often than not these also included members of the

---

43 John Kearney, *From the quiet annals of Daingean: articles on the history of a parish in north Offaly* (Daingean, 2006), p. 40. In addition, in the parish of Ferbane two new churches were built in 1820 and 1832. See Brendan Ryan, *The dear old town: a history of Ferbane in the 18th and 19th centuries* (Ferbane, 2002), p. 71. **44** House of Commons, *Accounts and papers: miscellaneous (Ireland) 3 Feb.–12 Aug. 1842*, vol. xxxviii (London, 1843) p. 3.

clergy). By the early 1840s, with the opening of Repeal reading rooms, agents were faced with a more organized and educated tenantry. At Edenderry, for example, a Repeal reading room was opened in 1842 in response to one established by Lord Devonshire's land agent Thomas Murray. The Repeal reading room, according to Myles Keon, was where 'obedience to the law is taught' and that a 'thirst for knowledge is spread among the people'.[45] A ladies Repeal club in Parsonstown was said to have numbered forty-six members in 1843, who were also active in promoting reading.[46] It was against such a backdrop that Lord Charleville was anxious to provide (and perhaps control) the education for his tenants at Tullamore, which he believed would be best achieved by 'moving for the total extinction of the hot bed of disloyalty and irreligion, the college of Maynooth'.[47] Perhaps of more importance here is that Repeal rent, or the O'Connell tribute as it was more commonly known – contributions to the building of schools, churches and other public buildings – exhausted already hard-pressed local funds with the result that the collection of the estate rental suffered. When it came to paying either the agent or the priest, tenants were cast between a rock and a hard place. As a result, tension existed between agents and the clergy, and this became evident when the Famine struck in 1845. Prior to the granting of Catholic Emancipation agents had enjoyed wholesale control over the tenantry. Indeed, this control meant that those like John Drought of Lettybrook could secure the support of an entire townland or parish at election time.[48] However, it should be noted that by the mid-1830s several land agents in King's County were themselves members of the Repeal party, something which brought them into conflict with their colleagues on other estates. Such divisions may explain why they were reluctant or unwilling to come together as a body to avert the crisis which the Great Famine brought.

The dragooning of the tenantry to vote for their landlord's wishes at election time was another essential requirement of the land agent and one which preoccupied much of his time.[49] Prior to 1829 it was also the agent's responsibility to ensure that 40s. freeholders were registered for election, something they had to do every seven years and at least one year prior to an election.[50] Naturally this added to their workload, while tenants naturally resented the interference and the visit of the agent. However, some tenants were quite happy for the agent to interfere at election time and often used it to their own advantage when whole townlands combined their votes in order to barter for the division of land or to

---

45 *KCC*, 25 June 1845. **46** *LE*, 21 Jan. 1843. **47** See 'Address to the electors of King's County, Nov. 1832' (Charleville papers, T/3069/D/2). **48** John Drought to Laurence Parsons, 24 May 1817 (BCA, E/34/19). **49** See Henry Hatch to William Trumbull, 15 Nov. 1757 (PRONI, Blundell papers, MIC/317). **50** Colonel Westenra to Mr Marlow, 29 Feb. 1824 (PRONI, Rossmore papers, T2929/3/48). Emancipation had come at a price and the number of freeholders entitled to vote at election had dropped from 191,000 to just over 14,000. See Michael Beames, *Peasants and power: the Whiteboy movements and their control in pre-Famine Ireland* (New York, 1983), p. 140.

gain new leases.[51] By the mid-1830s when the representation of King's County in the House of Commons was wrestled from the hands of Colonel Bernard and Lord Rosse, the heavily contested nature of politics meant that land agents were further pressed by their employers.[52] Following the passage of the Act of Union in 1801 the county's representation in parliament was dominated by the earls of Rosse and the Bernard family. This representation was punctuated by Hardress Lloyd (1807–18), who had married Alice, sister of the second earl of Rosse, in 1797. The first challenge to this oligarchy came in 1831 when, although unsuccessful, the liberal candidate, John Craven Westenra (1798–1874), second Lord Rossmore, offered voters a new voice.[53] Another election was called in June 1832, in which the repeal candidate Nicholas Fitzsimons (1807–49) of Broughall Castle was elected.[54] Lord Rossmore was finally returned as MP for the county in 1835 alongside Fitzsimons, smashing the power of Rosse and Bernard in an election that was billed as the 'tithe election of Ireland'.[55] According to Rossmore every effort had been exerted in 'breaking down an ascendancy phalanx as strong at least as that which I overturned in Monaghan'.[56] This may have been done at some expense to law and order as the election resulted in outrage and violence.[57] With an increased electorate in 1837 (there were 1,900 entitled to vote) Rossmore and Fitzsimons were again returned. Colonel Bernard contested the 1841 election but was defeated by Sir Andrew Armstrong (1785–1863) of Gallen House, Ferbane. This remained the representation for the county until 1852, when new candidates, styling themselves Liberal-Independents, Patrick O'Brien and Loftus Bland, received between them over 3,000 votes.[58]

The loss of electoral power for landlord and agent alike was a severe blow. These contested elections represented further occasions when the agents' duties were deflected from matters of estate management. Edward Meares Kelly, a barrister at Parsonstown, believed that the 'owners of property will experience no difficulty whatever in inducing their tenantry to give them one voice, if that only be asked'.[59] According to Kelly such a move by the agent of an estate would allow

51 McCourt, 'The management of the Farnham estates', p. 556.   52 See the correspondence of various landowners regarding King's County politics BCA, E/17/1–21.   53 Rossmore led a controversial campaign from the late 1820s to reform the representative peerage system, Scottish and Irish, although this seems to have come to an end when he accepted a peerage in 1838. 54 Fitzsimons was a nephew of Count Magawley and married a daughter of Sir John Power, a Dublin distiller, in 1829. His brother was married to a daughter of Daniel O'Connell and thus he enjoyed significant influence in the Repeal party. See Patrick Meehan, *The members of parliament for Laois and Offaly, 1801–1918* (Portlaoise, 1972), p. 127, and Byrne, *Legal Offaly*, p. 32. 55 Alfred G. Richardson to Lord Rossmore, 5 Dec. 1834 (Rossmore papers, T2929/4/54). 56 Lord Rossmore, Sharavogue House, Roscrea, King's County to Mr McDermott, Emyvale, Co. Monaghan (PRONI, DIORC/1/6/19).   57 Richard Westenra, Rossmore Park, Co. Mongahan to Lord Rossmore, 12 June 1824 (Rossmore papers, T/2929/3/53).   58 Meehan, *The members of parliament*, pp 114–15.   59 Edward Meares Kelly, Parsonstown to Lord Downshire, London, 9 July 1837 (DP, D/671/C/12/683).

the landlord to know which of his tenants 'deserved favour and indulgence'.[60] Such sentiments were in stark contrast to the behaviour of Lord Digby who was chastized in the 1830s for the indifference displayed by his agent Robert Tarleton in pressing the tenants for votes.[61] Indeed, it may have been Digby that Lord Downshire had in mind when he informed the duke of Wellington that the 'representation of the King's County is at present in the hands of the Roman Catholic peasantry and of the agitators owing much to the neglect of the Protestant landlords'. Regarding his Edenderry tenantry, Downshire believed that if they could 'withstand the whole power of the priesthood and the system of terror that is protected in the country they will vote at county elections as their landlord requires'.[62] Digby, however, was an exception to the rule, and there were widespread allegations that tenants were evicted from their holdings in King's County because they had voted against their agents' wishes at election time.[63] In particular, Colonel Bernard was reviled by the tenantry owing to his political influence and the pressure he exerted over his Kinnitty tenants.[64] Bernard was a staunch opponent of the Repeal movement and was supported by William O'Connor Morris, who believed that the problems of agrarian crime stemmed from the movement, and by Lord Charleville, who argued that Repeal would 'entail on this country the greatest of all evils of a resident nobility and gentry'.[65]

Party politics heightened tension during elections, and a certain level of coercion was used by all. In 1837 when Garrett O'Moore, a landlord at Cloghan, declared himself a candidate, several houses belonging to Lord Rosse's tenantry were destroyed to prevent them from voting for their landlord's candidate.[66] George Garvey was accused by Alfred Richardson, Colonel Westenra's agent, of using Lord Bloomfield's horses and carriages 'in forwarding freeholders to Clonmel at the last election, all against the popular members'.[67] Three years later attempts to compel men to vote for the Repeal candidate resulted in a vicious affray at Tullamore.[68] And the intimidation continued on both sides. A large party visited Mount Bolus, near Frankford, prior to the election, to threaten men into giving up their registry tickets to the Roman Catholic clergy.[69] At Clondalla, in the parish of Kinnitty, a party, described as a mob, visited Peter

60 Ibid., 14 Aug. 1837 (DP/D/671/C/12/690). Kelly was firmly anti-repeal, hoping that the county would be well 'purified' of such support. **61** Viscount Oxmantown, 52 Portland Place, London to Lord Downshire, Hillsborough, Co. Down, 18 July 1837 (DP, D/671/C/684). **62** Lord Downshire to duke of Wellington, 9 Mar. 1841 (DP, D/671/C/12/777). **63** *Devon Commission*, p. 778. **64** 'Tell truth pamphlet against Thomas Bernard' (NLI, MS 29,806(202). **65** Viscount Tullamore to the electors of King's County (Charleville papers, T/3069/D/12). See also O'Connor Morris, *Memories*, p. 62. **66** Edward Meares Kelly, Parsonstown to Lord Downshire, London, 14 Aug. 1837 (DP, D/671/C/12/690). **67** Alfred G. Richardson, Parsonstown to Lord Rossmore, Cortolvin Hills, Mongahan, 29 Nov. 1838 (Rossmore papers, T2929/4/65). **68** 'Printed copy of resolutions passed at a meeting of the freeholders of King's County', 5 Apr. 1841 (DP, D671/C/12/781). **69** Neal Browne to Lord Morpeth, 28 July 1841 (OPKC, 1841/15/11345).

and John Donican and warned them to vote for 'their country' at the election. In an effort to prevent agents from harassing tenants into voting for their landlord or his preferred choice, Bernard Mullins, the high sheriff of the county, refused the use of military protection to agents when canvassing for votes.[70] In a further measure to prevent the outbreak of violence, election broadsheets were distributed to voters calling on them to 'injure no man or his property. Peaceful determination and union will accomplish all'.[71] Such efforts were in vain, however. According to Elizabeth Smith, the wife of a Co. Wicklow landowner, 'dreadful excitement' began the 1841 election in King's County where the priests were 'as busy as bees and this time they must succeed for no Conservative ever before tried to rescue the people from the degraded state they have fallen into'.[72] Describing the county's election as 'a perfect riot', she later noted:

> All Sunday the priests were thundering from their altars so 70,000 ruffians assembled regularly drilled, relieving one another and ill using in every way Mr Bernard's voters, who, however, makes an excellent show on the poll. A small body of police and military were unable to keep the peace. This will be the last liberal struggle. The Conservative wealth must prevail over the pauper radicals in the end.[73]

The issue of Repeal continued to divide land agents in King's County. Even those like Francis Berry, who did not show a public interest, were influential enough to prevent some landowners from contesting elections.[74] Among the most vocal was Alfred Richardson who employed a 'staff' at election time, ready on horseback to go to 'every part of the county, ready to start off if anyone came forward to oppose us'.[75] Repeal agitation intensified in 1842–3, culminating in monster meetings throughout the country.[76] Describing the Repeal movement in King's County, William O'Neill Daunt recalled the enthusiastic and well-attended meetings at Clara and Banagher in the early 1840s.[77] A monster Repeal demonstration was held in Tullamore in July 1843, with bands from Roscrea, Parsonstown, Killeigh, Banagher, Edenderry, Rhode and Philipstown. Those present (a somewhat exaggerated figure was estimated at 150,000 people) heard Daniel O'Connell speak of his disdain for agents, who in valuing land 'may as well consult butchers about keeping lent'.[78]

---

70 Edward Meares Kelly, Parsonstown to Lord Downshire, London, 14 Aug. 1837 (DP, D/671/C/12/690).   71 'Election broadsheet, 1841' (Charleville papers, T/3069/D/24). 72 'Diary of Elizabeth Smith, 24 Feb. 1841' (in private possession).   73 Ibid.   74 Alfred G. Richardson to Lord Rossmore, 24 Jan. 1835 (Rossmore papers, T/2929/8/18).   75 Ibid. 76 In 1843 when the Ferbane Repeal party expressed their sympathy at O'Connell's imprisonment among their members were the land agents James Devery and Alfred Richardson. See *FJ*, 5 Mar. 1839 & 3 Aug. 1844.   77 See W.J. O'Neill Daunt, *A life spent for Ireland* (London, 1896), p. 1. William Joseph O'Neill Daunt was born in Tullamore in 1807.

On the eve of the Famine the confidence of King's County tenants was high that the Repeal movement and its objectives would triumph. The case was championed by landowners Robert Cassidy, Nicholas Fitzsimons and John O'Brien. The main thrust of support, though, came from the Catholic clergy who wielded their dominance over the local population. In many parts of the county the priest now enjoyed greater control and exerted more influence than the agent or landlord. Significantly, at a local level problems of leasing, rents and improvements were foremost in the consideration of Repealers and outweighed issues regarding the legislature or parliament; at Edenderry, for example, Myles Keon, a Repeal warden, agitated for access to turbary (the right to cut turf or peat).[79] However, the success of Repeal was a costly price to pay for many tenants as the 'rent' to the party was another crippling blow to their economic well being. In many cases the visit of the 'Repeal rent' collector was more feared than that of the agent. Ironically, some land agents and landowners, supporters of the Repeal party, would later use the Famine as a means of clearing their tenants, particularly those in financial trouble. Thus, it seems, that support in previous years mattered little, as thousands were put to the road.

78 *Nation*, 22 July 1843.   79 See Reilly, *Edenderry, 1820–1920*, p. 60.

5 Pioneers of change? Agents and the advance of agriculture

The frequent failure of the potato crop in the years prior to the Great Famine was something that greatly worried land agents. Between 1700 and 1845 as many as twenty-seven failures of the potato crop were recorded. Contemporary commentators lamented that no year in Ireland was without the dread of impending disaster in the potato crop. Perhaps partly because many also doubled as farmers and depended on securing a good potato yield, land agents, in the first half of the nineteenth century, invested considerable time and energy into acquiring the latest agricultural knowledge. In addition, as we have already seen, the advance of agriculture was seen as a means of changing the manner and habits of the people and thereby helping their overall welfare. In the early 1720s Robert Molesworth had declared that 'the whole economy of agriculture is generally mistaken and neglected in this kingdom' and proposed measures to overcome this. A decade later efforts made by the Royal Dublin Society marked an important attempt to circulate new farming ideas throughout the country, but, as Dooley contends, their membership of only 300 'spoke volumes for the level of interest among the gentry'.[1] By the 1750s things were beginning to change somewhat.[2] Land agents were presented with agricultural works from Britain on best practice and husbandry, and many were now appointed primarily because they possessed agricultural knowledge. Indeed, so important was that knowledge that by the beginning of the nineteenth century William Marshall could declare that the main duty of an estate manager lay 'in the field' and that the management of an estate required the 'whole of any man's attention', thus lawyers were deemed unsuitable.[3] Irish landlords quickly realized that improving the habits of the people would ultimately increase the rental, and thus this became a key function of the agent. By the 1830s the agents' concerns were firmly invested in agricultural improvement. Indeed, it could be argued that land agents were responsible for changing the agricultural habits of an entire population, although in light of what followed it is questionable as to what extent their advice was heeded. King's County was fortunate in that a number of the leading proprietors were keen agriculturalists including Lord Downshire, who encouraged a 'committee of agriculture and planting' and shows of livestock throughout Ireland, and the second earl of Charleville who, unlike his father,

---

1 See Dooley, *A research guide*, p. 20. 2 Quoted in Feehan, *Farming in Ireland*, p. 93.
3 William Marshall, *On the landed property of England: an elementary and practical treatise containing the purchase, the improvement and the management of landed estates* (London, 1804), pp 338–9. Marshall believed that a land agent could not be found in the 'echelons of the law library'.

took a special interest in the agricultural improvement of the people of Tullamore.[4]

To educate the tenantry, agents chose a number of methods, including the establishment of agricultural societies, schools and the publication of circulars about the benefits of agricultural improvement.[5] Having studied the methods adopted by English, Scottish, Belgian and Dutch agriculturalists, and through their own experiments, land agents on the eve of the Famine suggested changes which should be adopted in Ireland. The leading agricultural experts of the day included a number of agents, among them Joseph Lambert of Co. Mayo, who believed that knowledge and science were the key to agricultural improvement. According to Lambert the Belgian system of agriculture was the model to which Irish farmers, agents and landlords should aspire.[6] Significantly, Lambert advised that the turnip was key to Ireland's development and would lead to the overall advancement of Irish agriculture.[7] Likewise, Thomas Bermingham, agent of the Clonbrock estate in Co. Galway, was another who visited Belgium in the early 1830s, publishing widely on his experiences there.[8]

One of the best-known proponents of agricultural advancement was William Blacker who was invited by Lord Gosford and Colonel Close in Co. Armagh to demonstrate the advantages of the Flemish system of farming. His observations were contained in the most celebrated agricultural survey of an estate from which many land agents took their lead.[9] The experiment, it appears, was largely successful and landlords elsewhere soon 'imported' their own agriculturalists, mainly from Scotland, to advise tenants. Indeed, it is thought that Blacker brought as many as sixty agriculturalists to Ireland, many of whom officiated in King's County.[10] These men brought with them ideas, not just confined to agriculture, but for more effective estate management in general. Indeed, it is

---

4 Green, 'Agriculture', p. 120. King's County was among the first to have an agricultural survey; proposed by Arthur Young in 1794 and completed by Sir Charles Coote in 1801. 5 See, for example, 'Printed address to the tenants of J.W. Maxwell's Killyfaddy estate in Co. Tyrone from Jas. McLannahan, the agent, 18 July 1836' (PRONI, D1444/2). 6 Joseph Lambert, *Agricultural suggestions to the proprietors and peasantry of Ireland* (Dublin, 1845), p. 51. 7 Ibid., p. 69. 8 See Thomas Bermingham, *The social state of Great Britain and Ireland considered with regard to the labouring population* (London, 1834). I am grateful to Dr Kevin McKenna for bringing this to my attention. 9 See William Blacker, *An essay on the improvement to be made in the cultivation of small farms by the introduction of green crops, and house-feeding the stock thereon. Originally published in an address to the small farmers on the estates of the earl of Gosford and Colonel Close, in the County of Armagh. With a preface, addressed to landlords, giving full information to those who may be inclined to adopt the plan recommended, as to the best mode of introducing it, and the results attending its introduction, together, with the expenses likely to be incurred thereby* (Dublin, 1845). 10 Feehan, *Farming in Ireland*, p. 93. See also Lindsay Proudfoot, 'Placing the imaginary: Gosford Castle and the Gosford estate, c.1820–1900' in A.J. Hughes & William Nolan (eds), *Armagh history and society: interdisciplinary essays on the history of an Irish county* (Dublin, 2001), p. 909. On many estates tenants were required to pay for the services of the agriculturalist and this may reflect why some did not pay much heed to this advice. See Feehan, *Farming in Ireland*, p. 103.

likely that the success of the Highland clearances of the 1820s and 1830s was preached to Irish landlords and agents, who, as we shall see below, put into practice similar policies in the decade prior to, and including, the Famine. About these Scottish agriculturalists, one contemporary glowingly observed that they were teaching 'the art of farming to the tenants, the alphabet of which they were only beginning to learn'.[11] Crucially, they were not alone in their endeavours. Other innovative approaches to agriculture included John Scott Vandaleur's 'model farm' at Rahaline, Co. Clare. Influenced by the British radical Robert Owen and his 'commune', in the 1830s Vandaleur duly reorganized his 6,000 acre estate under the direction of his agent, E.T. Craig.[12] Another who sought to change agricultural practice was John Pitt Kennedy of Donagh, Co. Donegal, later secretary to the Devon Commission in the 1840s. For much of his lifetime Kennedy devoted himself to the task of showing farmers by practical example how much could be achieved.

Anxious to learn from their Scottish counterparts, Irish agents also spent time in Scotland, studying native husbandry. One such agent was Charles Ryan who wrote about draining, sub soiling, ploughing, enclosing land, the use of manure and the growing of a variety of green crops. Ryan noted that it was by cropping their land 'so judiciously' that Scottish farmers were able to pay such high rents. In his opinion, Irish landlords would be much better off if they compelled farmers to do likewise.[13] Samuel Hussey was also exposed to Scottish agriculture when, aged seventeen, he managed a farm in the south of Scotland.[14] He later made two trips around Scotland writing about agricultural practices.[15] And there were a host of alternative opinions. Samuel Robinson, a King's County landlord and miller, supported the Belgian model of agriculture which also involved keeping no horses, feeding their cattle in houses, and the use of dry mould and manure.[16] He was supported in his opinion by George Nichols, architect of the Irish Poor Law Act in 1838, who believed that agricultural development in Ireland on the lines of Belgium was needed.[17] Other pioneers included John Andrews, Lord Londonderry's agent in Cos. Down and Antrim. A believer in the 'Deanston' system of agriculture, Andrews set aside ten acres of land to demonstrate to tenants how close cropping could be applied to small farms. His methods were quickly adopted by other agents and farmers around the country. Like those writing about best agricultural practice of the day, Andrews highlighted the need for the land to be properly and adequately drained and for sensible rotation to be applied, which would raise the productivity of the farm.

11 Quoted in Bryan McMahon, 'Sixty years of estate management in Ardfert', *The Kerry Magazine*, 10 (1999), p. 49. See also *Nation*, 4 Feb. 1843.   12 Bell & Watson, *A history of Irish farming*, p. 42. The Palatine communities in Kerry, Limerick and Carlow also achieved remarkable agricultural success. See Feehan, *Farming in Ireland*, p. 107.   13 Charles Ryan, *An essay on Scottish husbandry adopted for the use of the farmers of Ireland* (Dublin, 1839), p. 100. 14 Hussey, *Reminiscences*, p. 32.   15 Ibid., pp 33–4.   16 *The Nation*, 31 Aug. 1838. 17 Nichols, *Poor law Ireland*, p. 168.

As early as the 1770s ideas regarding the benefits of agricultural improvement had reached King's County. Lord Shelbourne's estate at Rahan, near Tullamore, was overseen by a bailiff and agriculturalist, a Mr Vancover, who was brought from Norfolk, England. Vancover was well schooled in the science of agricultural improvement and brought with him a ploughman, new ploughs, harrow and tackle to implement his 'Norfolk husbandry'.[18] He was described as being a 'sensible, intelligent, active man who went through all the manual part of farming in seven years apprenticeship to a great farmer in Norfolk'.[19] Vancover had singled out for improvement some 4,000 acres of bog on the Shelbourne estate. According to Arthur Young, who visited the Shelbourne estate at this time, the farm manager had commenced to grow turnips, a favourable decision he believed, as this was always the most viable option for poor soil.[20] Young's comments were significant given what was to happen in the 1840s and that King's County was/is noted for the poor quality of its soil, with a large part of the county covered by bog.

Nowhere in King's County was the championing of agricultural improvement more visible than on the Charleville estate at Tullamore where Francis Berry attempted to encourage the farming techniques adopted by Blacker and others. Indeed, so determined was Berry to adopt new farming methods among Charleville's 'backward' tenantry, that he brought a number of them to Armagh in 1838 to witness Blacker at work.[21] Among the new methods that Berry implemented at Tullamore was the growing of Italian rye grass and the introduction of new breeds of cattle; on one occasion he informed Lord Charleville that the 'young Devon bull would be a better beast than the one from England as he has more gentle blood'.[22] In the late 1830s the importation of Ayrshire cattle and other breeds ????? the extent to which farmers had learned from the international exchange of ideas.[23] Berry also acquired the services of a Scottish agriculturalist, James Kidd, who instructed tenants in drainage and brought expensive horses to work the land. In an effort to further encourage the tenantry Kidd organized agricultural shows, ploughing matches and sports days. In 1838, for example, a sports day held for the tenantry when the harvest was complete concluded with a dinner attended by over 200 people, at which the agriculturalist expressed the wish that the tenantry would 'continue to look up to him [the landlord] as their generous benefactor'.[24] Two years later another show under the auspices of the newly formed Tullamore Agricultural Society was attended by Dr Thomas Bewley, president of the Irish Agricultural Society. Also present at the dinner was Pat Egan of Deerpark, Croghan, who, along with other tenants, had visited the Gosford estate, observing the agricultural methods of Blacker at first-hand. Francis Berry believed that Egan's 'judicious management' of his thirteen-acre

18 Hutton, *Arthur Young*, p. 65.　**19** Ibid., pp. 65–6.　**20** Ibid.　**21** Francis Berry to earl of Charleville, 14 Nov. 1837 (Charleville papers, T/3069/B/38).　**22** Ibid.　**23** Feehan, *Farming in Ireland*, p. 101.　**24** *LE*, 3 Nov. 1838.

holding was proof of the benefits of encouraging small farmers. The success of the Tullamore society was further illustrated in the large attendance at the 1843 show, when prizes were awarded for the best cow, heifer, bull, pig and the growing of green crops including turnips, mangolds, clover, rye grass and trans-planted rape. Other prizes were offered for drainage and the best kept labourer's cottage, indicating that it was not just agriculture that was being changed.[25] Obviously, while such methods would have been unable to avert the impending blight and calamity it wrought, it is evidence nonetheless of how land agents spent much of their energies on the eve of the Famine.

Although Berry's success at Tullamore was laudable, many land agents, it seems, were naive in their assessment of the problems that farmers and small holders faced in terms of bettering their own position. Failing to take into account the problems that were endemic at the time, Joseph Lambert believed that active weeding was necessary, something which was frequently overlooked by potato growers. According to Lambert if farmers kept hold of the weed colts-foot, that 'most insidious enemy of the peasant', they would have better potato yields.[26] Land agents, agriculturalists and those writing about best farming practice all agreed that the growing and use of clover could benefit the Irish tenant farmer as it helped in the making of manure and also the production of turnips. In 1841 William Bence Jones, in an open letter to his tenantry in Co. Cork, argued in favour of growing green crops. 'Some of you I know cannot understand why I am anxious that the tenants should grow green crops' he noted, insisting that it was not for his amusement or that his 'head is full of English farming'. He further pointed out that the tenants were 'being ruined for the want of manure' and that English farmers all believed that 'dung is the mother of gold'.[27] Others suggested the use of guano and bones as a substitute for farmyard manure.[28] Indeed, dung was such a sought-after product in King's County that in February 1836 it resulted in a court case involving two men who were in dispute over the scrapping of manure off the public road.[29]

As a means of overcoming this poor quality soil in King's County, a host of agents undertook extensive works in drainage and improvement on the eve of the Famine.[30] A large-scale reclamation project was undertaken at the Charleville estate in 1836 after the Office of Public Works had recommended that 'large portions of your lordship's waste lands in King's County might be worked to a reasonable profit'.[31] At Edenderry, John Watson, a tenant on the Downshire estate, was optimistic that agriculture was improving, praising in particular the

25 Ibid., 7 Sept. 1844. 26 Lambert, *Agricultural suggestions*, pp 76–7. 27 William Bence Jones, *The life work in Ireland of a landlord who tried to do his duty* (London, 1880), p. vi. 28 Ibid., p. 79. 29 Bernard Cummins, Kinnitty to Lord Lieutenant, Dublin Castle, 8 Feb. 1836 (OPKC, 1836, 15/27/1). 30 See Atkinson papers (NLI, Ainsworth report on private collection, no. 120). 31 Capt J.F. Burgoyne, O.P.W., Dublin to Lord Charleville, 19 July 1836 (Charleville papers, T/3069/B/60).

work of Thomas Murray in overseeing a large-scale drainage project.[32] Murray was particularly proud of his achievements at Edenderry and had used the Scottish agriculturist and drainage expert, William Cope, to oversee the works.[33] Providing anecdotal evidence of how well the scheme had worked, he claimed that Lord Downshire had delighted in being told by a tenant that 'I am now drawing corn over land where two years ago I had two bullocks drowned'.[34] Drainage and widening of river beds, particularly at Clara and Tullamore, also greatly increased farm productivity, for which lords Charleville and Mornington were praised. At Tullabeg, near Rahan, the reclamation included land which in the past had been 'much injured by the bad rivers, which inundate the land when it rains'. Indeed, it was argued that 'two hours of heavy rain will cover 4,000 acres of land from this to the Shannon'.[35] On an individual basis agents also looked towards improvement and many were successful in their endeavours. At an exhibition held in Parsonstown in 1845, Thomas Manifold won second place for land over 200 acres, being praised for the way that he had cultivated land which prior to this was 'in a wild and uncultivated manner'.[36] Such efforts to improve land were also championed by the Irish Waste Land Improvement Society which was established in the 1830s, and which included land agents among its members.[37] In King's County on the eve of the Famine agents also undertook and oversaw a widespread forestation policy, involving the planting of several hundred thousand trees, including larch, Scots fir, beech and poplars.[38]

Another successful attempt to change agricultural habits were the efforts of the Rait brothers near Rhode, in the barony of Warrenstown. Travelling through Ireland in the 1830s, the Scottish Whig politician Robert Graham described their farming practices as 'the best in Ireland'. The Rait property, originally part of the Trimleston estates, was acquired by the brothers when they moved from Philipstown in around 1805, and was laid out in fields of twenty acres. To ensure effective management the Raits had three sets of offices located in different parts of his estate. Six of his staff were brought from Scotland to instruct local farmers in the best agricultural practice and 'Scottish' horses were chiefly used and were bred at the farm. The introduction of a threshing mill on the estate was also said to have given the Raits a distinct advantage. The practice of crop rotation was also in place where oats, barley, turnips, wheat, hay and grass operated on an eight-year cycle. George Rait, a native of Dundee, Scotland, clearly modelled his farming on English and Scottish models, and was not an admirer of the tartarian, a variety of oats more suited to the Irish climate than the Scottish. Chevalier barley, which originated in Suffolk, was also used, while

32 See Reilly, *Edenderry, 1820–1920*, pp 38–42. 33 Thomas Murray to Lord Downshire, 29 Apr. 1840 (DP, D/671/C/9/638). 34 Quoted in Reilly, *Edenderry, 1820–1920*, p. 42. See also Coote, *Statistical survey of King's County*, p. 85. 35 *Devon Commission*, p. 622. For opposition to such schemes see *KCC*, 19 Oct. 1853. 36 *KCC*, 15 Oct. 1845. 37 Feehan, *Farming in Ireland*, p. 102. 38 'A register of trees for King's County, 1793–1913' (PRONI, T/3617/1B).

6 Rathmoyle, near Rhode, home of the Rait brothers
(courtesy of Offaly Historical Society)

an Italian clover, *trifolium incarnatum*, was introduced but was said to have failed.
A quarry on the farm supplied ready lime to be used as manure, while also
providing excellent building and paving stones. However, improvements came at
a price. Rait's plans were developed only after a large clearance of 'small
unthriving tenants', which created a 'great deal of ill will'. George Rait was
eventually shot and wounded.[39] Others were not impressed with the endeavours
of the Scottish brothers, believing that their methods were expensive, and would
not succeed in the long term.[40]

Not content with the practical experience they gained in Scotland, England
and on the Continent, the library in an agent's house was also well stocked with
the latest suggestions on estate management and agricultural practice. Thomas
Murray acquired books on Dutch farming which he frequently gave on loan to
farmers at Edenderry and advised that they should be translated into a 'language
that the Irish farmer would understand'.[41] Despite not making much use of his
European trips, Murray encouraged tenants in his annual address to 'till well,
drain and deepen the soil'. Likewise, George Heenan frequently printed circulars
for the Rosse tenants on methods of improving agriculture. The Co. Kildare
distiller, Robert Cassidy who immersed himself in the management of his King's
County property, meticulously recorded the agricultural output of his estates as a

39 Henry Heaney (ed.), *A Scottish Whig in Ireland, 1835–38: the Irish journals of Robert Graham
of Redgorton* (Dublin, 1999), pp 224–5. Graham mistakenly refers to the Raits estate at
Rathmoyle as Rynnmoyle. 40 Thomas Murray to Lord Downshire, 20 Nov. 1839 (DP,
D/671/C/9/???). 41 Ibid., 4 Feb. 1839 (DP, D/671/C/9/593).

means of improvement and also for the management of his distilling business. His voluminous library at his home in Monasterevin included many books on agricultural matters.[42] Elsewhere, others followed suit. On the eve of the Famine, for example, a Co. Monaghan public library included among its collection twelve copies of James Smith's book, *Remarks on thorough draining and deep ploughing*, which had been published in Stirling, Scotland, in 1840.[43] Bringing the 'gospel' to a larger audience, landlords and their agents supported the establishment of agricultural schools and societies in order to better educate tenants. They were not alone in such endeavours; the editor of the *Leinster Express* recommended that agricultural schools should be set up so that 'for the purpose of grounding the rising generation in a sound practical knowledge of husbandry'.[44]

Agricultural schools and societies had operated in various parts of King's County since the early nineteenth century – the Kinnitty society established in May 1813 under the direction of Colonel Thomas Bernard and his agent Daniel Manifold among the earliest.[45] In 1830 Hugh Scully established a society at Philipstown, having sought the assistance of Robert Cassidy.[46] This society was particularly successful, as was evident in the use of new farming implements in the baronies of Warrenstown and Philipstown by the end of 1830s.[47] The barony of Philipstown was also said to have benefited from the latest agricultural knowledge that local agents received from the Dublin land agency firm, Stewart and Kincaid.[48] And while scepticism remained as to the benefit to be derived from agricultural improvement, the increase in corn, wheat, oats and barley sold in King's County during the period 1826–46 certainly indicates that advances had been made.[49] However, the failure of land agents and agricultural enthusiasts to coordinate these efforts hindered greater progress. For example, it wasn't until 1840 that a county society was formed, when the Manifold brothers were foremost in its promotion;[50] however, the evidence suggests that this society was largely ineffective. The absence of societies at a more local level also hindered progress and arguably agents, like Murray, did not put their foreign travel experiences to any great use when they returned.[51] In some cases, there was

42 For his agricultural statistics see Cassidy papers (NLI, Unsorted Collection). Also included are the works of Sir John Watshun, Mr Hawley & Mr Maxwell (eds), *Practical suggestions for a national system of agricultural statistics* (London, 1854); R. Garnett and sons, *Catalogue of illustrated reference list of agricultural implements and machines* (London, 1849) and John Paine Morris, *The valuation and calculations assistant containing various tables* (Dublin, 1850). 43 Theo McMahon, 'The Rose estate, Tydavnet, county Monaghan', *Clogher Record*, 18:2 (2004), p. 253. 44 *LE*, 3 Mar. 1839. 45 Coote, *Statistical survey of the King's County*, p. 78. 46 Hugh Scully, Philipstown to Robert Cassidy, 28 Sept. 1830 (NLI, Cassidy papers). 47 Devon Commission, p. 627. 48 See various correspondence in the Stewart & Kincaid archive. (This archive is now in private possession but consulted by this author when in the possession of Roscommon County Library.) 49 During this period a total of 418,000 barrels of wheat, oats, barley were sold at the main markets in the county. See *The parliamentary gazetteer of Ireland* (5 vols, Dublin, 1846), vi, p. 556. 50 Pey (ed.), *Eglish*, p. 109. 51 Thomas Murray to Thomas Parry, 3 Oct. 1838 (DP, D/671/C/9/576).

resentment towards the new societies which were 'looked upon as a landlord's movement'.[52]

Farmers were often reluctant to join these new societies and accusations of bias against them were frequent. Significantly, for the secret societies and agrarian conspirators operating in King's County, agricultural advancement was very much viewed with suspicion. In the barony of Ballycowan, Thomas Parker O'Flanagan openly criticized the agricultural society which 'purports to embrace the district, but it does not co-operate with it'.[53] At Clara agricultural improvement was said to be non-existent, despite its proximity to Tullamore and Moate where societies were active.[54] Others argued that agricultural societies would be better served by supplying poor tenants with seeds rather than spending money on educating the wealthy farmers. These societies were merely 'benefiting a class of men who already knew what to do'.[55] Even advocates of improvement were sceptical and slow to embrace change. Samuel Robinson, a successful cotton and linen manufacturer at Clara, bemoaned the land he had lost due to the improvements, while Maurice Collis believed that the improvement of one acre of land meant the destruction of two acres through burning and cropping.[56] These negative attitudes towards improvement were also shared by tenants, largely because those wishing to avail of such advice were bound by certain conditions with regard to their character, behaviour and land management. Even the celebrated Blacker was reluctant to offer any advice to tenants who were deemed to be breaking the code of conduct laid down by the landlord.[57] There may have been some truth in the belief that improvement served only to benefit the better class of tenants. In 1846, tenants at the Toler estate were treated to a dinner at Thornvale, George Garvey's residence, where the annual agricultural premiums, consisting of ploughs, wheelbarrows and harrows, were presented. Those in receipt of premiums, numbering forty, largely belonged to the large farming class, and were treated to a dinner of roast beef and pudding. On this occasion Garvey informed those present that the new landlord was concerned about making his tenantry happy and prosperous and that he would always endeavour to promote the good feeling between landlord and tenant. Many of the tenants expressed their delight with having grown turnips for the first time and the assistance received from Mr Jackson, the agriculturalist, and also from Garvey, who had supplied them with manure and seed.[58]

Of course opposition to improvement also came from land agents themselves. George Crampton, agent of the Carter estate at Eglish, argued that drainage would interfere with spring planting and that the interest on loans might serve only to increase the estates debt and speed its ruin.[59] This was true of the

52 *Devon Commission*, p. 627.   53 Ibid., p. 638.   54 *LE*, 21 Jan. 1843.   55 *Devon Commission*, p. 642.   56 Ibid., parts II & III, pp 246 & 643.   57 See Proudfoot, 'Placing the imaginary', p. 910.   58 *KCC*, 17 Feb. 1846.   59 Tom Yager, 'Mass eviction in the Mullet Peninsula during and after the Great Famine', *Irish Economic and Social History*, 23 (1996), p. 33.

Fortescue estate in Co. Louth where the agent or steward, William Galt, had brought the landlord to bankruptcy by insisting that he bought the newest farming implements and the best breed of horses, cattle, sheep and pigs.[60] But even the best intentioned of land agents were thwarted by the habits of rural farmers. Frustratingly, even within a county or barony, agricultural practices varied, particularly where many farmers were reluctant to adopt 'outside' or 'landlord' ideas. The situation was best explained by James Caird, who writing in 1852 about the situation in England, but which was equally applicable to Ireland, noted that:

> the successful practices of one farm, or one county, are unknown or unheeded in the next. On the one side of a hedge a plough with five horses and two men, and on the other side of the same hedge, a plough with two horses and one man, are doing precisely the same amount of work.[61]

Regrettably, however, there were also too many landlords and agents who did not wish to embrace agricultural improvement. One of the best examples in King's County was the refusal of significant landlords to develop drainage and reclamation projects. John Hussey Walsh argued for government involvement in schemes to reclaim waste land which in turn could be allotted to impoverished people.[62] Although individual schemes were carried out – such as those at Eglish, where the Revd Joseph Barnes was involved in a 'remarkable' land reclamation project and quarried rocks and fenced large tracts of land – many were reluctant to adopt such measures.[63] The success of these schemes contrasted with the reality in other parts of the county. In areas such as Ballycommon and Mount Lucas over 10,000 acres of bog lay uncultivated and housed a considerable number of paupers.[64] The landlord William Trench of Shinrone, who although educated in the benefits of agricultural improvement, informed the Devon Commission that he would not encourage tenants to carry out drainage works.[65]

Despite all of this, there is ample evidence to suggest that land agents actively strove to improve agricultural practices on the eve of the Famine. In addition, it is also notable that many did not abandon their efforts of agricultural advancement during the calamity. There were those who instructed farmers on the growing of dock leaves to help fatten their pigs. Others introduced new breeds

60 Padraig O'Neill, 'The Fortescue's of County Louth', *Journal of the County Louth Archaeological and Historical Society*, 24:1 (1997), p. 16. **61** James Caird, *English agriculture in 1850 and 1851* (London, 1852), pp 498–9. **62** Ibid., p. 634. **63** Pey (ed.), *Eglish*, p. 18. By carrying out drainage and reclamation works at Ballyegan, Bernard Mullins was said to have created 'excellent pasture for live stock' which was said to be particularly well suited to the grazing of young horned cattle. See J. Feehan and G. O'Donovan, *The bogs of Ireland* (Dublin, 1996), p. 39. **64** Coote, *Statistical survey of the King's County*, p. 104. **65** *Devon Commission*, p. 586.

of sheep and cattle in an effort to promote a move from tillage to pasture. 'The progress that not a few of them have made in adopting the newest, best and most profitable system of agriculture' was seen as enough reason to continue the Parsonstown and King's County Farming Society during the Famine. Crucially, however, their attempts were stifled by three successive poor harvests from 1839 to 1841, resulting in a downturn in the economy. Already hard-pressed, farmers (and by extension landlords) dismissed the idea of outlaying capital into agricultural improvement and drainage.[66] The subsequent decline in rentals (as witnessed for those that survive for King's County) confirm this. Moreover, the competition for land in King's County was so intense that the landless cared little for the quality of the land they received, and thus were loath to adopt a more scientific approach to farming.[67] By the mid-1830s there was widespread opposition to any attempt to embrace grazierism, something which would define King's County well into the twentieth-century. For many land agents their efforts were futile and fell on deaf ears, and as Cormac Ó Gráda has suggested the agricultural society meetings of the 1840s were mainly 'jamborees' without substance.[68]

By 1845 those who owned estates in King's County, and moreover those who managed them, were clearly in difficulty. The economic downturn and, in many cases, the refusal of landlords to reduce their expenditure in the face of falling rents meant that many were on the verge of bankruptcy. Even had the Famine not intervened, it is probable that by the late 1840s many of these landlords would have disappeared. In addition, a number of other factors led to the chaotic management of estates. The third earl of Norbury left King's County when his house at Durrow was burned in 1843, as did William Magan when his mansion, Clonearl House near Philipstown, was burned two years later. The question remains: would increased social disorder have contributed further to their decline? The evidence for King's County from the late 1830s onwards suggests that it was growing unabated, as it was in neighbouring Tipperary. This was reflected in a government report of 1839 that concluded that it was 'next impossible' to live in King's County without being sworn into a secret society.[69] These secret societies were agrarian in outlook, their aim being to maintain the status

66 Ó Gráda argues that landlords expended as little as 3 per cent of their income on agricultural improvement. See Cormac Ó Gráda, 'The investment behaviour of Irish landlords, 1830–75', *Economic History Review*, 23 (1975), p. 139. However, the level of income expended on agriculture by landlords did not reflect the interest which existed in promoting new methods and techniques.   67 Of course another great hindrance to the spread of agricultural knowledge were the middlemen, who, taking what they could from their undertenants, were reluctant to reinvest any capital or time.   68 Ó Gráda, 'Poverty, population and agriculture, 1801–45', p. 129. Feehan contends that it was a 'reluctant revolution' and even those who did adopt new practice did so hesitantly. See Feehan, *Farming in Ireland*, p. 93.   69 *The State of Ireland since 1835, in respect of crime and outrage, which have rendered life and property insecure in that part of the Empire*, HC 1839 [486] xi, i, p. 526.

quo with regard to access to land, especially conacre, the maintenance of rents at an affordable level and the prevention of evictions or clearances that were facilitated after 1838 by the passing of the Irish Poor Law Act.[70] As it was, agents and their fellow estate employees found themselves the targets of increased agrarian outrage. On individual estates they attempted to combat growing disorder in an increasingly desparate manner. For example, on the Downshire estate Thomas Murray evicted any tenant who was found to have been involved in crime or belonged to a secret society.[71] As a body though, agents were ineffectual; they made no coordinated attempt to deal with either the growth in crime or the need to improve the lot of their tenantry, particularly the lower classes. They were ill-prepared for the social catastrophe that was to begin in 1845. Ultimately, this spelled disaster for the thousands in their care.

---

70 Conacre was more prevalent in some counties than others. Although operating upon the same principals, in some counties it adopted a different name, e.g., 'mock ground' in Clare, 'stang' in Wexford and 'rood land' elsewhere. See Nally, *Human encumbrances*, p. 249.   71 Thomas Murray to Lord Downshire, 2 Mar. 1840 (DP, D/671/C/9/627).

6 The coming of the blight: reaction and relief

> Landlords use no tyranny, keep your trumpeters at home, tenants gather all your corn into your farmyards; also threaten agents, land jobbers, moneylenders and millers.[1]

This passage taken from a threatening letter posted near Tullamore in September 1846 indicated the widely held public resentment towards landlords, agents and others in King's County almost one year after the first reports of blight were reported. As the previous chapters have shown, resentment towards the modernization of estate management had led to increased agrarian tensions from the 1830s onwards. The underlying causes were overcrowding – leading to subdivision – continued demographic growth, impoverishment and over-reliance on conacre for the growing of the potato crop. Landlords were also becoming increasingly wary, and in some cases paranoid, about the middleman system. The appearance of *phytophthora infestans* (or the potato blight as it was more commonly known) in September 1845 was a phenomenon that had not been experienced in Ireland or indeed in Europe before.[2] Although several failures of the potato crop had occurred in Ireland in the previous half century, none were as prolonged, or on the same scale, as that of the blight that struck in the mid-1840s. While the effects of the blight were not evenly felt throughout the country, it has been argued that the crisis caused by crop failure in King's County during the 1840s 'had proportionally a greater impact than in some of the western counties'. For example, excess mortality in Donegal was estimated at 10.7 per thousand while in King's County that rate was 18 per thousand people.[3] Over the course of the next six years or so, different communities would be affected to varying degrees by hunger, disease and blight. This chapter, while examining the impact that the Famine had on the various classes, evaluates how land agents in King's County coped with the crisis in the early years from 1845 to 1847.

In his memoirs published half a century after the Famine, William O'Connor Morris captured the physiological impact that the starving people had on him, recalling that 'the lean and wolfish faces of many of those are stamped on my mind even as I write now'.[4] O'Connor Morris inherited the family estate, near Pallas, at the height of the Famine and had first noticed the potato blight in September 1845 while partridge shooting, when the 'sickly smell of corruption'

---

1 Enclosed in 'Neal Browne, resident magistrate, Tullamore to lord lieutenant, Dublin Castle, 25 Sept. 1846' (OPKC, 1846, 15/25911).   2 For more on the origins of the potato blight see P.M.A. Bourke, 'Emergence of potato blight, 1843–46', *Nature*, 203 (Aug. 1964), pp 805–8.
3 O'Neill, 'The Famine in Offaly', p. 681.   4 O'Connor Morris, *Memories*, p. 128.

7 William O'Connor Morris (1824–1904) of Mount Pleasant
(courtesy of Offaly Historical Society)

assailed his nostrils.[5] A month later Lord Ponsonby's local agent at Philipstown, Joseph Grogan, reported to the Dublin land agency Stewart and Kincaid his initial reactions:

> the crop is still in the fields in stacks and can't be got into the haggards as it is raining same every day and night and the corn has received some damage in the stacks. With regard to the potatoes at the first time I wrote

5 Ibid., p. 129.

to you there was not the least appearance of damage on them but at this moment there appears to be great damage to the potato crop in this county or any other part that I am in the habit of travelling along the canal line but it is damaged more or less and the people appears (sic) to be greatly alarmed on that account.[6]

The coming of the blight, as highlighted by Grogan, coincided with heavy flooding in many parts of the country, thereby exacerbating the problem for farmers and labourers alike.[7] In King's County, as fields lay flooded and crops destroyed, reactions to the blight varied greatly. There were all types of theories propounded for the cause of the blight, some more far-fetched than others. At Philipstown Dr Cowell suggested that the 'great rains and changes in the atmosphere' were responsible,[8] while John Plunket Joly, the son of the Church of Ireland rector of Clonsast, recalled that the blight occurred when 'the north wind brought the Dublin smoke'.[9] Historians have since shown that the blight originated from the eastern United States or possibly from the northern Andes region of South America and had spread to Europe by 1844.[10]

Initially agents such as Joseph Grogan were optimistic that the damage would be minimal, that the blight would soon abate, and they saw little reason to panic.[11] Writing to Stewart and Kincaid at the end of September: 'I have tried my own [potatoes] which I thought were safe and I found that they were damaged. The white potatoes has suffered more than any other kind but I expect when they are digging out that they will not be as damaged as people think'.[12] Three months later he cheerfully reported that tenants were following his advice about how to lay out a potato pit and that 'the potatoes are not getting any worse thank god'.[13] However, others were not so optimistic. Daniel Manifold, Colonel Bernard's agent at Kinnitty, feared the worst and that the blight would result in widespread Famine.[14] These predictions were quickly proved true when James F. Rolleston reported a riot in Dunkerrin over the shortage of potatoes and requested troops to be sent as the 'rot is more or less extensive' and the people were in an awful condition.[15] Even in these initial stages of the Famine the worst

---

6 Joseph Grogan to Stewart and Kincaid, 16 Oct. 1845 (S & KA).   7 'Diary of John Plunket Joly, 2 Oct. 1845' (NLI, MS 17,035). [Hereafter cited as 'Joly diary NLI'].   8 Dr J. Cowell, Philipstown to relief commissioners, 8 Nov. 1845 (RLFC, 2/Z15408).   9 Quoted in Ciarán Reilly, *John Plunket Joly and the Great Famine in King's County* (Dublin, 2012), p. 25.   10 James S. Donnelly Jr, *The Great Irish potato famine* (Stroud, 2001), p. 41. See also Jacqueline Hill & Cormac Ó Gráda (eds), *The visitation of God?: The potato and the Great Irish Famine* (Dublin, 1993), p. 52.   11 Joseph Grogan to Stewart & Kincaid, 29 Sept. 1845 (PRONI, Molesworthpapers, D/1567/F/1/17/77).   12 Ibid., 16 Oct. 1845 (S.&.K.A.)   13 O'Neill, 'The Famine in Offaly', p. 685.   14 Sir Andrew Armstrong reiterated these sentiments warning that 'there will be more than the usual destitution this year'. See 'County lieutenants report, King's County, Nov. 1845' (RLFC, 2/441/15).   15 James F. Rolleston, Franckfort Castle, King's County to Lord Lieutenant, Dublin Castle, 16 Oct. 1845 & 20 Jan. 1846 (OPKC, 1846,

was feared and thousands were reported to have emigrated to Dundee and other centres in Scotland where work was said to be plentiful.[16] Curiously, however, the winter markets in King's County reported good returns – there were over seven hundred barrels of corn sold at Clara market – while the 'great May fair' of 1846 at Ballycumber produced 'plentiful supplies of pigs and stocks and generally good prices were got'. In addition, the Mullingar market was said to be abundantly supplied with potatoes from King's County.[17] All of this of course begs the question about access to food, even in the early days of the calamity.[18]

Arguably, landlords and agents may have been too far removed from the lower orders to understand that the alleviation of distress was immediately necessary. This was suggested by O'Connor Morris who believed that 'the memory of the distress of 1818–22 led many of the county's proprietors to believe that the failure of the potato crop would be short lived'. In his opinion, this was 'not heartlessness but the dangerous ignorance of a class kept apart from the classes beneath it'.[19] At Lusmagh Henry L'Estrange witnessed the early ambiguity of a destroyed potato crop amid an abundant oat crop and reported that unless relief works were put in place the labouring class would not be able to afford to buy the latter.[20] Significantly, the real problem in early 1846 was the scarcity of seed potatoes for the following season.[21] Although there had been frequent failures of the potato crop in the past, it is probably true to say that, in general, this generation of land agents were at a loss as how to react. This was equally true of their employers and nowhere was it more obvious than the case of Lord Rosse, lord lieutenant of King's County, who mishandled the initial investigations into the effect of the potato blight in the county. Rosse, it appears, misinterpreted the reports that were sent to him, which included, among others, an informative account by Francis Berry. According to Berry a third of the potato crop was lost and he feared 'excitements if not disturbances' would result if there were further crop failures.[22] Rosse subsequently reported to Dublin Castle that he believed that only a third of the crop was injured and that not more than a ninth of the potato crop would be lost.

15/21049 & 15/1453). See also *Times*, 27 Oct. 1845.   **16** *KCC*, 31 Dec. 1845. Another report noted that large numbers were emigrating from the barony of Clonlisk and from Philipstown. See *Times*, 17 Oct. 1845.   **17** *KCC*, 6 May 1846. See also *Papers relating to proceedings for the relief of distress, and the state of Unions and Workhouses in Ireland. Seventh series, 1847–48* [919] [955] [999], p. 29.   **18** Extracts from the diaries of Lydia Goodbody (in private possession). O'Neill has argued that there was a certain level of comfort, evident in the deposits in the banks in Parsonstown and Tullamore in 1846 and 1847. See O'Neill, 'The Famine in Offaly', pp 684 and 721.   **19** O'Connor Morris, *Memories*, p. 88.   **20** O'Neill, 'The Famine in Offaly', p. 687.   **21** This was later confirmed by the constabulary of the police at Ballymacwilliam, in the barony of Warrenstown, who reported that the poorer classes had not sown potatoes in conacre because of a want of seed. See 'Constabulary returns on the potato crop, 24 May 1846' (RLFC, 2/41/11).   **22** Francis Berry to Lord Rosse, 21 Nov. 1845 (RLFC, 2/441/15).

While the reality of the situation was lost on the county's major landowners, responsibility also lay with the new landlord class of merchants, shopkeepers and farmers who had emerged in the previous decade. An examination of the records of the Brosna Drainage Scheme of the 1840s, for example, highlights the large number of shopkeepers and merchants who had invested in King's County in the decade prior to the Famine, buying small parcels of land and letting them at exorbitant prices. These people cared, or knew, little of the plight of the people that populated their minute holdings. In addition, the number of landed estates in King's County that were under the care of institutions, schools and colleges militated against any cohesive relief mechanism among agents. Although many of these estates were relatively small, they contained a large population on which some degree of management was necessary.[23] For example, tenants on the estates of Mercers Hospital were described as being 'generally comfortable', although there was regular conflict between agent and tenant over the payment of rent.[24] The Commissioners of Education, another of the large landowners who generally left tenants to their own devices. To oversee the running of these properties the commissioners appointed a secretary who brought to the board, the queries and problems of the various agents who were appointed to individual estates. Although styled as agents these men were allowed to make a profit from the return of rent and cared little for the tenantry in their care. At Banagher, where tenants held at will, the agent Philip Drought exercised little control nor indeed offered any advice on improvement; accounts were settled bi-annually and no agriculturalist was sent to educate the tenantry.[25] The fortunes of tenants residing on the lands of the Erasmus Smith schools were not much better.[26]

Meanwhile, in an effort to come to terms with the impending calamity, agents in King's County began to issue instructions to tenants on caring for potatoes and on how to prevent the spread of disease, and, as in the case of Grogan, they also advised on the construction of storage pits.[27] George Heenan, Lord Rosse's agent, allowed tenants 3½d. for their rotten potatoes, provided that they would pit those potatoes which were deemed to have escaped the blight. Frederick

---

23 The fate of these tenants living on estates owned by institutions/schools has been largely overlooked by historians to date. See also 'Rent-ledger and miscellaneous accounts of the estate of Henry Palmer, King's County, 1794–1812' (NLI, MS 14,284). 24 *Devon Commission*, p. 615. 25 Ibid., p. 79. The largest estate in Ireland at the time belonged to Trinity College Dublin who held over 195,000 acres and was among the largest landowners in the British Isles. The King's County estates included 2,271 acres at Clareen which were given as a bequest by the provost of the college, Richard Baldwin, in 1758. These estates were said to be among the worst managed in Ireland. For more on the management of these estates see Robert McCarthy, *The Trinity College Estates, 1800–1923: corporate management in an age of reform* (Dundalk, 1992). 26 *Report from Commission of board of education in Ireland on schools founded by Erasmus Smith*, HC 1810 [194], x, appendix 2, pp 22–7. On the eve of the Famine the school owned 10,452 acres located in counties Tipperary, Limerick, Sligo, Westmeath, Galway, Clare and King's County, with an annual rental of £6,717. 27 Joseph Grogan to Stewart & Kincaid, 21 Dec. 1845 (S & KA).

8 William Parsons (1800–67), third earl of Rosse
(courtesy of Offaly Historical Society)

Ponsonby's agent, James Devery, reported that the disease in the potato crop was very general at Cloghan but sent Swedish or common turnip seed and oats to the tenants. Devery warned that although the potatoes looked healthy and promised a good yield, 'so speedy is the change and so rapid its progress' one could not foretell the future.[28] As we shall see below, the problem, as elsewhere, was that there seemed to have been plenty of food to feed the starving but no channels or goodwill to distribute it. Despite the distress, food continued to be exported, causing great consternation among the lower classes. George Crampton reported that as an agent of several estates, including William Carter's property at Eglish, he had received threats about the exportation of corn.[29] Significantly, as a result of such threats and violence some landlords and their agents refused to oversee the importation and distribution of relief. W.B. Armstrong of Garrycastle House, near Banagher, suspended the importation of Indian corn and meal because he feared for his safety and felt he could not prevent the food being stolen. 'As government have left everything to private enterprise they will be sadly disappointed as individuals will not import where not satisfied of

---

28 'Cloghan report'. 29 William Carter, Castle Martin, Kilcullen, Co. Kildare to relief commissioners, 22 Mar. 1846 (RLFC, 2/Z5616).

protection and safety' he noted.[30] Elsewhere, agents were anxious to learn as to
what their counterparts were doing to avert the disaster. In particular they
watched to see what the professional land agencies were engaging in (although
some merely did so as a means to learn better methods of forcing payment of
rent or how those agencies handled eviction and clearance).[31]

Francis Berry was one of the first agents to take the initiative in calling for
relief works in an effort to alleviate distress. In the spring of 1846 he pleaded
with Lord Rosse to initiate public works and to build roads from Tullamore to
the nearby villages of Durrow and Killeigh. Prior to this Rosse had urged
caution, noting that the people should repot the potato seeds and wait for the
next harvest. While it appears that Rosse was frequently ignorant of the plight
of the lower classes (as late as July 1846 he claimed that there was little distress
in the county),[32] his family gave generously to the Parsonstown relief committee
and also contributed to other committees where their estates were located.[33]
Such efforts were applauded by Sir Randolph Routh, who oversaw the distribution of relief in Ireland, and who believed that Rosse's 'excellent judgment and
character' would do much for the state of the county.[34] However, there were
others like the Revd Henry Tyrrell at Kinnitty who believed that Rosse was
'taking care of his own' in contrast to neighbouring landlords who employed
great numbers and increased wages, and that 'all according to their ability have
done the same'.[35] By and large King's County landlords made similar gestures or
at least involved themselves in some form of activity that suggested their
concern for the plight of the destitute.[36] But there still existed the need to do
more. Horatio Darby, addressing the Parsonstown Farming Society, urged
members to practice 'self denial', pull together and give as much employment as
possible.[37] Some answered the call: Henry L'Estrange's daughter provided work
for 100 women spinning and knitting at Moystown, while Thomas Manifold
offered to mill flour free of charge for the Kinnitty relief committee.[38]

---

30 W.B. Armstrong to relief commissioners, 20 Oct. 1846 (RLFC, 3/2/15/20). 31 Martin
Kelly, Athlone to Thomas Roberts, 19 Sept. 1848 (OPW/NUI Maynooth Archive & Research
Centre, Strokestown Park Archive). 32 Earl of Rosse to relief commissioners, Dublin Castle,
4 July 1846 (RLFC, 3/1/1266). 33 Lord Rosse to William Stanley, 6 Jan. 1847 (RLFC,
2/441/41). 34 *Correspondence explanatory from failure of potato crop in Ireland*, p. 456.
35 Revd Henry Tyrrell to lord lieutenant, Dublin Castle, 13 Oct. 1846 (RLFC, 2/441/41).
36 For example, William Poole, a landlord and middleman at Clonsast, inquired whether relief
for labourers with large families could be given in addition to public works. See William Poole to
relief commissioners, 11 Nov. 1846 (RLFC, 3/2/15/36). See also *KCC*, 17 Mar. 1847. 37
Ibid., 21 Oct. 1846. 38 Henry L'Estrange to relief commissioners, 2 Feb. 1847 (RLFC,
3/2/15/21). Ironically, some years previously Manifold was one of those who protested against
the importation of foreign goods to King's County when he was one of several millers in the
county who presented a petition to the House of Lords calling for the importation of flour to be
suspended in an effort to protect local interests. See *House of Lords debate*, 18 Mar. 1842, vol. 61,
c835.

By the summer of 1846 the crisis in King's County was deepening, and for many agents reality now dawned. According to one report 'all the horrors of starvation will be experienced by half at least of the population'.[39] Remarkably, as the Revd Henry Tyrrell of Kinnitty noted, although potatoes were no longer available for human consumption and provisions were dear the people remained 'quiet and patient'.[40] However, there were areas outside Kinnitty where the destitute were less patient. Those most in need decided to pawn whatever possessions they had and their desperation was seen in the establishment of pawn shops in Banagher, Tullamore and Parsonstown.[41] The Revd Robert Healy of Eglish appealed for help as there was 'no employment for the destitute and no food to appease the cravings of hunger'.[42] It was a similar situation at Clara where Lydia Goodbody noted that there was 'general humiliation on account of the failure of the potato crop'.[43] It was clear to many observers that this was a population on the brink of disaster. A threatening notice posted at Philipstown in October 1846 warned that if the poor were not soon supplied with relief that they would 'resort to harsh measures'.[44] By December many in the town were reported to be surviving on boiled turnips.[45] That same month the Edenderry workhouse, built to provide shelter for 600 inmates, was accommodating nearly 1,800 'wretched souls'. The Edenderry board of guardians petitioned the government for help, noting that 'distress daily increases among all classes of the poor'.[46] It was hardly unexpected, given the Revd James Colgan's admission that 'families are in a pitiable condition'.[47] It may seem strong then, in the midst of such deprivation, that Thomas Murray oversaw a collection for a memorial statue to the late Lord Downshire who had died in September 1845.[48]

Significantly, there was at this stage little collective effort made by the gentry or their agents to alleviate distress even though they had begun to realize that this was no ordinary crisis.[49] Conscientious agents had to contend with the miserliness of merchants, shopkeepers and meal jobbers and those who stocked piled goods to increase prices.[50] There were varied responses on how to deal with such

---

39 Quoted in O'Neill, 'The Famine in Offaly', p. 686.   **40** Revd Henry Tyrrell to William Stanley, 13 Oct. 1846 (RLFC, 2/441/41).   **41** William J. Smyth, 'The role of towns and cities in the Great Irish Famine' in John Crowley, William J. Smyth & Mike Murphy (eds), *Atlas of the Great Famine* (Cork, 2012), p. 248.   **42** Quoted in Pey (ed.), *Eglish*, pp 114–15.   **43** 'Diary of Lydia Goodbody, Nov. 1846' (in private possession).   **44** Ibid., 21 Oct. 1846.   **45** Ibid., 2 Dec. 1846.   **46** *Correspondence relating to state of union workhouses in Ireland*, p. 21, HC 1847 [766] [790] [863] lv. 27, 141, 231.   **47** Revd James Colgan, Edenderry to relief commissioners, 31 Mar. 1846 (RLFC, 3/1/1098).   **48** *LE*, 24 Oct. 1846. This report noted how a full-length statue of Downshire was erected in Edenderry 'ordered by his Edenderry tenantry'. It can, the paper noted, 'be seen for miles on the approach roads to the town. Little if any distress has been felt among the tenantry'.   **49** Neale Browne to lord lieutenant, Dublin Castle, 25 Sept. 1846 (OPKC, 1846, 15/25911).   **50** In March 1846 Pat Kelly, a member of the Ordnance Survey working at Eglish, outlined the problems in that locality, highlighting the general behaviour of the local community: 'the people of the parish are bordering on starvation but to their detriment food jobbers are withholding food and will not help their neighbours'. See *LE*, 7 Mar. 1846.

9 Statue of Arthur Hills, third marquis of Downshire, erected by his Edenderry tenantry, 1855 (courtesy of Offaly Historical Society)

destitution. The Edenderry board of guardians proposed the establishment of more soup kitchens.[51] By January 1847, after being refused permission for such a plan, the guardians took a stronger stance and questioned the mode of relief that was being granted. Dr Richard Grattan, a poor law guardian, believed that while drainage and other public works schemes were beneficial, they were not capable of feeding the masses.[52] This lack of soup kitchens and food depots was highlighted by Francis Berry, who headed the Ballycowan, Geashill and Killoughy relief committee: 'our poorhouse is full; nay it has 201 more than it

51 *Correspondence relating to state of union workhouses in Ireland*, p. 22. Their suggestion it seems was not acted on to any great extent in other areas. In fact very few soup kitchens were ever established in King's County, with the exception of, for example, those at Brosna, Clonmacnoise, Cadamstown and Dunkerrin. 52 Ibid., p. 23.

was intended for. The wretches would merely commit a crime to have themselves put in jail'. Berry and his wife provided soup for the poor of Tullamore from recipes given by Lady Charleville.[53] Unfortunately, such benevolence was limited.[54] However, quite frequently, their efforts were thwarted by the tenants' lack of education. When one landowner procured a shipload of rice, 'universal dissatisfaction was expressed regarding the new food, because it crunched under the teeth of the eaters. They had devoured it uncovered'.[55]

Thus, the early stages of the Famine in King's County were characterized by haphazard attempts at relief by agents and landlords, as they tried to come to terms with the deepening crisis. A typical nationalist interpretation of landlords and agents during the Famine in King's County contends that they did little to alleviate the plight of their tenants;[56] this is too much of a generalization. Certainly it was the case that some agents feared the effect that providing relief might have in attracting paupers from other localities. For example, Thomas Murray feared the prospect of paupers and beggars flooding into the town of Edenderry. Such a prospect seemed likely in light of John James Pomeroy's request for Indian corn for 2,500 souls on his brother's estate at neighbouring Carbury, Co. Kildare.[57] Murray's fears prevailed throughout the county. A Board of Works' engineer criticized landlords for acting 'like the besiegers of a town in starving them [smallholders and cottiers] out' in an attempt to place the impoverished on the relief list.[58] Such criticism was, it appears, warranted, and landlords and their agents in some instances added to the problem. Petty squabbling in parishes and baronies about who was responsible for various areas also hindered relief. This squabbling was essentially about boundaries and administration, on which agreement could not be reached. For example, Lord Rosse was instrumental in the establishment of relief committees for each barony and took it upon himself to organize them. However, several areas were left without assistance. There was considerable resentment with Rosse's refusal to divide the barony of Lower Philipstown into three relief districts after an attempt at establishing a committee at Croghan failed.[59]

Elsewhere local rivalries and a reluctance to establish a single relief committee for each of the baronies of Ballycowan, Geashill and Kilcoursey delayed the provision of relief to a large part of the county's population.[60] It was unrealistic

---

53 Francis Berry to relief commissioners, 8 Dec. 1846 (RLFC, 3/2/15/12).   54 Despairingly, by this stage Lord Rosse admitted that little over six weeks of provisions remained in the county and feared for the outcome: *Correspondence explanatory of measures adopted by Her Majesty's Government for relief of distress arising from failure of potato crop in Ireland*, HC 1846 [735] xxxvii, 41, p. 456.   55 Freeman-Attwood, *Leap Castle*, p. 85.   56 Ryan, *A land by the river of God*, p. 130.   57 John James Pomeroy to relief commissioners, 30 Mar. 1846 (RLFC, 3/1/1126).   58 Ryan, *A land by the river of god*, p. 130.   59 Lord Rosse to relief commissioners, Nov. 1846 (RLFC, 3/2/15). By 1848 eighteen committees were formed throughout the county.   60 Ibid., 7 Apr. 1846 (RLFC, 3/1/1266).

to expect that the one committee established for these three baronies would be able to carry out the necessary work. This was particularly true of the barony of Geashill, where Henry Norewood Trye reported that the lack of relief gave rise to the suffering of a 'miserable and mutinous' population.[61] There, the Revd Wingfield Digby refused to raise funds for the baronies of Ballycowan and Kilcoursey and so set up his own relief committee in 1846. Likewise, Henry Sheane set up a committee at Lusmagh to relieve the plight of over 1,000 starving tenants, but the committee split from that at Banagher over the appoint-ment of a chairman.[62] Other squabbles were of a personal or a religious nature; at Parsonstown, Captain Thomas Cox tried to keep the Catholic priest, the Revd Spain, from becoming a member of the relief committee.[63] This failure to organize properly in order to systematically engage with the crisis and the relative degree of pettiness over geographical considerations led to fundamental difficulties that might have been avoided had landlords, agents and others worked together. The success of interdenominational collaboration at Clonbullogue, where in September 1846 the Revd Henry Joly and his Roman Catholic counterpart, the Revd Dunne, managed to raise subscriptions and tend to those most in need, were, unfortunately, isolated cases.[64] Such collaboration may have been suggested by Joly's friend, Christopher Hamilton, agent of the Gifford and Tyrrell estates (which Jasper Robert Joly later inherited through marriage), who actively sought the assitance of the local Roman Catholic clergy during the Famine in maintaining 'some degree of social control on the estate'.[65] While there were agents such as George Heenan and Francis Berry who engaged in relief, there were equally those who were apathetic. For example, John Hussey Walsh noted that there was an 'inability' or 'reluctance' on the part of agents in the barony of Lower Philipstown to subscribe to relief efforts.[66] This reluctance was shared by George Garvey who believed that there was no need to overspend. When the Nenagh poor law guardians proposed £4,000 for relief works in Upper Ormond (which also impacted on King's County), Garvey was the only dissenting voice, arguing that twenty-five per cent of that figure would be plenty. His objection was revealing when he went on to state that there would be 'no publicity in giving a larger sum'. This case highlighted the major problem – there was too much emphasis on frugality when investment might have saved more lives.[67] Had landlords and agents been prepared to collaborate in relief measures at barony level rather than concentrating on their own estates, more progress might have been made in terms of the relief of hardship.

61 Henry Norewood Trye, secretary, Geashill relief committee to relief commissioners, 7 Nov. 1846 (RLFC, 3/2/15/29). 62 Henry Sheane to William Stanley, 4 Nov. 1846 (RLFC, 2/441/41). 63 Capt. Thomas Cox to Revd John Spain, n.d (RLFC, 3/2/15/8). 64 Joly Diary NLI, 5 Nov. 1846. 65 Ballinderry papers (In private possession). 66 John Hussey Walsh to relief commissioners, 9 July 1846 (RLFC, 3/2/15/32). 67 Daniel Grace, *The Great Famine in Nenagh Poor Law Union, County Tipperary* (Nenagh, 2000), pp 74–5.

Moreover, too few land agents were appointed executive members of relief committees; positions, it seems, were filled by members of the 'class specified' by the relief commissioners' guidelines – primarily Church of Ireland and Roman Catholic clergy. Indeed, Francis Berry, one of the few agents who chaired a relief committee and who was described by Lord Rosse as 'a man of excellent character', only did so because of the lack of a resident gentry.[68] Agents who knew the local community would have been better placed to serve on relief committees. This may have compensated for the lack of landlord representation.[69] However, in a number of cases agents did not possess sufficient knowledge to impart to the tenantry. George Heenan, for example, did not, it seems, adequately inform the tenantry about how to use or prepare Indian meal, which ultimately made the situation worse as tenants then ate the meal unprocessed.[70] This lack of knowledge meant that starving tenants soon lost trust in the agent and looked elsewhere for help. Tenants on the Tyrrell estate near Castlejordan, for example, bypassed the agent when petitioning for relief.[71] Widespread frustration among the lower orders and increased hardship meant that secret societies and mobs – often one and the same – involved themselves in attempts to secure food. There were dangers with the transporting of meal and other foodstuffs along the canals because of the 'nightly depredations', meaning that the carts were often attacked.[72] When the relief works at Clareen were cancelled in June 1846 the labourers protested, stating that 'they would not die like cowards, all we want is work so as not to be allowed to starve. If we don't get that we will be obliged to procure food with the bayonet'.[73] That same month 150 tenants visited Lord Rosse's demesne looking to have over 40 men put to work, and if not they threatened to go to Parsonstown and take what they could. The threat was obviously taken seriously as a special guard, coordinated by the agent George Heenan, was formed among the townspeople who pledged their support to prevent disturbance.[74] The incident also displayed the deference of the local community towards their landlord even in times of severe want. As food and provisions became scarce, predictably the crime rate rose. Special guards like those established at Parsonstown were not enough to stop a famished population.

68 Earl of Rosse to relief commissioners, 14 May 1846 (RLFC, 3/1/2290). 69 For example, Richard Gamble who served as treasurer and secretary of the Killoughy relief committee, which at its height catered for over 2,300 people, criticised absentees such as Charles Molloy and Henry Kemmis, calling on them to contribute 'if they had the welfare of the country at heart'. See Richard Gamble to the Killoughy proprietors, 1848 (NAI, Gamble papers, M 3493). 70 George Heenan to relief commissioners, 27 June 1846 (RLFC, 3/1/3740). 71 Louisa Gifford to Christopher Hamilton, n.d (Ballinderry papers, in private possession). 72 In June the Revd Walsh of Lusmagh dispersed a crowd of 800 men gathered in search of food and employment, but who possessed it was feared menacing intent. See W.B. Armstrong to relief commissioners, 20 Oct. 1846 (RLFC, 3/2/15/20). 73 Ibid. 74 Lord Rosse to lord lieutenant, Dublin Castle, June 1846 (OPKC, 1846). A list of those who pledged support to the Defence Committee is included in the file.

By 1847 an average of eight robberies a day were reported in King's County, while many more went unrecorded.[75] It was little wonder then that J.W. Armstrong sought police protection, stating that he was willing to import 1,000 tonnes of corn or meal to his mills at Banagher if such could be given.[76] A number of flour carts were attacked at Lemanaghan, Ballycumber, while further plunder and intimidation occurred in Ferbane where whole fields of turnips were stolen.[77] Elsewhere, crowds gathered to protest about flour leaving the country.[78] In most cases their protests fell on deaf ears.

Travelling through the county in 1847 Alexander Somerville noted that the people of Parsonstown had broken the bridge leading from the town to prevent meal, intended for exportation, from reaching Shannon Harbour. Without any pity, Somerville noted that 'the peasantry here are very ignorant', failing to mention that they were also starving.[79] Even those fortunate enough to avail of a place on the public works schemes were said to be among the most wretched. John Keegan's recollections of those working on schemes in the barony of Clonlisk reflected this:

> It is melancholy to witness the bad effects which the relief works and the doling out of the wretched Indian meal have on the morals and feelings of the unfortunate peasantry. That delicate and commendable pride, which made them formerly conceal their wants, is gone, and has given place to a shameless clamour for relief and 'yellow meal'. Poverty, grinding poverty, and starvation have broken spirits, humiliated and debased them.

While Keegan's account once again raises the issue of culpability, the journal of James Dillon, the county coroner, offers another remarkable insight into the social conditions of the time and further illustrates the world in which the land agent worked.[80] Dillon conducted well over a thousand inquests in King's County during the Famine – perhaps only a fraction of the deaths that occurred in the county at this time. In carrying out inquests Dillon was joined by land agents George Heenan and John Corcoran in his duties and his journal highlights some of the deprivations which the inhabitants of King's County endured during the late 1840s, while also provoking questions about some unexplored aspects with regard to the Famine. Many of the deaths for which

75 *Correspondence relating to measures for relief of distress in Ireland (Board of Works series), January–March 1847*, HC 1847 [764] 1.1, p. 110. **76** J.W. Armstrong to General Routh, 17 Oct. 1846 (RLFC, 2/441/41). See also OPKC, 1846 15/29325. **77** *FJ*, 11 Dec. 1846; 2 Mar. 1847 & 2 Feb. 1848. The term 'vailing' was used to describe digging up of potatoes and turnips illegally during the Famine. **78** Neal Browne, Tullamore to Dublin Castle, Nov. 1846 (OPKC, 1846, 15/30075) **79** K.D.M. Snell (ed.), *Letters from Ireland during the Famine of 1847* (Dublin, 1994), p. 171. **80** 'Journal of James Dillon, King's County Coroner, 1846–53' (ORC).

Dillon held inquests may well have been as a result of suicide. According to the coroner's verdicts many people were reported to have 'casually' fallen into water and bog holes. These included John Stapleton who 'fell into' the Grand Canal at Sragh, near Tullamore, in May 1846; three months later Michael Connell 'casually' drowned in the Cushina river near Clonsast, while Charles Fitzgerald at Edenderry committed suicide in 1849 by hanging himself from a tree. There were others too, like Thomas Brien of Doon, who died from the 'overuse of ardent spirits' but, of course, the vast majority succumbed to hunger, fever and cold. Most were simply recorded as having died from the 'visitation of god'. In some instances inquests were carried out on only 'part of the body', indicating perhaps that animals had eaten the corpse.

As distress grew, crimes became more aggressive and progressed from attacking food carts to threatening and attacking landlords and agents. In December 1846 William Lloyd, a landlord, was shot dead at the door of his home in Parsonstown after having served an eviction notice on several tenants who had failed to pay their rent.[81] Another landowner, Owen Power, was murdered in April 1847 in a riot near Parsonstown that had its roots in the issue of access to conacre.[82] The ubiquitous threatening letters – the preferred method of intimidation in Famine Ireland – increasingly were addressed to land agents and their staff. A notice posted on the door of Busherstown House, the residence of George Minchin, threatened the landlord with death if he did not change the system of managing his property. As a result Minchin quit the country, which of course naturally affected those under his direct care.[83] Likewise, Philip Fanning, an agent at Clonlisk, was attacked because his occupation was deemed 'obnoxious'.[84] It was allegedly a characteristic shared by John Watson, sub-agent of the Holmes estate, who suffered repeated attacks following his instruction to tenants that 'the less they said the better for them'.[85] In 1846 a petition from tenants at Ballyboy complained that 'the gentry of our parish are negligent in our regard and the farmers who could not go to the helm of relief and shout for work and hire, they will not because they are wallowing in the riches of this world'.[86] Again, these sentiments also raise the issue of culpability – that large farmers did very little to relieve the plight of their less well off cottier neighbours.

As the Famine wore on, land agents soon turned their attention to these once 'snug farmers' and middlemen. In March 1847 many of the tenants on the

---

81 *The sessional papers presented by order of the House of Lords*, 10 and 11 Victoria, Session 1847, p. 71. 82 Ibid., p. 39. 83 *KCC*, 10 Dec. 1845. Indeed, King's County ranked the ninth highest in Ireland in 1846 for the number of threatening letters which were sent. See also *A return of all murders that have been committed in Ireland since the 1st of January 1842*, HC 1846 [220] xxxv, 293. 84 *Returns relative to Homicides (Ireland)*, HC 1846 [363] xxxv, 273, p. 3. 85 John Watson to George Greeson, 10 Jan. 1842 (Greeson papers). See, for example, *Return of assaults, incendiary fires, robbery of arms, administering of unlawful oaths, threatening letters, malicious injury to property and firing into dwelling, 1845–46*, HC 1846 [369] xxxv, 181, p. 17. 86 'Ballyboy petition' (OPKC, 1846).

Holmes estate at Shinrone pleaded with the agent, George Greeson, for
leniency:

> We the under mentioned tenants on the Kilcommon estate having been
> served with processes for arrears of rent submit their cases severally to
> your consideration hoping that in the present cases you will not take
> proceedings against them as this year in particular is turning out a year
> of severe hardship for the potatoes. We expected [we] could hold the
> summer's provisions for ourselves and for families. Should you proceed
> against us generally we do not know what we will do in the present trying
> circumstances, so we humbly hope your honour will consider us in the
> present cases for which we are duty bound to pay.[87]

How Greeson acted on this occasion is not recorded, but by 1849 many of the
large farmers on the estate had been evicted. It was little wonder then that
threats towards land agents and estate personal continued unabated. Edward
Russell, Thomas Bernard's bailiff, was assaulted by disgruntled and starving
tenants.[88] A landlord named Smith and his steward at Annville were threatened
that they would be murdered if they did not employ more people, while a sub-
agent Quinn was fired at by two men at Killishin, near Philipstown, as he carried
out his duties for the absentee Mr Dillon of Dublin.[89] Amid continued outrages,
the *Nenagh Guardian* newspaper, which was also widely circulated in King's
County, queried whether 'anything could be done to put a stop to such proceedings?'[90] Evidence of the fear that existed among land agents can be seen from the
fact that George Garvey now required an armed escort at all times and carried a
double-barrelled pistol in his possession. He survived a number of attempts on
his life during the Famine.[91]

Despite the high levels of destitution and the breakdown in law and order,
Henry Sheane, agent of the Bell estate at Banagher, noted the complete reluctance
of the poor to enter the workhouse, many of whom would sooner 'die in the ditch
rather than go there'.[92] However, many were soon left with no choice. By this stage
Famine relief schemes were deemed to have been largely ineffective.[93] When the
dredging of the River Shannon scheme at Banagher ended, hundreds of starving
workers streamed into the town in the 'most pitiable condition'.[94] The problems

87 'Petition of Michael Dooley, James Bourke, John Flannery and others to George Greeson, 23
Mar. 1846' (Greeson papers). 88 *KCC*, 11 Mar. 1846. 89 *Times*, 4 Jan. 1847.
90 *Nenagh Guardian*, 11 Nov. 1846. 91 Ibid., 8 & 15 Mar. 1848. 92 Henry Sheane to relief
commissioners, 23 July 1846 (RLFC, 3/1/4653). 93 Peter Gray, *Famine, land and politics:
British government and Irish society* (Dublin, 1996), p. 133. These schemes were first introduced
in January 1846 following the passing of the Public Works (Ireland) Act in the House of
Commons. 94 Henry Sheane to relief commissioners, 14 July 1846 (RLFC, 3/2/15/22). A
similar situation was reported at Kinnitty. See John Stothard to John Burke, 27 May 1846 (NAI,
Quit Rent Office papers, 2B/39/29).

at Banagher were said to have been exacerbated by the 'ways and customs of the people'. According to Sheane the 'labouring poor rented plots at £20 an acre, built an average of twenty cabins per acre and refused to leave hovels in search of work'. These problems mirrored those experienced by Frederick Ponsonby's agent at Cloghan, James Devery, who complained that despite a relief committee being set up for the parish of Gallen, nothing had been done and he requested that he should be sold Indian meal from the store in Banagher in order to feed the poor of the area.[95] Devery hit on a crucial point when he lamented that all the able-bodied workers in the district were employed at 'fair wages' but that their earnings were not enough to purchase food for their families, probably owing to the inflated price of provisions being charged by merchants and others.[96] There were, of course, other reasons propounded for this continued malady. In February 1847 a reporter in King's County, claiming that the tenant farmers were 'unwilling to work', which probably should have read 'unfit to work', went on to state that there was an 'appearance and colour [on] their faces which is sickening to behold' and that 'unless these people are supplied with seed and the means of sowing it the land will lay waste'.[97] There were also cases whereby some landlords and agents refused to allow tenants to apply for or receive relief. This was often a case of pride before a fall. For example, John A. Burdett, a landlord at Coolfin, near Ferbane, stated that he would not allow any of his tenants to take relief because, as their landlord, he was responsible for them.[98]

However, not every landowner buried his head in the sand like Burdett. The earl of Portarlington urged his agent John Sadlier to promote better agricultural practices among his tenants in an effort to relieve distress.[99] Believing that local farmers could also be helped by agricultural instruction, the Revd Henry Joly did likewise, enlisting the services of a Mr Cronly from Rathangan, Co. Kildare. Described simply as a 'teacher of land', Cronly instructed farmers in Clonsast in dealing with the potato blight and in adopting new farming practices.[1] On the Joly estate a large variety of crops were grown including cabbage, curled cale, cauliflower, orange and Belgian carrots, broccoli and Dutch turnips. On their home farm fruits planted included cantaloupe melon, peaches, pears and artichokes, which were said to have grown 'quite well'.[2] Moreover, the potato varieties they grew, such as the 'Bangor' and 'Oxford noble', were less affected by blight than the dreaded 'lumper'. These initiatives remained isolated ventures, and it was not until the spring of 1847 that King's County landlords and agents met at Tullamore as a united body to discuss the plight of the tenantry. This meeting, chaired by Francis Berry, discussed the best and the

95 James Devery to relief commissioners, 2 June 1846 (RLFC 3/1/2784). **96** Ibid. See also Donnelly Jr, *The Great Irish potato Famine*, pp 68–9. **97** Quoted in Ryan, *A land by the river of god*, p. 130. **98** Pey (ed.), *Eglish*, p. 111. **99** *KCC*, 3 Feb. 1847. **1** Joly Diary, 24 Nov. 1846 (NLI, MS 17,035). On other occasions Joly gave seed potatoes to the poor or those adversely affected by the blight. **2** Ibid., 17 Feb. 1847.

most productive way forward in assisting the small farmers in the sowing of oats and the planting of potatoes.[3] Again, crucially, there existed a major problem in this regard as the small farmers were said to be holding back oats and other crops from the markets in the hope that they would get a better price in the future.[4] However, despite these moves to grow alternative crops, many farmers soon returned to the potato crop.[5]

Under increased pressure and more frequently the target of violence, agents became critical of their landlord employers. George Garvey told a meeting in Moneygall, called to help those who were starving, that although it wasn't the duty of the magistrates to provide employment they should reach into their pockets. In particular, he called upon the Revd William Minchin to make a liberal contribution to the relief of destitution. Minchin replied that because he had a large family to support and having already provided employment he was not in a position to do so. He subsequently left the meeting when Garvey reminded him that it was in his interest to give employment and that he only paid his workers 6*d.* per day, far below what some landlords were offering. As a means of influencing others to join the relief effort, Garvey offered to supply one tonne of grain from his own supply, and that Lord Bloomfield and Mrs Holmes would do likewise.[6] But some landlords had their own stereotypical impressions of what they perceived to be a lazy tenantry unwilling to help themselves, none more so than Lord Rosse, who believed that the tenant farmers of King's County were 'unsuited to work' and thus perhaps relief works were not the best method of solving the crisis. For him smallholders were 'little accustomed to work' and thus would be reluctant to join the public work scheme.[7] However, the overall figures of those employed on relief projects in the county contradicted somewhat the foregoing statements – the numbers rising from 718 at the beginning of July 1846 to over 3,750 by the end of that month.[8] By the end of 1847 this number had risen to 12,557.[9] Significantly, nearly twenty per cent of those employed were from the barony of Ballyboy, which had a number of merchant/shopkeeper landlords who were unable or perhaps reluctant to offer assistance directly to their tenants.

While the administration of relief was largely controlled by landlords and the clergy, many agents were active in the operation of Board of Works schemes, such as drainage, the building of roads and the development of canal harbours and

3 Offaly Historical & Archaeological Society, *Farming in Offaly* (Tullamore, 1987), p. 14.
4 Richard Woods to relief commissioners, Dublin Castle, 4 Dec. 1845 (NAI, RLFC 3/1/114).
5 The potato acreage planted in King's County tripled from 6,500 in 1847 to 20,001 in 1848. Indeed, King's County farmers produced more potatoes per tonne than their counterparts, for example, in Co. Cork in 1847 and 1849.   6 *Tipperary Vindicator*, 19 Mar. 1846. He also established a soup kitchen at Laughton near Lord Bloomfield's residence in Moneygall. See George Garvey to relief commissioners, Mar. 1847 (RLFC, 3/2/15).   7 Lord Rosse to William Stanley, 6 Jan. 1847 (RLFC, 2/441/41).   8 *Commissioners of Public Works (Ireland), fourteenth report*, HC 1847 [762] xvii, 457.   9 *Return of Advance under 10 Vict., c.32. PP, 1847–8, lvii.*

bridges. Agents such as W.J. Reamsbottom at Ballycumber and Paul Fawcett at Rahan spent much of their time overseeing drainage work on the River Brosna, a scheme that was initiated in 1846, and that gave employment to thousands of labourers in the baronies through which it passed.[10] In total, more than 16,500 acres of land were drained in King's County during the Famine. Ultimately, while the scheme improved the value of holdings and estates through which it passed, it also providing much-needed relief work. The careful management of the scheme by engineers and officials of the Board of Works allows for an examination into the work undertaken in the county during the Famine. More importantly, it illuminates on the work of local agents, without who's cooperation such projects could not have been completed. By 1851 the works on the scheme included the construction of a short under watering cut at Moystown; the deepening of the bed of the River Brosna; the building of a weir 500 feet long; the underpinning of Mr Callaghan's mill and the building of a new bridge with three arches. At Ballycumber 1,050 feet of the River Brosna had been opened to an average of six feet in depth, while similar work was undertaken on the River Tullamore. P.J. Klashen reported that it was pleasing to see 'hundreds of acres which were two years ago impassable swamps now tilled and providing crops'. He continued that 'instances are now to be found in many parts of the county where crops had been obtained from such lands, the value of which in one year has been sufficient to repay the whole expense of relieving them from flood'.[11]

Other agents looked to the drainage of land as a means of providing relief and improving the estate. A total of forty-six landlords in King's County applied for advances under the Land Improvement Act of 1847–8.[12] But even the large-scale employment of people was threatened by the inability of agents and tenants to come to agreement over who was entitled to compensation. Tenants affected by the drainage scheme were required, in the presence of their landlord and two independent witnesses, to give their assent to works being carried out on their holding. Naturally, there was widespread allegations of fraud on the part of agents who did not remit the money to their tenants, thus leading to the reluctance of others to cooperate.[13]

What was the fallout for agents in light of their inability or in some cases their reluctance to deal with the crisis? While William Wilde, for example, was complimentary of Thomas Murray's management of the Downshire estate,

---

10 The scheme commenced under the Acts 5 and 6 Vict., c.89–8 and 9 Vict., c.69 and 9 Vict., c.4. The rivers drained included Brosna, Frankford, Clodiagh, Tullamore, Ballyboughin and Cloghatanny. **11** 'Supplemental report to the commissioner showing the present state of the works, the expenditure of the works executed and the total cost of completing the district, Dublin, 1851' (NAI, Office of Public Works, 24194/51). **12** *Correspondence relative to expenditure of advances under Land Improvement Act (Ireland), 1847–8* [423] p. 41. **13** As each landlord was required to send a list of the tenants likely to be affected by the works, the records offer another vista on landholding and indeed is an important genealogical resource for the Famine period.

noting that 'the general appearance of comfort in this district at once bespeaks the encouragement of the landlord and the admirable care of the resident agent', the evidence suggests he was somewhat disingenuous.[14] As noted above, destitution in the Edenderry area was so acute that the workhouse was grossly overcrowded, and while Wilde was complimentary, history has been less so. Indeed, as already noted, writers such as Carleton have portrayed their fictional agents as being men without heart or compassion. Not all were intentionally so and perhaps do not deserve the criticism and odium directed at them as a class in the post-Famine period. First, as has been shown above, there were those who assisted tenants either by direct estate relief or else through their work on committees. In addition, there were, for example, agents such as John Long, sub-agent at the Holmes estate at Ballycumber and Clara, who was apprehensive about carrying through his employers' instructions that would have resulted in evictions for non-payment of rent. Writing in June 1847, Long noted that he had visited the tenants and found them 'all unable to pay anything at present as a great number of them are living on the relief store and if you will forbear till next month I hope you would find no great difficulty to get it'.[15] Obviously, the benevolence of some land agents spared many the fate of eviction.

Remarkably, there were also agents who were relatively successful in collecting rents in these straightened times. For example, Abraham Bagnall, agent on the King estate at Ferbane, although working in the highly troubled barony of Garrycastle, collected almost £3,000 in rent during the years 1845 to 1850.[16] Notably, in the face of large-scale eviction, George Heenan was successful in collecting rent from the tenants on the Rosse estate. Such successes by agents must have been welcomed by their employers, particularly in light of the comments of George Greeson's bailiff, John Carty, who wrote in 1847 that most of the landlords of the county were happy to receive half the rental as there was 'no money in this country'.[17] Naturally, one must consider that the evidence in the forgoing paragraph is based on limited surviving sources relating to the collection of rent in King's County during the Famine. It is probably safe to conclude that the ability of these agents to collect rents was atypical. Much of the other documentary evidence points to resistance and refusal on the part of individual estates, sometimes more organized in a locality, but never coordinated by an anti-rent movement at county level. Undoubtedly, the failure of agents to collect rents was dictated by the inability, or reluctance, of tenants to pay them, but there were cases of large farmers and middlemen who may have taken advantage of the situation in order to avoid payment.[18] In 1850, looking back at the

14 Wilde, *The beauties of the Boyne*, p. 35.   15 John Long to George Greeson, June 1847 (Greeson papers).   16 'Account book of Revd Henry King 1835–50' (NLI, MS 4121). 17 John Carty, Kilcommon to George Greeson, 17 May 1847 (Greeson papers).   18 For a brief mention of this see O'Neill, 'The Famine in Offaly', p. 684.

early years of the Famine, Robert Cassidy contended that there had been a combined effort, spearheaded by large farmers on his estate at Killyon, not to pay rent from 1846.[19] In September of the same year Lord Rosse reported his alarm at the 'vicious confederacy' to restrict the payment of rent.[20] A similar situation existed at Brosna where William Lucas reported in 1846 that his tenants were refusing to pay rents and that he could not secure the services of a bailiff unless the latter was to be offered protection.[21] The protection must not have been forthcoming, however, as Lucas was himself murdered in late 1848. The Roman Catholic clergy also urged tenants not to pay rents and to hold part of their crops for their own subsistence. Some of the more radical priests such as the Revd Devine at Eglish used the opportunity to condemn landlords as 'exterminators', advising people to treat them with contempt.[22]

The opposition to the collection of rent might have been a lot more determined had agents and landlords in the early years of the Famine not addressed the situation by granting abatements or forgiving arrears of rent. For many agents, receiving something from tenants was better than nothing. In October 1845 George Crampton, agent on William Carter's estate at Cloncarbin in the parish of Eglish, cancelled a large amount of arrears and promised to return again in December and make further reductions.[23] Similarly, William Trench of Cangort Park, near Shinrone, remitted to his tenants the hanging gale that was due.[24] The following month Bernard Mullins, of Ballyegan, reduced his rental by one fourth, earning him the title of 'a good landlord'.[25] Lord Ponsonby's agents made reductions in rent on the 'town properties' at Philipstown. Abatements were also granted to the 'improving' tenants on the rural portion of the estate. As a result the *King's County Chronicle* described the Ponsonby family as the 'most indulging and humane landlords [who] have seldom or ever ejected any tenants even when years of arrears have been due'.[26] Some agents believed that it was not in their interests to harass tenants, particularly in a time of distress. Just as John Long appears to have done at Ballycumber, the bailiff Meara did not push tenants on the Holmes estate at Kilcommon, instead allowing them time to gather the rent, convinced that once fair days were over 'those who have not paid would not until the harvest'.[27]

Leniency was also requested and many agents were forced to grant abatements following threats to their lives, as the case of James Haslam at Drumcullen

19 Robert Cassidy to Thomas Redington, 21 Apr. 1850 (OPKC, 1850, 15/351). **20** Lord Rosse to lord lieutenant, Dublin Castle, 7 Sept. 1846 (NAI, CSO, Registered papers box 1389, no. 415292). See also *Morning Chronicle*, 17 Oct. 1847. **21** William Lucas to lord lieutenant, Dublin Castle, 14 Oct. 1846 (OPKC, 1846, 15/27953). **22** Robert Cassidy to lord lieutenant, Dublin Castle, [n.d.] (OPKC, 1849). **23** *KCC*, 22 Oct. 1845. Crampton was a native of Co. Mayo and secretary of the Belmullet relief committee, in one of the worst affected areas of the country. See George Crampton to relief commissioners, 11 Aug. 1846 (RLFC, 3/1/5337). **24** *KCC*, 12 Nov. 1845. **25** Ibid., 10 Dec. 1845. **26** Ibid., 17 Mar. 1847. **27** Ibid., 1 June 1845.

highlighted.[28] Others, of course, were forced to take action. At Moneygall the agent Stephen W. Minchin carried out a number of evictions on his brother's estate at Cooraclevin but did allow the evicted tenants the growing crops in an effort to encourage them to emigrate. Many of the tenants owed upwards of three years rent.[29] By now, and significantly in King's County, it was not just large landowners who were evicting tenants. In December 1846, Joseph Dwyer, a Co. Dublin merchant, who owned just twenty-five acres near Parsonstown, evicted fifteen families, amounting to over 100 people.[30] The scenario was somewhat similar with the middlemen. Largely because they had themselves rents and arrears to pay, middlemen were often less sympathetic to the plight of their under tenants. In June 1846, for example, a middleman near Shinrone took matters into his own hands and forcibly evicted his tenants, setting fire to their cabins.[31]

In the midst of all this suffering there were those who continued with their traditional lifestyles. Francis Berry wryly commented that 'there are three sets of people making fortunes – the corn and flour merchants (Lord John Russell's pets), the coroners who hold inquests on dead bodies and the coffin makers'. Notably, he did not mention that his own extended family would have benefited from transporting the relief stocks along the Grand Canal to Tullamore, Banagher and Shannon Harbour or that his employer, the earl of Charleville, had escaped the ravages of the Famine by going to live in Berlin.[32] Amid letters and appeals for relief, it appears remarkable that the Revd Henry Tyrrell, secretary of the Kinnitty relief committee, looked for funding from the relief commissioners to carry out repairs on his glebe house at Kinnitty.[33] Likewise, John Plunket Joly appears to have been unperturbed by the Famine, or the suffering which must have occurred in the barony of Coolestown in which the family's estate was located. Joly's description of everyday life in King's County during these years contrasts greatly with the scenes of destitution and the daily pleas of the relief committees. In general Joly appears to have been ignorant of the plight of the masses. For example, at the beginning of 1847 he notes in his diary: 'That year is all over, a good one it was, that the next may be as good'.[34] The entry contrasts sharply with the experiences of the Quaker Lydia Goodbody at Clara who recalled a year that was:

---

28 A.W. Gamble to lord lieutenant, Dublin Castle, 1846 (OPKC, 1846, 15/32629). **29** *KCC*, 16 Aug. 1848. Previously, his brother, Charles Henry Minchin, was threatened with death if he did not change the management of his estate where he employed over fifty people. See *Times*, 8 Dec. 1845. **30** Quoted in the *Waterford Chronicle*, 31 Dec. 1846. **31** John Kelly, Shinrone to lord lieutenant, Dublin Castle, 21 June 1846 (OPKC, 1846, 15/4723). **32** Quoted in Mary Molloy, 'Tullamore during the Famine' (Unpublished manuscript, ORC), p. 23. **33** Revd Henry Tyrrell, Kinnitty to relief commissioners, 23 June 1846 (RLFC, 3/1/3562). **34** See Reilly, *John Plunket Joly*, p. 7.

fraught with circumstances the most remarkable ... the almost total failure of the potato crop which blossomed beautifully with every appearance of abundance but in one night a blast had visibly taken place which caused the plant gradually to decay from the uppermost part of the stalk down to the root ... Famine now exists beyond what can be remembered by the oldest man.[35]

Her experiences, however, did not reflect those of the King's County gentry at large. In his memoirs William O'Connor Morris recalls that he had been left the owner of an 'embarrassed legacy' during the Famine and that his family had done much to relieve the plight of their tenants despite not having the resources to do so.[36] Yet in January 1846 the *King's County Chronicle* reported on the lavish dinner that was hosted at the family home of Mount Pleasant to celebrate the coming of age of William himself. It was reported that upwards of 160 people enjoyed the meal that was served and 'a merry and well prolonged dance, in which our national character for fun was well kept up'.[37] Likewise, in February 1847 a lavish dinner was celebrated and attended by upwards of 150 people at Thomastown House for the coming of age of Francis Bennett.[38] Two years later, the *Tipperary Vindicator* reported that whole districts were being cleared of smallholders and landless labourers at the same time as Francis Bennett was throwing a feast for all the tenants at his estate, at which it was once again reported that nothing was spared.[39] Elsewhere, a 'Ball and Supper' were celebrated at Tisaran, the home of Edmund L'Estrange, in August 1846, while Mr Armstrong of Balliver gave a picnic on a 'magnificent scale' at Strawberry Hill House.[40] Great festivities were celebrated on New Year's Day 1849 for Colonel Westenra's tenants at Sharavogue at which the celebrated Cunningham, a piper, played and Mr Potter, the land steward, presided.[41] Despite the acute financial difficulties experienced at the Charleville estate a number of festivities greeted the coming of age of the third earl in the early 1850s.[42]

While the Famine undoubtedly interrupted the 'Big House' building boom in Ireland it did not deter landlords and agents from embellishing their houses and demesnes. It could be argued that by doing so they provided much-needed employment and therefore relief. From 1840 to 1845 the Parsons carried out large-scale improvements at Birr Castle, which included a 'bell ceiling', a mock gothic structure housing the great telescope and iron gates set into the gate keep of the castle.[43] Then, from 1846 to 1848, came the construction of the 'Vaubanesque' fortifications at Birr Castle, while plans were also put in place in

35 'Diary of Lydia Goodbody, Jan. 1847' (in private possession). 36 O'Connor Morris, *Memories*, p. 92. 37 *KCC*, 14 Jan. 1846. 38 Ibid., 4 Feb. 1847. 39 Ibid., 5 Sept. 1849. 40 Quoted in Ryan, *The dear old town*, p. 67. 41 *LE*, 13 Jan. 1849. 42 See, for example, *KCC*, 7 July 1852. 43 'Designs for Birr Castle by Mary, countess of Rosse and/or Colonel Wharton Myddleton' (BCA, *c.*1800–45, O/30).

1850 for two gardens to be set out in front of the castle.[44] During the Famine it was noted that visitors to the castle enjoyed 'pretty good fishing' as there were large quantities of fish in the lakes.[45] Many years later Laurence Parsons, sixth earl of Rosse (1906–79), noted that his great-grandparents spent most of their time engaged in relief work and that astronomical pursuits only began in earnest after 1848.[46] The rather contradictory contemporary evidence suggests that Birr Castle was a recognized international scientific centre during the Famine, and many visitors travelled there to see the great telescope, including Lord Stanley and the Prince Imperial, son of Napoleon III.[47] Rosse was certainly not alone, and the leisure pursuits of the ascendancy appear to have been largely undisturbed by the onset of Famine. In particular, the Ormond and King's County hunt, which numbered several agents in their ranks, continued to meet regularly during this period.[48] Other sporting pastimes included pigeon racing and cock fighting, and indeed one meeting of the latter at Annaghmore, near Drumcullen, was attended by over 1,000 spectators.[49] Examples of leisure and entertainment in the midst of Famine are also to be found in the aforementioned Joly diaries, showing an altogether different perspective of the Famine at local level.[50]

This chapter has charted the initial reaction of land agents, and by extension their employers, to the Famine from 1845 to the beginning of 1847, contextualizing the socio-economic conditions within which the crisis developed. No reference has been made to the impact of the workhouse system or indeed to evictions. This is largely because both issues became much more prominent from 1847 – traditionally regarded as the worst year of the Famine – onwards, and will be dealt with in the next chapter. The crisis caused by crop failure in King's County was not unanticipated. Remarkably, in his annual speech to the Parsonstown Agricultural Society in 1843, Lord Rosse drew attention to the twin social evils of over population and subdivision and warned that:

> A year of scarcity would at length come, and with it, a visitation of the most awful famine, such as the history of the world affords very many examples of, a famine followed by pestilence, when the utmost exertion of the landlords of Ireland, of the government, and of the legislature, aided by the unbounded generosity of the people of England, would be totally inadequate to avert the most fearful calamities.[51]

44 Ibid. (BCA, O/32–34, c.1850).   **45** Quoted in Malcomson, *Calendar of the Rosse papers*, p. 73.   **46** Ibid., p. xxviii.   **47** Ibid., p. 72. The third earl received numerous illustrious honours for his work on the Great Telescope including honorary degrees at Oxford and Illinois; the order of St Patrick; the French Legion d'Honeur and membership of the Russian Imperial Academy. **48** See, for example, *KCC*, 24 Mar. 1847 & *Nenagh Guardian*, 17 Jan. 1849.   **49** Quoted in Pey (ed.), *Eglish*, p. 119.   **50** See Reilly, *John Plunket Joly*.   **51** Quoted in Margaret Hogan, 'The Great Famine, Birr and District', transcript of lecture at Dooley's Hotel, Birr, 11 May 1996 (ORC).

He hardly expected that within such a short period the calamity that he spoke about would arrive in King's County and the country as a whole. In the early stages, agents as a body were unprepared and disorganized (as Rosse suggested would be the case in general). At first they tried, albeit to a limited extent, to use various relief schemes to alleviate some of the hardship. Evidence suggests that on many estates abatements and rent reductions were granted, although there were others where a much less sympathetic approach was taken. However, their actions were sometimes dictated by the growth in agrarian disorder. The evidence also suggests that levels of evictions reached a plateau in 1845 to 1846 before escalating in the years that followed. When a policy of granting abatements and reductions failed to encourage tenants to pay their rents (or part thereof), agents adopted a more hardline approach to estate management. As described at the beginning of this chapter, agents such as Joseph Grogan were optimistic that the damage would be minimal and that the blight would soon dissipate.[52] However, he, and others, gradually began to realize that this was no ordinary crisis.

52 Joseph Grogan to Stewart & Kincaid, 29 Sept. 1845 (PRONI, Molesworth papers, D/1567/F/1/17/77).

7 Eviction and clearance

Travelling through Ireland in the summer of 1847, Alexander Somerville lamented that it was an opportunistic time for evictions, perhaps suggesting that agents and landlords were using the social conditions as a pretext for clearing their estates of the cottiers and smallholders who had obstructed improvement in the past and who had been continually in arrears.[1] Somerville's comments also coincided with the renewed vigour of land agents to press for rents and arrears and to oversee the distress of animals and crops. Such policies had much to do with already straightened times for landlords. The statistics for King's County show that evictions increased rapidly over the ensuing years. In most cases landlords had not received rent or arrears since 1845, and in some cases even before that. As there was no sign of an improvement in social conditions, agents adopted new and more stringent estate management policies.[2] The catalyst for those policies was the introduction of the 'quarter acre' or 'Gregory clause' in 1848, which stipulated that holders of more than a quarter of an acre of land could not be deemed destitute and thus not entitled to relief. This was also at a time when public opinion in Britain was changing towards Irish landlords, as the country became swamped with Famine refugees. The *Illustrated London News* and other journals now depicted landlords as 'extremely selfish, negligent, ignorant, profligate and reckless'.[3] The disastrous failure of the potato crop in 1849 placed landlords and tenants alike in an even more precarious situation. By August of that year, according to Lydia Goodbody of Clara, there was 'scarcely a green potato stalk to be seen' in King's County.[4] The same writer also noted that 'every living animal is disappearing from around the cottages; there being no food for them so that pigs and fowl of all kinds become scarce'. Moreover, heavy frost and rain in King's County had a disastrous effect on the harvests of 1848 and 1849 and a general depression in agricultural prices followed.[5] The continued potato blight threat meant that by 1850 landlords and their agents held little hope of any immediate recovery. Tensions, in light of continued hardship and rising levels of evictions, reached new heights and culminated in the murder of three land agents, adding to those who were murdered pre-1847.

Realizing that there was little immediate prospect of recovery, and perhaps ultimately to provide a pretext for the clearance of impoverished tenants from

---

1 Quoted in Snell (ed.), *Letters from Ireland*, p. 19. 2 See, for example, Joseph Grogan to Stewart and Kincaid, 21 Feb. 1844 (PRONI, Molesworth papers, D/1567/F/1/17/10) in which he noted that 'it is very difficult to get any money from the people' at Philipstown. 3 Quoted in Norman A. Jeffares & Peter Van Der Kamp (eds), *Irish literature in the nineteenth century* (2 vols, Dublin, 2007), ii, p. 8. 4 'Diary of Lydia Goodbody, 28 Aug. 1849' (in private possession). 5 *KCC*, 15 June & 10 Sept. 1849. See also James S. Donnelly Jr, 'Production, prices and exports, 1846–51' in Vaughan (ed.), *A new history of Ireland*, p. 292

his estate, the earl of Rosse introduced a new set of estate rules in January 1847. These rules addressed many of the underlying social problems and agrarian issues that had led to estate management difficulties in the past. Some rules were directed towards the improvement of holdings but it is clear that these could only be carried out by tenants who could afford them. For example, tenants were directed to replace thatch roofs with slate, for which Rosse was willing to provide half the cost. A further clause stipulated that these improvements could only be carried out with the prior sanction of his agent, George Heenan. Rosse also noted in the rules that any tenant who was ejected would be compensated for improvements, thereby avoiding public censure. Significantly, in an effort to prevent further subdivision of land, middlemen were prohibited from subletting or allowing the erection of a building on the estate without prior approval from the agent. Tenants were prohibited from 'burning' the land or from working it on a 'land jobbing' or shared basis. Rosse's aim was to create more economic and viable holdings. To this extent, the rules promoted voluntary emigration, allowing the agent to permit tenants in distress to sell their crops and fixtures (to presumably more prosperous neighbouring tenants) before departure. The 'estate rules' concluded that both the agent, Heenan, and the agriculturalist, Lyle, would be visiting the farm of every tenant to view its management in what appears to have been an in-depth audit of the estate at the height of the Famine. Rosse contended that his rules were based on best estate practice and on regulations set out on other estates, which were 'considered among the best managed, and it is hoped they will afford the industrious tenant the up most amount of encouragement that can be reasonably given'.[6] It is probable that Rosse had clearances in mind before he published these stringent rules. He was certainly aware of the negative publicity that had followed the much-publicized evictions on the Gerrard estate in Co. Galway in 1846.[7] Such was the public condemnation of these clearances that other landlords who engaged in evicting tenants were said to be guilty of 'Gerrardising' the people.[8] Rosse, however, was astute enough to realize that if he issued the rules beforehand he could argue that evictions were justifiable on the grounds of the tenants' failure to adhere to them.

According to Robin Haines there were many who believed that Ireland's improvement could only be brought about by a revolution in landholding and the permanent ejection of smallholders and squatters.[9] This was reflected in the

---

6 'Rules for the management of the Rosse estate' (BCA, J/3). See also *KCC*, 3 Feb. 1847. 7 For more on the Gerrard eviction controversy see 'Cases of tenantry eviction: letters and comments from newspapers, 1840–47' (NLI, 5A 3234) and S. Redmond, *Landlordism in Ireland: letters on the eviction of the Gerrard tenantry a portion of which appeared originally in the* Freeman's Journal (Dublin, 1846). 8 Lord John Russell believed that clearances were among the greatest evils perpetrated on the Irish and was said to have been particularly shocked by the Gerrard evictions. See Gray, *Famine, land, politics*, p. 152. 9 Robin Haines, *Charles Trevelyan and the Great Irish Famine* (Dublin, 2004), p. 454.

decision a year after the beginning of the Famine when an act to regularize ejectments (rather than to stop them altogether) had been introduced by the
government.[10] By now there was increased pressure on the various relief schemes
and much debate centred on how landholding structures could be altered in order
to alleviate congestion. Spearheading this in March 1847 that *Times* newspaper
advocated exclusion from relief to all who held more than one rood of ground.[11]
Later that month the *Morning Chronicle* warned that such a scheme would create
many hardships.[12] Within a few months the soup kitchen scheme was terminated
and the government reverted to the poor law system 'as the principal means of
affording relief to the destitute'.[13] There had been various amendments that June
of 1847, including the provision that those who were not able bodied were to be
relieved either in or out of the workhouse. However, the most significant legisla-
tive development was the introduction of the so-called 'Gregory clause'.
Introduced to parliament by William Gregory, a Co. Galway landlord and MP for
Dublin, it included measures to protect landowners from the increased burden of
local taxation in the form of rates caused by people claiming poor relief who were
not entitled to it.[14] Interestingly, when the law was introduced it had no precedent
in the English poor law system and was only objected to by a handful of politicians.
Indeed, even members of the Repeal party, including Morgan John O'Connell,
the son of the 'Liberator', Daniel, were in favour of the proposed measures. This
was despite the fact that, to all concerned, the act meant only one thing, summed
up by James S. Donnelly Jr, who concluded that:

> the purpose of this clause was to arm landlords with a weapon that would
> enable them to clear estates of pauperized smallholders who were paying
> little or no rent. Only by surrendering their holdings above one rood to
> the landlord could these tenants qualify themselves and their families for
> public assistance. Although not all the consequences of the quarter-acre
> clause were fully appreciated in advance, its enormous potential as an
> estate-clearing device was widely recognized in parliament.[15]

Donnelly's assertion mirrored contemporary belief that the act would allow for
the 'complete clearance of the small farmers of Ireland'.[16] As David Nally has
more recently suggested, the Gregory clause was simply 'a war on dwellings'.[17]

It soon became evident that landowners were using and abusing the quarter
acre clause to rid their estates of smallholders, cottiers and the landless. There
was a sense of bitterness on the part of landowners and others who were
expected to provide relief for the host of undertenants who did not belong to

10 Kinealy, *This great calamity*, p. 218.   11 *Times*, 1 Mar. 1847.   12 *Morning Chronicle*, 31
Mar. 1847.   13 Donnelly, *The Great Irish potato Famine*, p. 101.   14 Kinealy, *This great
calamity*, p. 218.   15 Donnelly, *The Great Irish potato Famine*, p. 102.   16 Gray, *Famine, land,
politics*, p. 278.   17 Nally, *Human incumbrances*, pp 161–2.

anyone and who were seen merely as 'squatters' on the land. In some cases the lack of sympathy for their plight was striking. For example, in 1848 John Persse Grome, a Parsonstown poor law guardian and landowner, told a meeting of the board that it was 'truly ridiculous to be wasting so much of their valuable time in talking over so much unimportant matters. It was all sympathy for paupers, beggars and brats and in what way they were to be made comfortable, as they had not been used to cabins and hovels of the meanest and filthiest kind from their birth; such talk was really monstrous and absurd', and while all the pity was for the beggars 'there was no sympathy for the landlords and gentlemen of the country, at whose expense these persons were to be fed sumptuously'. In conclusion, he wished to hear no more of such talk.[18]

Grome was not alone in his outburst or feelings towards those most in need. In May 1849, Dr Richard Grattan provoked consternation and received widespread condemnation when he informed the Dublin Central Relief Committee that the Edenderry board of guardians had passed a resolution in an effort to avert crowds of paupers, from Galway and other Famine-stricken counties, from inundating the town. In order to do so they had decided to transfer paupers found in the town to Dublin: 'The people of Edenderry are determined not to have the frightful scenes of other places enacted there, of hundreds of corpses lying unburied on the roads and ditches and devoured by dogs' he concluded.[19] Such attitudes prevailed elsewhere. Lydia Goodbody noted how Clara had escaped the worst effects of cholera simply because 'watches were put up on all the approach roads and no one infected got past'.[20] The same was true of Tullamore where Dawson French, a land agent, was engaged 'in clearing the town of nuisances and the diseased'.[21] Outsiders were not wanted in Parsonstown either where farmers attending the weekly market complained to Lord Rosse that their stalls had been taken by 'others' who frequent the town.[22] At Killoughey, Richard Gamble warned tenants that any person 'in the habit of giving lodgings to strangers, strollers and persons of bad character' were to be refused relief from the committee.[23] Charity, it appears, was far from the minds of many. A more sinister reaction to the issue of poverty and distress can be seen in the response to eviction and clearance, again highlighting the issue of culpability. In 1850 the *Times* newspaper reported that the eviction of nine families from the earl of Portarlington's estate in Queen's and King's County was 'for the general benefit of the community'.[24] The belief here was that as the tenants owed more than seven years rent they were never likely to recover, and thus were deemed a burden on the local community.

18 'Parsonstown Board of Guardians, Minute Book, 1848'; quoted in Sandra Robinson (ed.), *The diary of an Offaly schoolboy, 1858–59: William Davis* (Tullamore, 2010), p. xxx.   19 *FJ*, 28 May 1849.   20 'Diary of Lydia Goodbody, Apr. 1849' (in private possession).   21 *KCC*, 5 Oct. 1853.   22 Ibid., 22 Nov. 1848.   23 'Resolutions of the Killoughy Relief committee, 1847' (NAI, Gamble papers, M3499).   24 *Times*, 26 Aug. 1850.

The foregoing sentiments reflected a much wider change in the mindset of the public at large as the Famine wore on. In many ways land agents had an unenviable task of pressing for rent and arrears and were placed under particular pressure to do so by their employers. By the late 1840s it was debt and not death that most land agents were concerned with. Where an agent was deemed to be too lenient on the tenantry he was quickly replaced. On the other hand, there were those such as Henry Odlum, William Johnson's agent at Tullamore, who believed that tenants had been shown too much leniency during the Famine. For him, appeals for reductions in rent were 'really a peremptory demand'. According to Odlum, if the landlords of the county were to grant abatements there should be in the very least 'an appearance of unanimity among them'.[25] However, there appeared to be little unanimity among landlords and their agents and while there were those such as William O'Connor Morris who granted twenty per cent reductions at Mount Pleasant, George Garvey who was instructed by his employer on the Lettybrook estate to forgive rents, and R.L. Moore, the marquis of Drogheda's agent, who granted abatements to over 200 tenants, as the Famine progressed these seem to have been the exception rather than the rule.[26]

But still, King's County land agents were singled out on occasion for their benevolence. For example, the 'exemplary treatment' (presumably the reduction of rents) shown by the agent of Mrs W. Nunn, near Parsonstown, was highlighted by the *Nation* newspaper, which hastened to add that they infrequently acknowledged landlord charity.[27] Another example was William White, a bank manager and agent of the L'Estrange estate at Moystown, near Ferbane, who informed tenants in December 1849 that he would reduce their rents and was willing to pay the poor rates on their behalf.[28] Despite their many acts of benevolence, the continued plundered of landlord stocks and houses left many land agents feeling disillusioned. In October 1849, the *Economist* newspaper remarked that 'not one fourth of the crop lifting plunder in King's County goes reported. This week alone tenants on the Mount Pleasant and Rathrobin properties carried off everything they could'.[29] In addition, agents were horrified that their generosity was not rewarded with votes in the hotly contested general election of 1847, which saw continued support for Repeal candidates.[30] It was perhaps little wonder then that agents turned to eviction as a means of restoring order to the estates.

25 William Johnson, Grove House, London, to Lord Charleville, July 1848 (Charleville papers, T/3069/D/31). 26 See *LE*, 10 Nov. 1849; *KCC*, 3 Oct. 1849 and *Times*, 22 June 1848. 27 *Nation*, 8 Dec. 1849. 28 Quoted in Ryan, *The dear old town*, pp 78–9. 29 *The Economist*, 20 Oct. 1849. 30 Others who had shown remarkable charity and kindness were also the victims of violence and intimidation. In 1850 the Revd Francis Turner of Banagher was outraged when his house was attacked and robbed, despite his daily exertions to help the poor. See *KCC*, 23 Jan. 1850.

Eviction statistics have always troubled historians and it is probable that the true extent of the clearance of people during the Famine will ever be known.[31] Adding to this problem is the fact that many who were evicted were later allowed re-enter their holding or were relocated to another site, confusing somewhat the statistics. In 1849, King's County had the highest rate of eviction in Leinster when some 619 families, numbering 3,255 individuals were evicted.[32] Of these as many as 123 families (or 631 people) were later readmitted as caretaker tenants. Indeed, this was a feature of many evictions that took place in the county, and, with the exception of 1849, more than one-fifth of evictees were later readmitted. To understand the problems associated with eviction and the re-admittance of tenants during the Famine period it is necessary to understand the various land laws that existed and which, to a large extent created confusion and as a result unrest. Most tenants in nineteenth-century rural Ireland were granted holdings by the landlord as either freehold or leasehold. The latter gave the tenant security for the lives of the people mentioned in the lease; freehold, on the other hand, generally lasted forever. A larger proportion of tenants still operated on a tenancy at will, which could be terminated at any period by either of the parties involved and offered no protection from the law.[33]

The rising level of evictions in 1848 prompted the inhabitants of King's County to present a petition to the House of Commons in 1849, through a Mr Reynolds and Roche, to alter the law of landlord and tenant in Ireland.[34] Their petition obviously fell on deaf ears as a year later King's County again had the highest level of eviction in Leinster with 652 families evicted, amounting to 3,346 people.[35] The figures included middlemen and strong farmers who were now being actively forced out by the agent.[36] It was natural that agents turned their attention in particular to the expulsion of middlemen, as it greatly facilitated their wider eviction policies. In 1847, Lord Rosse hinted at this eviction of middlemen: 'there is another cause which will contribute to render outrages more frequent; that in many cases the immediate lessee having paid poor rates for small tenants who have paid no rent, he will eject; and he will do so with less

31 For this debate see for example O'Neill, 'Famine evictions' in King (ed.), *Famine, land and culture*, pp 29–70. 32 In total the province of Leinster had 3,353 families evicted. *Return by provinces and counties (compiled from returns made to the Inspector General, Royal Irish Constabulary) of cases of evictions which have come to the knowledge of the constabulary in each of the years 1849 to 1880 inclusive*, H.C. 1881 (185) lxxvii, 725, pp 3–23. 33 After 1816 a landlord could bring the case either to a civil bill court or a superior court; civil bill was no more than £20 value of the holding; in either case the tenant had to owe one year's rent. It allowed for the speedy eviction of a tenant who was in arrears . See William Dwyer Ferguson, *A treatise on the practice of the Queen's bench, common pleas and exchequer of pleas in Ireland, in personal actions and ejectments* (2, vols, Dublin, 1842). 34 *House of Commons debate, 1 & 5 March 1849, vol 103, c9 & 66*. 35 In 1850 270 families (1,516 people) were readmitted in King's County. 36 *House of Commons debate, 1 & 5 March 1849, vol 103, c9 & 66*. T.P. O'Neill has estimated that as many as 40 per cent of tenants with land valued at over £50 were ejected between 1847 to 1848. See O'Neill, 'The Famine in Offaly', p. 710.

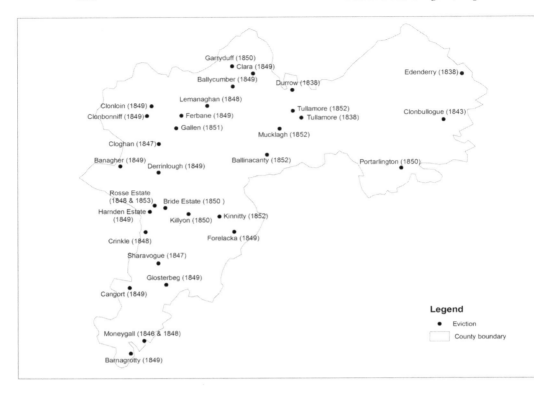

2 Locations of major evictions in King's County during the Famine

compunction'. The law, he believed, facilitated the rapid removal of tenants.[37] Of course a significant amount of evictions did not come to the attention of local or national newspapers, and as the constabulary were not required to keep records until 1849, the true extent of the clearances during the Famine may never be known. More often than not the newspapers reported only sensational cases involving large numbers or where extreme cruelty had been used.[38] In King's County the years 1848 to 1849 witnessed a considerable amount of evictions involving small numbers of people, which ultimately saved agents from public admonishment. These included the eviction of six families at the Westenra estate at Sharavogue, eight families on the O'Moore estate at Cloghan, six families on the Bennett estate at Annaghmore and five families on the Cox estate at Clara, among hundreds others.[39]

37 Ibid. 38 One such report from December 1849 involved the eviction of tenants at Tubrid, near Ferbane, where the bailiffs had been armed with pitchforks, hatchets and vitriol in an attempt to consume all the premises by fire. See *The Nation*, 8 Dec. 1849. 39 'Return of all notices served upon the relieving officers of poor law districts in Ireland by landowners and

Elsewhere, agents upped the ante and continued their eviction policies with particular vehemence. In December 1848 George Greeson oversaw the removal of thirty-one families at Lemanaghan, near Ballycumber, levelling five houses in the process. Of those evicted twenty-six families were subsequently allowed to re-enter their properties as caretakers. Many of these tenants had not paid rent for three to five years. [40] In March 1849 twenty-seven families, comprising 126 people, were evicted from Forelacka, Kinnitty, for arrears of rent.[41] Two months later, at George Walpole's estate at Glosterbeg, near Brosna twenty families were evicted.[42] Henry Sheane evicted tenants at the Bell estate at Banagher who were over five years in arrears and were deemed 'unsatisfactory tenants as their buildings were very much dilapidated'.[43] In 1850 A.L. Bride, a small landowner in the south of the county, evicted forty-eight families and levelled eight houses. Having experienced considerable resistance from his tenants over numerous years Robert Cassidy commenced a large clearance of his estate in 1848. Among those evicted included William Donahue of Ballinree and his sons, who were feared to be troublesome tenants, simply because they were unable to read or write. Some of those evicted by Cassidy were also middlemen. For example, Michael Fitzgerald and his under tenants who owed four years rent ($£104$) were evicted, as was Dan Carry, who owed $£78$, and Pat Walsh, who owed $£148$.[44] Having been denounced from the alter by Revd Devine, Cassidy later complained to the bishop of Meath, but to no avail. Pouring scorn on Cassidy, Devine advised his congregation that they should 'hoot and groan' at landlords and their agents as they passed on the road.[45] In his defence Cassidy argued that 'the condition of the landholders has generally much improved, the arrangements made for the last few years has greatly benefited the landholders tenure and terms so much so that abatements made during the disastrous seasons since 1846 have been on many estates discontinued and the tenants do not complain'.[46] The evictions continued into January 1850 when more tenants were cleared. Little mercy was shown. One under-tenant by the name of Williams was said to have had five children dying with fever when the evictions were carried out. This particular clearance was ironic to a certain extent, as many of those removed had

others under the act 11 & 12 Vict., c.47 'involving tenants of King's County estates' in *An act for the protection and relief of the destitute poor evicted from their dwellings*, HC 1849 [1089] xlix, 315. **40** *KCC*, 6 Dec. 1848. In August 1849 Greeson evicted a number of families at Grogan and Lebeg, part of Miss Anne Holmes' estate. On this occasion no mercy was said to have been shown from Greeson who took one man lying in bed with fever and put him on the ground. See *KCC*, 8 Aug. 1849. **41** Pey (ed.), *Eglish*, p. 121. **42** *Leinster Express*, 19 May 1849. Six families, a total of thirty-nine people, were evicted and their homes levelled at the Harden estate near Parsonstown, while three families, numbering twenty persons, were evicted from the Revd William Minchin's estate at Barnagrotty. **43** 'Irish Rent Book, Banagher District, 1849–1878' (NLI, MS 16, 164). **44** Robert Cassidy to under secretary, Dublin Castle, 21 Aug. 1850 (OPKC, 1850, 15/351). **45** 'Note on evictions carried out by John Deany of Cloneen', nd (OPKC, 1849, 15/450). **46** Robert Cassidy to Robert Murray, Provincial Bank of Ireland, 19 Dec. 1854 (NLI, Cassidy papers).

championed their landlord during the heady days of Repeal, of which he was a firm supporter. Such support mattered little when creditors had to be paid and rental arrears multiplied.

It was something that was replicated by Sir Andrew Armstrong, a Repeal MP for King's County. In 1851 forty-two families, comprising 220 people, were evicted and twenty-one houses levelled on his estate at Gallen.[47] Prior to this, in November 1850, a large notice in the *King's County Chronicle* advertised the 'extensive sale of elegant modern household furniture', announcing that Armstrong was going to live on the Continent.[48] Several local land agents watched the break-up of the Armstrong estate with interest and were, it appears, in a position to buy up large tracts of the land, thereby cementing their position in local society. Evictions made the land all the more attractive for potential buyers. It was clearances of this nature that it prompted the *Nation* newspaper to denounce what it termed 'landlord crime'.[49] There may have been some truth in the charge, as in some instances, including some in King's County, tenants were evicted although they did possess the means to pay the rent. Others were evicted because they had been misguided by the influence of local agitators who claimed that 'there would soon be a new act called Tenant Right introduced where a tenant need not pay the rent he owed and that Daniel O'Connell had left an order in his will for the British government to have it passed at once'. As a result of such misguided belief, the *King's County Chronicle* reported that 'many of the ignorant lower order are under the impression and are withholding the rent accordingly'.[50]

As already highlighted, for a variety of reasons a large number of clearances, executed over longer spells, escaped the censure of the local newspaper editor. In 1850–1 Jasper Robert Joly, agent of the Gifford estates at Castlejordan, near Edenderry, issued quit notices to several tenants. Three years later even more tenants were ejected by Joly.[51] In December 1850 Francis Berry brought ejectments before the petty sessions at Tullamore amid little or no controversy.[52] Likewise, the actions of the Goodbody brothers at Clara provoked little negative attention or outrage. Despite playing such a central role in the provision of relief across Ireland with their Quaker brethren, their actions towards tenants in King's County in the late 1840s is somewhat contentious. In August 1849 several cabins were thrown down by the Goodbodys in advance of the building of their country house near Clara. The following year the brothers, Marcus and Jonathon, bought 532 acres at Ballydoogan, near Clara, for £4,126 in the Incumbered Estates Court, and evicted twenty-five tenants (possibly as many as 150 people) who received 'only small sums to take them to America'.[53]

As a final example of eviction, the clearances on the Rosse estate in 1848

47 'Constabulary returns of evictions 1850' (NAI, 6482.117 (3/02/4)).   48 Quoted in Ryan, *The dear old town*, p. 104.   49 *Nation*, 20 Nov. 1847.   50 *KCC*, 5 Jan. 1848.   51 Ballinderry papers (in private possession).   52 *KCC*, 1 Jan. 1851.   53 *Nation*, 10 May 1851.

indicated that the introduction of the new estate rules had an agenda, this being to facilitate the clearance of tenants in arrears from the estate. In 1848 arrears, on a total rental of over £8,000 on the 'Inner' portion (the town and surrounding areas) of the Rosse estate, amounted to £2,894.[54] In light of this George Heenan made a concerted effort to press harder with the collection of rent. He treated various classes of tenants differently, as undoubtedly was the case with agents elsewhere. Ultimately, he met with little difficulty in clearing the smallholders. At the townlands of Newtown and Fadden, near Parsonstown, eighty-two families were evicted in one month alone. In the village of Crinkle, where arrears amounted to almost £209, one quarter of the tenants were given notice to quit.[55] Tenants at Lumpcloon, whose plight was exacerbated by heavy flooding in 1847, were also removed.[56] Sarcastically, and referring to clearances on the Rosse estate, the *Freeman's Journal* noted that 'the sheriff and his men in Clonbonniff and Clonlion today continue the good work. They are to evict more families, besides the above of Derrinlough on the day after'.[57] Particularly vexing for Heenan was that a number of tenants, such as James Goldrick at Paulduff, had 'gone away', taking with them their crops and animals and leaving the estate in arrears. In the country as a whole, widespread evictions such as these were becoming all too common and 'a vast social change' was taking place in Ireland.[58] However, Heenan was reluctant to evict what he termed 'quite solvent' tenants, giving them every opportunity in 1848 to sell their harvest to pay their rents, informing Rosse that he did not 'think it judicious to press them at present'.[59] The agent's methods seem to have paid off and by the end of 1848 he had collected almost £4,000 in rent and arrears on the 'Inner' estate and over £5,000 on the 'Outer' estate.[60] But the evictions continued into the 1850s when Heenan cleared a further thirteen families, comprising sixty-five persons.[61] In addition, the earl of Rosse's brother, Laurence Parsons, permanently evicted eight families, amounting to thirty-two people, and levelled all their houses.[62] It seems that what Lord Clanricarde, an extensive Co. Galway proprietor, declared at the end of 1848 rang true for landlords in King's County: 'the landlords are prevented from aiding or tolerating poor tenants. They are compelled to hunt out all such, to save their property from the £4 clause'.[63] Archbishop MacHale criticized Irish landlords for throwing tenants upon 'dunghills'.[64] Indeed, the numbers 'hunted out' could have been far greater had the hut levellers and crowbar brigades not received daily threats on their lives. L.P. Curtis has claimed

54 For management purposes the Rosse estate was divided into 'Inner' and 'Outer' portions. **55** 'Rental of the Inner Estates, 1848' (BCA, Q/100/A). **56** 'Rental of the Outer Estates, 1848' (BCA, Q100/ B). **57** *FJ*, 22 Sept. 1849. **58** *Illustrated London News*, 16 Dec. 1848. **59** 'Rental of the Outer Estates, 1848' (BCA, Q100/ B). **60** Ibid. **61** 'Police returns for evictions, King's County for the quarter ended June 1851' (NAI, Official papers, 1851/28). **62** Ibid. **63** See 'Marquis of Clanricarde to earl of Clarendon, 31 Dec. 1848' quoted in Woodham-Smith, *The great hunger*, p. 364. The £4 clause made landlords liable for the poor law rate on all land under that valuation. **64** *Times*, 13 May 1850.

that in most cases bailiffs exaggerated the violence towards them; in King's County, however, it was far from imagined.[65] In August 1850 Robert Cassidy claimed that 'so much intimidated are the bailiffs about Parsonstown that they will not attend [an eviction] unless paid a large fee'.[66] In other locations bailiffs and process servers were regularly prevented from carrying out their duties. For example, in January 1850, when James Enraght of Lusmagh distrained crops from a tenant named Ryan, 300 men assembled and swore they would not let them proceed. The standoff was only halted by the arrival of the police.[67]

Such resistance coincided with the growing disdain for the workhouse system in King's County. As Donnelly argues, even before the quarter acre clause made the situation worse, conditions within the workhouse had underlined the woeful defects of the poor law system as the main instrument of confronting the effects of Famine.[68] Evicted and destitute tenants flocked to the towns and workhouses looking for assistance. But conditions were so bad in Tullamore workhouse, for example, that on occasion the dead were not buried – one report noting that 'within the last week the bodies of two persons remained for three days unburied, their friends having no means to purchase coffins and the church wardens had no funds available for that purpose'.[69] Agents such as Richard Gamble, himself a poor law guardian, knew there would be a price to pay; in 1848 he informed the absentee proprietors of Killoughey that the poor of the barony had only the means to last until December and called for a liberal subscription on their part.[70] His call fell on deaf ears and the peace and stability of the barony was threatened, most notably after what became known as the 'Killoughey barracks affray', where two policemen were murdered by an angry mob who were resisitng the movement of distressed corn.[71] As Lydia Goodbody recorded, this was 'awful work with the police and the country people who were running away corn from the landlords'.[72] Significantly, this incident also highlighted the use of outside help in subverting the will of agents and their staff. According to Andrew Gamble, a party calling themselves the 'Wicklow Rangers', armed with pitchforks, were operating in the barony of Ballyboy. Gamble warned that 'if it is not checked in its infancy the collection of rents will become a matter of utter impossibility with persons allowed to gather at night for unlawful purpose'.[73] The use of outside help was also evident in the combi-

---

65 Curtis, *The depiction of eviction in Ireland*, p. 21.   66 Robert Cassidy, Monasterevin to under secretary, 21 Aug. 1850 (OPKC, 15/351).   67 John Duncan, Parsonstown to under secretary, Dublin Castle, 30 Jan. 1850 (OPKC, 15/61).   68 Donnelly Jr, *The Great Irish potato Famine*, p. 103. There were three union workhouses in King's County in 1847; Edenderry, Parsonstown and Tullamore, while Nenagh, Co. Tipperary and Mountmellick, Queen's County, also catered for a large proportion of the county's population.   69 *KCC*, 12 Apr. 1848.   70 Gamble papers (NAI, M 3493).   71 See Smith, *The Killoughey barracks affray*.   72 'Diary of Lydia Goodbody, 14 October 1849' (in private possession).   73 A.W. Gamble to Thomas Redington, 20 Sept. 1847 (OPKC, 1847, 15/510).

nation of men from Queen's County and Tipperary who took part in the cutting and carrying away of turf on the lands of W.H. Bird at Cloghan.[74]

By now Tullamore workhouse was described as having no order or discipline, and it was becoming increasingly hard to find someone to occupy the master's role.[75] Local land agents, it seemed, were powerless. While Francis Berry was active on local relief committees and became chairman of the Tullamore board of guardians in March 1850, there was little he could do when faced with a system that could not cater for the swelling numbers of destitute and homeless.[76] Similarly, Parsonstown workhouse was said to have been overcrowded with some 1,058 paupers and the guardians were reprimanded for failing to provide adequate provision for the inmates.[77] Further investigations alleged that the nurses were stealing the children's rations, which contributed to the high rate of infant mortality.[78] The Parsonstown guardians were also rebuked for frequently failing to meet, owing to a shortage of committee members – the earl of Rosse stated that he would attend only on a day that there was not quorum.[79] Acting as clerk, Robert Johnston Stoney, Mr Oakley's land agent, was burdened with the weekly chores of administration, including the purchasing of provisions, the distribution of rations and dealing with the queries of the workhouse master. Contemporary reports by visitors to the workhouse would indicate that either Stoney was inept or that the situation had gotten out of hand. The latter is more likely to have been the case. In 1849 the earl of Fitzwilliam sent James Massey, chief agent of his Irish estates, to visit Parsonstown workhouse in which several of his Cloghan tenants had sought refuge. Noting the terrible conditions of the house, Massey was appalled to find that the food was 'not sufficiently nourishing and they are looking very ill and appear much reduced'.[80] As a means of coping with the destitution in the workhouse (and to relieve individual estates) agents such as Stoney used their power as guardians to oversee the emigration of a large number of young women from King's County, the majority of whom were sent to Sydney, Australia, in 1849 and 1850.[81]

Conditions inside and outside King's County workhouses led to high mortality rates. As disease spread, it killed more people than starvation. Across Ireland diseased paupers flocked to dispensaries, many of which had been established in the early 1830s to deal with the cholera epidemic. Again, this system was wholly inadequate to deal with the problem. In King's County in 1845 there were only twelve dispensaries catering for a total population of 147,000 people, an average of 12,238 persons per dispensary.[82] With the appearance of dysentery,

74 Richard Pennefather to Dublin Castle, n.d. 1846 (OPKC, 1846, 15/11297). **75** O'Neill, 'The Famine in Offaly', p. 695. **76** Murphy, *Tullamore Workhouse*, pp 80–1, 115. **77** *KCC*, 5 Jan. 1848. **78** O'Neill, 'The Famine in Offaly', p. 701. **79** *KCC*, 16 Jan. 1848. **80** James Massey to Earl Fitzwilliam, 6 Feb. 1849 (Sheffield Archives, Wentworth Woodhouse Muniments G/37/100). **81** See Trevor McClaughlin, *Barefoot and pregnant? Irish famine orphans in Australia* (2 vols, Victoria, 2001), ii, pp 200–12. **82** *Report from the select committee of*

fever and dropsy in 1849 these buildings could not cope. At Parsonstown, for example, 756 people died, and in one week there were 101 reported deaths in the workhouse.[83] By 1851 the inability to bury people as quickly as they died again became a matter of concern for Francis Berry who feared that this would lead to further disease in Tullamore.[84] Thus, the board of guardians appealed to Lord Charleville to provide a suitable site for a new cemetery, which was subsequently granted.[85] The reappearance on a number of occasions in the 1850s of blight also threatened the survival of the most marginal in society. In February 1851, Joseph Sutherland, a small farmer at Gurteen, warned that 'if the next crop fails the small farmer may die altogether'.[86] By August the destruction of the potato, including new varieties such as Wellingtons, Long Black and Pinks, was widely reported in King's County.[87] More blight was reported in August 1852 when the potato prospects were considered 'not good'.[88] Fourteen months later the disease of the potato crop was once again prevalent in the county.[89]

The population of King's County decreased by 23.6 per cent, or some 34,781 people, during the period 1841 to 1851. Of this number, workhouse records in the county list 6,288 deaths during the Famine. There were 5,667 uninhabited houses, and villages such as Ballinagar, Clonony and Brosna simply disappeared.[90] This desolation to rural communities naturally raises questions about the role or assistance offered by land agents. Did they turn a blind eye or were they simply overwhelmed by the scale of the calamity? Emigration greatly contributed to population decline in King's County, although it is impossible to provide accurate statistics for this period. As early as 1848 newspapers such as the *King's County Chronicle* advocated assisted emigration as a means of solving the problems and advised the people to 'prepare yourself for emigration'.[91] Despite this, King's County landlords did not engage in assisted emigration on the same scale as practised by others – most notably the fifth earl Fitzwilliam (Wicklow), Charles Wandesforde (Kilkenny) and the third marquis of Lansdowne (Kerry).[92] The aforementioned landlords had controversially deemed emigration a more practical solution than having to pay the poor law rates. John Ross Mahon of the Dublin land agency firm, Guinness and Mahon,

the House of Lords on the laws relating to the relief of the destitute poor and into the operation of the medical charities in Ireland, together with the minutes of evidence taken before the said committee, HC 1846 [694], p. xxvi.   **83** 'Minute Book of the Parsonstown board of guardians, 1849' (Offaly County Library).   **84** *KCC*, 30 Jan. 1852.   **85** Ibid., 16 Jan. 1851.   **86** Frazer, *Tenants no more*, pp 82–3.   **87** *KCC*, 20 Aug. 1851.   **88** *Times*, 9 Aug. 1852.   **89** Ibid., 16 Oct. 1852.   **90** O'Neill, 'The Famine in Offaly', p. 701.   **91** *KCC*, 14 June 1848.   **92** Other assisted emigration schemes were undertaken by the fourth marquis of Bath (Monaghan); the third Viscount Palmerston (Sligo); Colonel George Wyndham (Clare); Sir Robert Gore Booth (Sligo); Francis Spaight (Tipperary) and the third Viscount de Vesci (Queen's County), who between them assisted as many as 80,000 people in emigrating See Gerard Moran, *Sending out Ireland's poor: assisted emigration to North America in the nineteenth century* (Dublin, 2004), pp 36–8.

summed up this belief, writing that assisted emigration schemes were a 'conclusive solution to the management of landed estates'.[93]

At the Ponsonby estate at Cloghan, a scheme of assisted emigration was overseen by James Devery in 1847, at a cost of £350, and involved about seventy-five people.[94] It remains unclear whether this scheme was proposed by the incoming landlord, Earl Fitzwilliam, whose agent in Wicklow, Robert Chaloner, carried out one of the largest schemes of assisted emigration during the Famine, or by the outgoing owner, Lord Ponsonby.[95] In November of the same year, George Fawcett, an absentee landlord living in Dublin, encouraged his tenants in King's County to sell their holdings and emigrate, and he offered to pay their passage, but few took up his offer.[96] Owing to the labour demand for young women in Australia, Colonel Westenra assisted ten young women from Sharavogue with their parents, all fully equipped with clothing.[97] Elsewhere, a concerted effort on the part of the earl of Portarlington's agent to clear the estate was evident after 1848. As the estate was overcrowded with under-tenants, John Sadlier initiated a scheme of assisted emigration. Unlike on other estates, where whole families were shipped out, single men and women were the preferred choice on the Portarlington estate. In total, provision was made for the emigration of 140 tenants.[98]

However, there were also those who left voluntarily because they could afford to do so, or because they were given an incentive. Sometimes finance was raised with the benevolence of land agents. Henry Sheane organized a private subscription in Banagher to assist a man named Stephens, his wife and seven children to emigrate.[99] In May 1848 another five families sought the means to emigrate from Cloghan.[1] According to James Massey, the farms of those who emigrated were 'thrown to the adjoining tenant for your lordship will perceive the small holders are the worst off'.[2] Others were anxious to go and, according to John Long, were endeavouring to sell their places and quit for America.[3] Emigration benefitted many of those who remained. The competition for land continued, and can be seen in an instance, one tenant, upon leaving for America, selling his interest in eleven acres for £57.[4]At Ballylin, the Revd Henry King helped a number of tenants in arrears to emigrate.[5] Anxious to relieve the burden of the workhouse

---

93 Quoted in Arthur Gribben, *The Great Famine and the Irish diaspora in America* (New Jersey, 2000), p. 141.   94 'Cloghan report'.   95 See, for example, Jim Rees, *Fitzwilliam tenants listed in the Coolattin Estate emigration, 1847–56* (Wicklow, 1998).   96 *Tipperary Vindicator*, 8 Nov. 1847.   97 Ibid., 16 Nov. 1853.   98 'Diary of an agent of earl of Portarlington, 1847–1858' (NAI, MS 6168 (1). See also O'Shea, *Prince of swindlers*.   99 *KCC*, 19 Jan. 1848.   1 Frederick Ponsonby, Dublin, to James Massey, 12 May 1849 (WWM, G/37/11).   2 James Massey to Earl Fitzwilliam, 6 Feb. 1849 (WWM, G/37/100).   3 John Long to George Greeson, June 1847 (Greeson papers).   4 The chief constable of the police at Shinrone, John Kelly, reported that many people were anxious to give up land in return for a passage to America. See John Kelly, Shinrone to lord lieutenant, Dublin Castle, 17 Apr. 1846 (OPKC, 1846, 15/9563).   5 'Account book of Revd H. King, 1835–50' (NLI, MS 4121).

the Tullamore board of guardians also facilitated the emigration of several families, including, for example, the Nerchall's, who were given £20 by the board to emigrate.[6] No doubt people left in droves from King's County, a fact aptly captured by a *Times* newspaper article:

> [emigration is] almost daily enacted in this town (Parsonstown) on the departure of the long car to meet the Grand Canal passage boat on its way to Dublin. The office from which it leaves is generally for some short time before its leaving, surrounded by a crowd of emigrants and their friends, the latter of whom with trifling expressions of grief, largely mingled with shouts of exultation, take leave of their friends and pursue them with loud promises of soon joining them in their distant homes.

Significantly, the writer lamented that those departing were increasingly the young and sturdy farmers, and the families of the few remaining 'snug farmers', perhaps suggesting that it was those who could afford to emigrate who did so.[7] A more sinister aspect of this wave of emigration was that many who were preparing to leave were attacked and robbed when it became known that they had acquired the passage money to go.[8]

Social memory in King's County associates clearances from estates with a corresponding rise in workhouse numbers. Even at the time of the Famine, landlords were aware that people did not want to be housed in a workhouse.[9] The association of workhouses with mass evictions fuelled the anti-landlord, anti-agent rhetoric of the post-Famine period as did the loss of huge numbers through emigration, whether assisted or voluntary. While many of those who emigrated continued to benefit the local community they left, through the sending home of remittances – by 1850, for example, in Lusmagh it was claimed that 'there is not a man in the parish who does not have a son or a daughter sending money home'– they also brought with them a baggage of resentment.[10] The effects that these dramatic social changes had on the smallholders, cottiers and the landless undoubtedly fuelled their resentment against a system that offered little protection. As physical symbols of this system it is hardly surprising that landlords, their agents and other employees became frequent targets of aggression during the Famine.

---

6 'Minute Book of the Tullamore board of guardians, 12 Nov. 1852' (Offaly County Library). 7 *Times*, 12 June 1852. 8 *KCC*, 26 Feb. 1851. 9 Robert Cassidy, Monasterevin to under secretary, Dublin Castle, 21 Aug. 1850 (OPKC, 15/351). 10 Quoted in Denis Kelly, *Famine: gorta i Lusma* (Lusmagh, n.d.), pp 8–9.

8 Levelling the score: the murder of land agents

Murders do not take place where the rents are fair and the tenures long.[1]

The clearances of 1848 to 1849 followed on from earlier evictions during the period 1845 to 1847 when some pitiful incidents were recorded. For example, in January 1847 an eviction of tenants was carried out on the Westenra estate at Sharavogue in the midst of a heavy snowfall. According to the Revd McMahon 'a wretched mother with her three children' were left lying in the snow as her 'unfortunate husband whose name is Redmond was trying to remove furniture from the ruin'.[2] The number of ejectments in King's County before the higher courts (those outside the bounds of the local assizes) increased almost seven-fold from 1846 to 1847. Indeed, from 1846 to 1853 it has been estimated that there were 117 evictions per 1,000 agricultural holdings in King's County; only Cos. Leitrim, Waterford, Tipperary and Limerick had more.[3] The clearances were also evident in other statistics, most notably the change in the number and size of holdings. Here the largest decrease appeared to have been among the holders of between five and fifteen acres and indeed more than 2,500 of these holdings disappeared. Further consolidation of land was evident in the increase of over 1,200 farms of thirty acres, one of the largest such increases in Ireland. By extension the creation of even larger farm units – for the promotion of large-scale grazing – ultimately led to resentment in the years that followed.

The treatment of the aforementioned Redmond family and thousands more resulted in a backlash against agents. James S. Donnelly Jr has argued that despite the clearances and evictions that occurred during the Famine there was remarkably little resistance and still less shooting by tenants.[4] This was not the case in King's County where four landlords, seven agents and four other estate employees were murdered between 1838 and 1852.[5] Of these, four were agents murdered between 1845 and 1852. These figures do not include others such as James Stapleton, who although agent of the Pepper estate in Co. Tipperary was murdered for taking a tract of land at Ballymacurrough, near Kinnitty, in June 1844. Nor does it include James Gleeson and Patrick Mortimer, the aforementioned constabulary officers murdered at Killoughy in October 1849 following the seizure of crops that had been taken for non-payment of rent.[6] Such was the level of assassination attempts on land agents in the county that in April 1847 the *King's County Chronicle* thought it necessary, when reporting on the shooting of

---

1 *Nation*, 30 Oct. 1852.   2 'Cases of tenantry eviction: letters and comments thereon from newspapers, 1840–47' (NLI, 5A 3234).   3 O'Neill, 'The Famine in Offaly', p. 646.   4 Donnelly Jr, *The Great Irish potato Famine*, p. 139   5 John Julian, Parsonstown to under secretary, Dublin Castle, 20 Aug. 1850 (OPKC, 15/352).   6 See Smith, *Killoughy barracks affray*.

John Wilson of Cloneygowan, to highlight that he was neither a landlord nor an agent.[7] The murder of land agents was merely the most serious manifestation of the violence directed against that occupation during these years; had would-be assassins more success, the figures would have been considerably higher.[8] But what was the context in which agents were attacked and murdered in King's County and what were the possible motivations involved in individual cases?

In 1845, John Mayne, who managed the estates of Sir St George Ralph Gore, ninth baronet (1841–87), located in counties Limerick, Galway and King's County, was the first land agent to be murdered in King's County during the Famine. Unfortunately, there appears to be few contemporary reports or evidence surrounding his murder. Mayne's successor, appointed the following year, was Charles Trench Cage, regarded as 'a gentleman most respectfully connected'.[9] When he arrived as agent in King's County he began an extensive 'remodelling' of the Gore estate in what has been described as the 'broom syndrome', where tenants were quickly cleared.[10] Reviled by the tenants, he was murdered at Ferbane in October 1849 following the eviction of four families and the serving of several others with ejectment bills. The *King's County Chronicle* noted it was 'one of the most daring and atrocious murders carried out in this blood stained county', the latter adjective suggesting the extent of violence there.[11] The Gore estate consisted of the townlands of Endrim and Creggan, near the village of Ferbane in the barony of Garrycastle, amounting to just over 1,100 acres. By the mid-1840s it seems that rents were not being paid by tenants and it was next to impossible for the agent to collect the same. When Cage arrived at Ferbane he spent a few months renovating the school that had been built for the tenants' children. Mayne's murder obviously played on his mind and he carried a percussion gun stick on all occasions when going over the estate. His bailiff, Molloy, had been warned that if Cage came to live at Endrim he would be murdered. On Sunday 12 October 1849, he left Endrim cottage to attend service at Ferbane. Riding a horse belonging to a farmer named Patrick Spollen, he was accompanied by a tenant, Patrick Cahern. Significantly, he had the sum of £11 8*s*. in his pocket, which remained untouched after the attack.[12] Somewhere near Ferbane he was ambushed. He returned fire at his would-be assassins but was fatally wounded. Despite the incident taking place on a very public road, with several witnesses, the assassins were never convicted. John Julian, the county solicitor, believed the cause of Cage's death lay in his endeavours to remove the smaller class of tenants and to consolidate their farms into more viable units. There was conflicting evidence

7 *KCC*, 21 Apr. 1847. 8 Revealingly, in 1847 Lord Crofton, a Co. Roscommon landlord, noted that 'although I am beyond their reach, my agent, Mr Brown is in a perilous situation'. See Lord Crofton to under secretary, Dublin Castle, 5 Dec. 1847 (OPKC, 1848). 9 *Economist*, 20 Oct. 1849. 10 Quoted in Ryan, *The dear old town*, p. 75. 11 *KCC*, 14 Oct. 1849. 12 Ibid., 17 Oct. 1849.

presented about Cage's management policy. By some he was considered strict towards 'bad tenants' but liberal and encouraging to others. In 1848 he had evicted a number of tenants and taken possession of over 100 acres. Unable to secure tenants for this holding he farmed it himself, therefore becoming more odious to the local community.[13] A number of suspects were arrested. An approver, Thomas Johnston, named three men – Patrick Kelly, Bernard Gunning and Edward Farrell – as the assassins.[14] Julian argued that the evidence of Johnston and another approver, Hugh Egan, 'a miserable cratur', would not be sufficient to go on trial. They were so destitute that when they were placed in Mullingar gaol they had to be given new clothes for the trial.[15] The prosecution's case collapsed because the magistrates were unable to give credit to the evidence of the informers which was, to say the least, conflicting.[16]

It was a fate to befall many murder trials in King's County during the Famine. Following the murder, David Fitzgerald and his son William were appointed as agents of the estate and also of Gore's property in Co. Limerick. Fitzgerald adopted a policy of conciliation by negotiating with tenants who had the 'disposition to act properly' and abatements were duly given. In January 1850 he carried out a survey of the tenants in the presence of Gore, and having assessed their character, agreed in some instances to give abatements and in others to increase the size of the tenant's holdings. At this stage some degree of stability seemed to have been brought to the estate. However, seven months later, when Gore went back to Ferbane with William Fitzgerald, none of the tenants would meet with them. Fitzgerald believed that the return to Ferbane of three men who had been implicated in the murder of Cage had contributed to the change in the tenants' mindset. He believed that it was now necessary to seize crops and animals to assert his authority, for which police assistance was required.[17] Fearing for their safety, neither the agent nor his son chose to live at Ferbane and infrequently visited the estate, preferring instead to place responsibility in the hands of Molloy, the bailiff.

The third agent to be murdered was Robert Pyke, in August 1850. Pyke had been originally employed at Robert Cassidy's estate at Killyon as an engineer to instruct on proper drainage and other means of improvement. He was subsequently brought in as agent to replace John Corcoran who Cassidy believed was too lenient with tenants. Like Cage, his eviction policy on the Cassidy estate made him unpopular with the tenantry. However, his employer saw his murder as being part of a much wider anti-rent conspiracy and that 'a system of low party business which is spread over all that part of the county from

13 John Julian to under secretary, Dublin Castle, 15 Oct. 1849 (OPKC, 1849, 15/483).
14 Brendan Ryan, *Policing in West Offaly, 1814–1922* (Tullamore, 2009), p. 20.   15 John Julian to under secretary, Dublin Castle, 5 Mar. 1850 (OPKC, 15/126).   16 John Gilbert King and Robert Lauder, Ferbane to under secretary, Dublin Castle [nd] (OPKC, 15/68).   17 David Fitzgerald to T.N. Redington, 29 Aug. 1849 (OPKC 1849, 15/405).

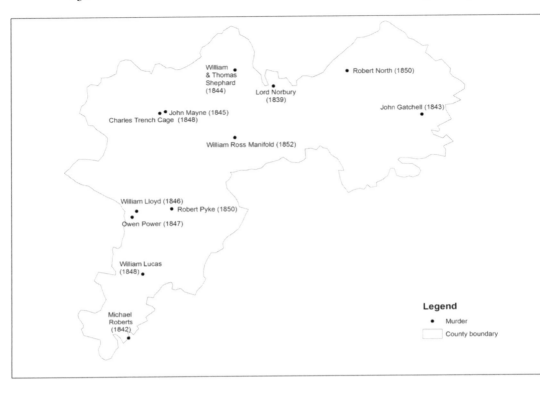

3 Locations where landlords and land agents were murdered in King's County, 1830–60

Knockhill to Mr Darby's of Leap and thence to Ferbane' was responsible for the murder. Cassidy did concede that the tenants on his estate probably had no part in the murder 'yet they rejoice and believe it is a move in their favour'. But significantly he also warned that if there were further attempts to seize crops there would be more murders of that nature and revealingly concluded that his tenants would prefer to be shot or hanged than to go to the workhouse in Parsonstown.[18] Pyke's murder caught the attention of the national press, with the *Times* noting that not since the murder of Norbury in 1839 had there been 'a more audacious, horrible or revolting murder than that of the agent Pyke'.[19]

Once again the motivation for the crime can be traced to the agent's estate management policy and his confrontation with tenants who had refused, or were unable, to pay their rents after the harvest of 1846. Again, like Heenan on the

18 Robert Cassidy, Monasterevin to under secretary, Dublin Castle, 21 Aug. 1850 (OPKC, 15/351). 19 *Times*, 8 Aug. 1850.

Rosse estate, he seems to have been selective in terms of who he granted abatements to – namely those who were 'in a position to pay rent' at a later stage. In 1848 and 1849 Pyke undertook measures to remove those who could not maintain themselves, pay the rent or till their lands to their advantage. At this stage he was reputed to have boasted: 'there is not a ruffian in the country able to shoot me'.[20] Again, he too was murdered on a public road during harvest time when there were large numbers of people working in the fields. According to one contemporary account at least fifty people had witnessed the murder but none could be found that would testify to what they had seen.[21] Cassidy was adamant that the murder of his agent would not deter him in executing ejectment decrees. In an effort to prove that 'the law is stronger than faction and that even murder will not prevent the rights of property being carried out' he continued with eviction.[22] To show an example he visited Killyon and was present at the eviction of eleven families.[23] John Corcoran was reinstated as agent, an unenviable position it seems, as when Cassidy went over the rental books he lamented that all seemed 'very gloomy'.[24]

One of four brothers employed as an agent in King's County, William Ross Manifold of Cadamstown was murdered in 1852. He was agent for the O'Connor Morris estate in the barony of Ballyboy. Like Cage and Pyke contemporary accounts depict him as being a benevolent land agent, although the writers in each instance obviously displayed a hint of bias. The *King's County Chronicle* described Manifold as 'a gentleman of unusually kind habits and disposition and that it was not in his power to injure or oppress a single human being'.[25] Indeed, it was reported that he resigned as baronial chief constable because of the harsh measures he was expected to take with the rate payers. It was further claimed that his benevolence was the reason why many of the inhabitants of the Parsonstown Poor Law Union had not ended up in the workhouse.[26] However, such a eulogy was obviously not shared by all. The background to the murder of Manifold is more complex than that of Cage or Pyke and although no motive was ever proven, several were offered. Capt Carew Shapland Morris took over the O'Connor Morris estate in 1851 having purchased it in the Incumbered Estates Court. Newspaper reports claimed that the previous owner had already collected whatever rent he could from the tenants and that Carew Shapland Morris instructed his agent, Manifold, to collect the rents again. William O'Connor Morris contradicted a report in the *Leinster Express* which laid part of the blame with him for the murder. He refuted that both himself and Carew Shapland Morris had laid claim to the rents on the estate and concluded: 'by expressing admiration of the many excellent qualities of the gentleman who has

20 Pey (ed.), *Eglish*, p. 123.   **21** Alexander Somerville, *The whistler at the plough: containing travels, statistics and descriptions* (Manchester, 1852), p. 95.   **22** Robert Cassidy, Monasterevin to under secretary, Dublin Castle, 21 Aug. 1850 (OPKC, 15/351).   **23** Pey (ed.), *Eglish*, p. 124. **24** 'Diary of Robert Cassidy, 1850' (NLI, Cassidy papers).   **25** *KCC*, 21 Oct. 1852.   **26** Ibid.

thus been suddenly taken away. He had been the agent of the former and was the agent of the present proprietor of the estate, and I believe gave the greatest satisfaction to both his employers'.[27] However, in later years O'Connor Morris put forward another explanation for the murder when he wrote: 'the agent of the purchaser was most unhappily shot – whether this was the crime of the injured tenants has never been proved to this day; but even if it was, a wrong had been done, and someone in the Incumbered Estates Court was unwittingly to blame'.[28] Andrew Gamble, who was employed as agent on the O'Connor Morris estate prior to Manifold, also challenged assertions that he had harshly treated the tenants.[29] At any rate, some of the tenants refused Manifold's request for the rents and he duly took action against seven of them, issuing eviction orders, and having served these he was shot while returning from Tullamore. He had in his possession £47 and ejectment papers, none of which were taken.[30]

What is significant, if the report in the *Times* is to be believed, is that 'not one Catholic attended the funeral of Manifold at Ballyboy'. In the days following the murder 'few of the peasantry showed themselves and the few that did, showed their apathy and indifference to what had just occurred'.[31] Two Dunne brothers who had been ejected from their holding near Mount Pleasant became the immediate suspects. Though the government offered £100 for information, none was forthcoming. The murder also appears to have drawn a sincere response from the gentry. At the end of October Lord Rosse called a meeting of the magistrates of the southern baronies of the county to inquire into the murder.[32] On this occasion the magistrates pledged a further £300 reward for the apprehension of the culprits, a sum that was later raised to £600. Eventually, information was forthcoming and Thomas McCormack was imprisoned for the murder; his house was located at the end of the demesne wall at Pallas, close to the scene of the murder.[33] Whether McCormack was involved or not in the murder was never proved. In local lore Manifold told several tenants, including McCormack, that they would be shortly required to surrender their land to which McCormack allegedly replied that the agent 'might not be around very soon to oversee such a plan'.[34] Significantly, the names of the above murdered agents (and that of John Gatchell in 1843) survive to the present day in 'Cage's bridge', 'Pyke's tree', 'Gatchell's bush' and 'Manifold's hole', the reputed scenes of the atrocities. Indeed, until the end of the Irish War of Independence in 1921 Manifold's hat hung at Killoughy RIC barracks.

That contemporary opinions on the management of land differed was evident from the reports that emerged after the aforementioned murders. Around the same time as the murder of Manifold the *Nation* newspaper commented that

---

27 Ibid., 27 Oct. 1852.   28 O'Connor Morris, *Memories*, p. 125.   29 *KCC*, 13 Apr. 1853.
30 Ibid., 21 Oct. 1852.   31 *Times*, 27 Oct. 1852.   32 Ibid., 2 Nov. 1852.   33 *KCC*, 2 Feb. 1853.   34 Ibid., 3 Mar. 1853.

'murders do not take place where the rents are fair and the tenures long'.[35] The motivation behind the murders of Cage, Pyke and Manifold possibly indicates why a nationalist newspaper would reach this conclusion. Besides agents, landlords also became the targets of a disgruntled tenantry. The most notorious and well-documented murder of a landlord during the Famine was the case of Major Denis Mahon at Strokestown, Co. Roscommon, in November 1847.[36] Mahon's murder received international attention and was commented on from Westminster to the Vatican. Yet there were others whose murders did not receive the same amount of attention. In King's County two landlords were murdered, one of whom, William Lucas of Brosna, acted as agent of his own estate. It has been noted previously that Lucas had difficulty collecting his rents from 1846 and, as a result, the following year he began to clear recalcitrant tenants from the estate. Steadfastly, a number of these erected temporary huts and continued to reside there.[37] The incident generated some controversy and John Julian, the crown solicitor for King's County, regretted that these 'ejected' tenants at Lisduff had returned because 'it affects every person residing and having property in the neighbourhood'.[38] When Lucas was murdered in October 1848 Julian reported that it was by distress and civil bill process that he had got rent 'tolerably well'.[39] It mattered little that in the past he had reduced rents or that he had subscribed handsomely to the Seir Kieran relief committee.[40] It seems that Lucas had received a number of warnings that his life was in danger, but he continued to accompany his bailiff and was present at the levelling of fourteen houses at Brosna, which eventually sealed his fate.[41] Again, no one was ever convicted of the murder, but a man named John Scott later confessed to the crime as he lay dying of typhus in Tullamore gaol in May 1849.[42] The other landlord murdered in King's County was Roger North, near Croghan, in September 1850. Once again, the eviction of a number of tenants at Garyduff was perceived to be the reason for his murder.[43] North's murder mirrored that of Daniel Egan of Ballydonagh, near Dunkerrin, the son of a middleman, who having evicted a number of under-tenants was murdered in 1849.[44]

Of more relevance here is the litany of attacks on agents that took place during the course of the Famine. They were also the target of ubiquitous threatening letters. One of these letters to George Garvey reflected the perception that the lower orders had of agents and the gentry in general during the Famine: 'The poor will not starve while Garvey and other gentlemen have plenty of fat sheep'

35 *Nation*, 30 Oct. 1852. **36** Reilly, 'Agents, eviction and assisted emigration'. **37** Anne Lucas, Brosna to earl of Clarendon (OPKC, 1847, 15/638). **38** John Julian to Colonel Lloyd, 1 Dec. 1847 (OPKC, 1847, 15/ 637). **39** O'Neill, 'Famine Evictions', p. 35. **40** Ibid., p. 36. See also 'Subscribers of the Seir Kieran Relief Committee' (RLFC, 1846, 2/4441/41). **41** John Julian to Lord Rosse, Oct. 1847 (OPKC, 1847, 15/558). **42** *LE*, 2 June 1849. **43** 'Petition of J.H. Walsh, John Wakely and John Lucas, 16 Oct. 1850' (OPKC, 1850). **44** O'Rian, *Dunkerrin*, p. 141.

concluded one threatening notice. [45] Such sentiments may explain why a large number of the tenants at the Trench estate at Shinrone stole upwards of thirty sheep from Cangort Park, although these were later recovered by the constabulary.[46] In January 1848 James Devery, who chose to remain among the tenantry of the Fitzwilliam estate at Cloghan, was attacked and robbed of three stone of flour, oats and a donkey. On this occasion Devery's wife was also assaulted.[47] In May 1849 two bailiffs, Coughlan and Hinsey, were 'waylaid' and beaten at Frankford as they were returning from Tullamore having arrested a tenant of Robert Cassidy and brought him from Kinnitty to Tullamore to be lodged in gaol. Coughlan later died from the wounds he received, while Hinsey 'lay critical for some weeks'.[48] Patrick Fallon, agent of the Dowdall estate at Ballycumber, survived several attempts on his life. In February 1849 he was shot at when collecting rent and the following May 'a man snapped a gun at him several times' at Leabeg.[49] In July and December 1849 he was also robbed of the agency books near Ballycumber, suggesting that tenants did not want him to have records of their rental accounts.[50] The taking of estate books and records was a method adopted elsewhere; John Coughlan and William Read, two process servers at Ballinacur, near Kinnitty, were severely beaten and their books taken from them when they went to serve notices.[51] Of course such intimidation was not universally supported. When Colonel Westenra cleared a number of tenants at Sharavogue a threatening letter was sent to his wife, at which the tenants were said to have 'displayed horror and revulsion'. Presenting an address to her, the tenants praised the Westenra's 'many acts of kindness to the poor of your neighbourhood ... which will never be forgotten'. The address was signed by sixty tenants 'of all classes and creeds', while a reward of over £100 was offered to find the culprits of the letter.[52]

By June 1850 the north-east of the county, particularly the baronies of Warrenstown and Upper and Lower Philipstown, were said to be greatly disturbed by alleged Whiteboy offences.[53] By deeming them Whiteboy offences the authorities were suggesting some sort of conspiracy, where as in reality offences were sporadic and localized. If tenants in other counties stood by as evictions were daily carried out, those in King's County did not. Tenants on the Holmes and Bernard estates, for example, poisoned animals in response to a number of evictions at both estates.[54] The sons of James Delaney, a herd for Guy Atkinson of Cangort Park, were severely beaten by four men following

---

45 Ibid., p. 129.   46 *KCC*, 5 Jan. 1848.   47 Ibid., 12 Jan. 1848.   48 *Times*, 21 May 1849.
49 *KCC*, 23 May 1849.   50 Ibid., 4 July 1849 & 6 Dec. 1849. See also *LE*, 9 June 1849.
51 Pey (ed.), *Eglish*, p. 115. Elsewhere, in August 1849 shots were fired into the home of the landlord and agent Henry Drought at Oaklawn, Kinnitty, a day after he had evicted two tenants from nearby holdings. See *KCC*, 1 Aug. 1849.   52 *KCC*, 5 Jan. 1848.   53 John Hussey Walsh and John Lucas, Philipstown to under secretary, Dublin Castle, 4 June 1850 (OPKC, 15/285).
54 Ibid., 4 July 1849.

evictions.[55] Timothy Cloran, a caretaker at Capt. Richardson's estate, was shot at Rathbeg in March 1851, on the same day he presided over a number of evictions. On this occasion Cloran shot dead one of his assailants, Patrick Morgan. Cloran had been appointed to take care of a parcel of bog from which the previous caretaker was dismissed but was deemed 'to be obnoxious to the tenantry he dealt with'.[56] Thomas Day, bailiff of the Bennett estate, was attacked and beaten in a 'ferocious manner' in November 1852.[57] An attempt was also made to shoot J.G. Butler, a rent collector at the Westenra estate.[58] Edward Beecham, William J. Reamsbottom's clerk, was threatened with 'the death of Manifold and Cage' after having being present at the eviction of a family at Ballycumber. Prior to this, Reamsbottom, an agent at several estates, was said to have acted with 'lenience and upright character' in his duties.[59] In the weeks that followed the murder of Manifold in 1852, William White, the former manager of the Provincial Bank at Parsonstown, was appointed interim agent to collect the rent on the Rosse estate. Again, he too was quickly threatened that he would receive the same death as that of Manifold if he did not give up his office.[60] White, it appears, heeded the threat, because R.W. Townsend replaced him in December 1852 and by the following March he himself had resigned the position to George Garvey, perhaps further evidence of continued intimidation.[61] As a result of such sustained violence, landlords like Major Barry Fox of Annaghmore quit the county, deciding on absenteeism as a means of preserving their lives.[62]

Francis Bond Head was one of the few commentators of the day who highlighted the plight that many land agents faced, noting that many were 'now lying festering around you either with fractured skulls and broken limbs or with bodies perforated by bullets and shot'. According to Head, much of the trouble that land agents encountered stemmed from the scathing attacks of priests, and that their families were now mourning the irreparable loss after some had been shot while 'innocently cultivating land' or in 'domestic happiness seated in their own houses'.[63] Ultimately, it seems as if land agents were offered insufficient protection from either their employers or the law enforcement authorities in the carrying out of their duties. This was certainly the case of John Corcoran who complained to his employer Robert Cassidy that despite repeated threats he was not entitled to private protection by the police.[64] He was dependent upon his own appointed bailiffs, for example, to protect the livestock and crops distrained and indeed other property belonging to the landlord: 'the Killyon men have to patrol Thomastown and watch Eglish pound and leave your property and the furniture in your house much exposed to be carried away. If the Killyon men

55 Ibid., 15 Aug. 1849. 56 Ibid., 12 Mar. 1851. 57 Ibid., 3 Nov. 1852. 58 Ibid., 8 Dec. 1852 59 Ibid., 2 Feb. 1853. 60 Ibid., 3 Nov. 1852. 61 Ibid., 1 Dec. 1852. 62 'Minute book of Tullamore board of guardians, 23 Aug. 1850' (Offaly County Library). 63 Francis Bond Head, *A fortnight in Ireland* (London, 1852), p. 385. 64 *KCC*, 20 Oct. 1852.

were left in their own district we could at least call on them to prevent a violation of the peace'. The problem was that if the 'Killyon men' were in Thomastown other areas were left exposed; thus Corcoran reported that one tenant in particular, a man named Troy, was causing him numerous problems. Troy was aware when the men were on duty in Thomastown and openly carried off his distrained crops in the knowledge that he would meet with little resistance.[65] Ironically, as Corcoran was busy watching and distraining tenants in arrears he was also bitterly complaining that his own family had been badly treated by their landlord, Valentine Bennett of Thomastown. According to Corcoran such treatment would urge a man to look for the introduction of 'Tenant Right'. In his opinion Bennett had 'treated us worse than the worst pauper tenant' and had taken all the stock off their land despite Corcoran having spent over £500 in improvements and his father having paid the rent for over fifty years. However, the treatment of the Corcorans was probably politically motivated, the family having voted for the Liberal candidates at the 1852 elections; he was by his own admission penalized 'for giving a vote in accordance with the dictates of his conscience'.[66]

The murder of land agents in King's County represented the most notorious aspect of agrarian crime in the period under study. That seven agents in total were murdered not only suggests the conflicting attitude of tenants towards estate management policy, but also indicates just how dangerous the agency occupation could be during periods of economic crisis. Indeed, in 1852 Lord Annelsey's land agent in Co. Down, William Wann, complained that an insurance company had refused to insure his life because of his occupation.[67] Elsewhere, owing to the threats that he faced daily, Thomas Cooke Trench, an extensive land agent in Co. Kildare, took his own life in 1851.[68] Such hazards were portrayed by Carleton in the novel, *The Squanders of Castle Squander*, where the agency of an estate is passed over by one man who declares that he wishes to die a natural death, thus underlining the fear and danger that came with such an occupation in the mid-nineteenth century.[69] Manifold's murder in October 1852, being the last of the seven in King's County, also more-or-less coincided with the end of the Famine crisis and the beginning of an economic upturn that, with the exception of the early 1860s, was to last until the Land War era of the late 1870s. There were to be sporadic outbreaks of agrarian agitation in King's County from the Famine to the Land War; however, there was no further attempt on a land agent's life until 1875, when one was made on the life of John Exshaw, agent of the Head estate at Derrylahan, near Parsonstown following the seizure of crops for rent.[70] This was despite, for example, the

65 John Corcoran, Thomastown to Robert Cassidy, Monasterevin, 27 Aug. 1852 (NLI, Cassidy papers). 66 Ibid. 67 Quoted in Vaughan, *Landlord and tenants*, p. 138. 68 *Morning Post*, 15 Apr. 1851. 69 William Carleton, *The Squanders of Castle Squander* (Dublin, 1852), p. 259. 70 See *Times*, 1 Oct. 1875.

extensive clearances on the Digby estate at Geashill in the late 1850s by William Steuart Trench and his son Thomas Weldon Trench to make way for improvements. The late 1850s were very different times though, and these clearances were carried out during a period of economic prosperity.

9 Aftermath of the Famine: agents and the Incumbered Estates Court

That the Famine was mainly responsible for the ruin of many Irish landlords is pervasive in Irish historiography.[1] However, as James Donnelly and others have argued, the day of reckoning would have arrived whether the Famine had occurred or not.[2] For many agents it became increasingly impossible to collect rents and so accumulating debts drove several landed estates to bankruptcy. However, the scale of their debts, as revealed in their applications to the Incumbered Estates Court, were 'far too great to have been caused by the Famine alone'. Quite simply, years of extravagant living had finally caught up on landlords and the Famine was the proverbial 'last straw'.[3] Landlord indebtedness was not a new thing, as evidenced by the introduction by the government, earlier in the nineteenth century, of a series of statues to deal with insolvency. These included the establishment of a Court for the Relief of Insolvent Debtors in 1818; the Receivers Act, introduced in 1835, with two permanent Commissioners of Bankruptcy being appointed the following year.[4] For a variety of reasons these measures largely failed, and by the mid-1840s it seemed that the government could not overcome the problem of insolvency. By 1849, four years into the Famine, property with an estimated rental of £2 million in Ireland was under the control of the Court of Equity – the older debts caused by generations of lavish expenditure and costly litigation, the more recent by the fall in rents and rise in rates.[5] In King's County, for example, as many as seventeen estates were in chancery at this time. Thus, the government, Irish landlords and indeed their mortgagees were under considerable pressure to deal with the situation.[6] In the hope of finally solving the problem, the Incumbered Estates Act was introduced in 1849, and, as Cormac Ó Gráda has argued, the impact of the Famine on landlordism is difficult to separate from the creation of the Incumbered Estates court.[7] The act was designed to create 'a new and more efficient landlord'.[8] It was also designed to expedite the sale of incumbered property by making the legal process less complicated, something that had been called for four years previously by the Devon Commission, which had argued that every help should be given to facilitate quick sales in order to avoid lengthy and costly litigation cases.[9] Perhaps arising from that, in March 1845, Count Magawley, a

1 See Cormac Ó Gráda, 'Bankrupt landlords and the Great Irish Famine' in Cormac Ó Gráda (ed.), *Ireland's Great Famine: interdisciplinary perspectives* (Dublin, 2006), p. 59. 2 Ibid., p. 58. 3 Ibid., p. 56. 4 Tim O'Neill, 'Doing local history', *Journal of the Galway Archaeological and Historical Society*, 53 (2001), p. 55. 5 Ó'Gráda, 'Bankrupt landlords', p. 58. 6 Dooley, *A research guide*, p. 31. 7 Ó Gráda, 'Bankrupt landlords', p. 49. 8 Paul Bew, *Ireland: the politics of enmity*, p. 208. 9 Eriksson, 'Irish landlords and the Great Irish Famine', p. 3.

landlord in the barony of Ballyboy, petitioned Sir Robert Peel to encourage the government to facilitate and accelerate land sales.[10]

The necessity of such an act, as the Famine wore on, was aptly summed up by Percy Fitzgerald, a Co. Louth barrister, who noted that 'it was indeed time that something should be done ... the incumbrances had to be cut out with a knife'.[11] In particular, Fitzgerald criticized the actions of landlords, agents and middlemen for draining away the 'vitals' of their estates and for allowing arrears to mount. He was also vocal about their indifferent and sometimes cruel treatment of tenants. Over the next thirty years or so, a quarter of the land in Ireland changed hands as a result of the Incumbered Estates Act and land agents were to play a significant role in this development. Ironically, it may be argued, many land agents had been responsible for bringing estates before the court in the first place.[12] In King's County, as elsewhere, several landowners had depended on loans and mortgages provided by their fellow proprietors for survival.[13] When the time arrived for the loans to be repaid it spelled financial ruin. Under the terms of the act a property was defined as incumbered when the income from the rent did not suffice to service the interest charges or when the property was no longer acceptable as security for a loan.[14] The government hoped that the act would encourage outside investment; as George Boyce commented, 'to encourage free trade in land' and thereby create a much-needed stimulus to the economy.[15] In essence, however, such a plan failed and while much remains to be understood about the workings and success of the court, it did not live up to expectations. Indeed, only £3 million of the £20 million invested in 3,000 Irish estates from 1849 to 1857 came from outside the country. Nonetheless, the act resulted in the largest transfer of land in Ireland since the 1650s and thus made a significant impact on the ownership and management of landed estates.

From 1849 to 1855, 148 townlands in King's County (thirteen per cent of the total number) had land auctioned in the court, while sales of estates in the county up to 1853 amounted to £132,696.[16] Indeed, in the first fifteen months of the court's operation some 1,477 King's County cases were entered, evidence, perhaps, of the scale of bankruptcy among the county's landowners. For land agents operating in the county the sale of estates through the courts presented a new responsibility for them, while also providing challenges that many were

10 Quoted in Gray, *Famine, land, politics*, p. 84. His own estate was later sold under the Incumbered Estates Court in 1852. Count Magawley sold his estate at Frankford for seventeen and half years purchase or £11, 565. See *Times*, 19 Nov. 1852. See also Michael Byrne, 'The Magawley's of Temora and the Banons of Broughall, county Offaly', *Offaly Heritage*, 6 (2010), pp 128–78. 11 Percy Fitzgerald, *The story of the Incumbered Estates Court* (London, 1862), pp 3–6. 12 Quoted in Ó Gráda, 'Bankrupt landlords', p. 50. 13 Ibid., p. 58. 14 W.A. Maguire, 'Lord Donegall and the sale of Belfast: a case history from the Encumbered Estate Court', *The Economic History Review*, n.s., 29:4 (Nov. 1976), p. 572. 15 Quoted in Alvin Jackson, *Ireland, 1798–1998: politics and war* (Oxford, 1999), p. 77. 16 Ó Gráda, 'Bankrupt landlords', p. 53. See also O'Neill, 'The Famine in Offaly', p. 728.

unable to attend to, owing to various social backgrounds and circumstances. As a barrister in the court, Francis Longworth Dames, the son of a King's County landlord, would have been familiar with many of the cases that came before him.[17] These involved some of the largest landowners in the county – Sir Andrew Armstrong, Robert Blosse Lynch, Earl Fitzwilliam, Count Magawley, Garrett O'Moore, Earl Milltown and William O'Connor Morris. Thomas Spunner's estate at Shinrone was among the first in King's County to be sold in the court in April 1850, and this case highlighted many of the problems that the court would encounter, and the difficulties for all concerned. Although a relatively small holding (only 142 acres), a number of jointures and mortgages meant that the owner himself was forced to bring a case before the court. However, in what the *Morning Chronicle* described as a sale of 'ludicrous character', Thomas Spunner bought out all the creditors and jointures by paying £1,500 for the property or fifteen years purchase.[18] At Gallen, near Ferbane, Sir Andrew Armstrong was forced to sell part of his estate for £12,950 or twenty years purchase of rents of roughly £650 per annum.[19] Similarly, Earl Fitzwilliam sold his estate at Cloghan for seventeen years purchase of the rental – he had only bought the estate in 1847.[20] In 1852, the Revd William Minchin at Moneygall sold his estate before emigrating to Australia with his young family. The subsequent auction, held in the court house in Roscrea, was thronged with people taking an interest in the property; there were several mortgages, judgments and annuities charged on the estate when Richard Chadwick petitioned the court to force its sale.[21] Among the purchasers were Montague Blackett, a native of Northumberland.[22] Other landlords took advantage of their neighbours' misfortunes; Thomas L'Estrange purchased the townland of Ballyloughan, part of the aforementioned Fitzwilliam estate in 1853 for £5,000; James Drought purchased much of the O'Moore estate at Cloghan and even the county court solicitor, John Julian, was among the successful bidders. A new class of proprietor also emerged. J.J. Bird, a Dublin medical doctor, purchased part of Cloghan Castle demesne for £400,[23] while in 1851, 3,200 acres of the O'Moore estates at Cloghan were sold to Dr Robert Graves, one of the outstanding doctors of the nineteenth century. Prior to the sale of the estate, Garrett O'Moore had granted long leases, in some cases for ninety years, to 'respectable tenants', including the agents, James Devery and Daniel L'Estrange.[24] Wealthy millers and merchants who had made fortunes during the Famine, such as the Maxwell's of Ballinacard

17 Rob Goodbody, *Sir Charles Domville and his Shankill estate, county Dublin, 1857–71* (Dublin, 2003), p. 15.   18 *Times*, 15 Apr. 1850. See also *Morning Chronicle*, 15 Apr. 1850 and *Ipswich Journal*, 20 Apr. 1850.   19 Ibid., 28 June 1852.   20 Ibid., 18 Apr. 1853.   21 *Nenagh Guardian*, 4 and 11 Dec. 1852.   22 *Tipperary Vindicator*, 5 June 1852.   23 *Nenagh Guardian*, June–Dec. 1851 and Jan.–June 1852.   24 Sir William Hale-White, *Great doctors of the nineteenth century* (London, 1935), pp 126–7. Graves was a professor in the Institute of Medicine in Trinity College Dublin (1826–7) and was synonymous with the treatment of disease. His epitaph testified to such: 'He fed fever'.

and the Goodbodys of Clara, also bought large tracts of land in the Incumbered Estates Court. Both families subsequently had the noted architect, John Skipton Mulvaney, design lavish country homes for them as their fortunes increased in the 1850s.[25]

Agents were also among those who benefited from the sale of estates, none more so than the notorious 'prince of swindlers', John Sadlier, the earl of Portarlington's agent. Sadlier had commenced the agency in the late 1840s when the estate was described as resembling 'the immediate neighbourhood of some volcano'.[26] From 1849 to 1854 he purchased several estates in counties Tipperary, Cork, Waterford, Mayo, Galway, Kerry, Limerick and Roscommon at a value of £233,000 – some on behalf of clients, others for himself.[27] Elsewhere, the Manifold brothers were also in a position to purchase several tracts of land from their employers and neighbouring landowners, and indeed profited handsomely in the aftermath of the Famine. Others did likewise. George Garvey purchased several townlands in 1853, while Abraham Bagnall, agent on the King estate, purchased the townland of Rashina, part of the Armstrong estate, for £2,550.[28] In the same year, he also purchased part of the O'Moore estate at Cloghan Hill, almost 900 acres, for £5,200.[29] All of this, of course, points to the obvious wealth that land agents had accrued during the Famine and the favourable position many now found themselves in. On the other hand, the impact of the Famine on the personal finances of a few agents led to their demise and forced some into selling their own estates. For example, Charles Hamilton, agent of the Tyrrell estate near Edenderry (as well as the Colley Palmer and Harberton estates in Co. Kildare), was forced to sell his estates in the Incumbered Estates Court.[30]

Although those like John Julian, the crown solicitor, rejoiced in the tranquillity of King's County by 1850, a new wave of clearances began in the years that followed and coincided in many instances with the sale of land in the Incumbered Estates Court. One of the reasons for this was that insolvent landlords, hoping to sell their estates in the court, wanted to rid themselves of impoverished tenants so as to make the estate more appealing to potential purchasers, while those that purchased land cared little for those who were now out of lease; the eviction of tenants on the aforementioned Armstrong estate highlighted this. Equally, clearances were part of more stringent estate management policies – aimed at consolidating and enlarging smallholdings into more

25 National Inventory of Architectural Heritage, *An introduction to the architectural heritage of county Offaly* (Dublin, 2006), p. 95. **26** Ó Gráda, 'Bankrupt landlords', pp 51–2. **27** See O'Shea, *Prince of swindlers*. **28** Rolleston papers (NLI, MS 13,794 (1)). See also 'Sale of the estate of Andrew Armstrong, 25 June 1852' (NLI, O'Brien rentals). **29** 'The estate of the earl of Fitzwilliam, Cloghan, in the barony of Garrycastle, King's County sold under the Incumbered Estates Court, 15 April 1853' (O'Brien rentals). **30** Index of the estates sold in the Incumbered and landed estates court, 1850 to 1864 (O'Brien rentals).

viable units and ridding estates of middlemen. These policies were adopted, not only by new owners, but also by some landlords who had survived the Famine. Perhaps the most controversial clearance, and one that highlighted the complexities of land-related issues in the county, occurred in June 1852, with the eviction of fifty-six people from the crown lands at Kilcloncouse, near Kinnitty. In an effort to save face (and also to ensure that the eviction was final), all those cleared were assisted in emigration, at a cost of £363, first to Liverpool and then to New York; all, that is, with the exception of one man, Patrick Lowry, who for the strange reason that he had only one eye was deemed unfit for New York and so was sent to Philadelphia![31] According to the earl of Donoughmore the crown estates were the worst managed properties in Ireland. In 1829, leases on the 900-acre crown estate at Kilcloncouse (which had been confiscated from Colonel Grace in the 1640s) were granted to tenants for twenty-one years. Rents had been paid regularly until 1846 when twelve families, numbering sixty-eight persons, found themselves without any provisions and 'in most precarious state'. In April 1847, the commissioners acting for the Court of Chancery ordered the rent collector 'to give such indulgence in payment to each tenant as their circumstance may require', after a number of tenants had appealed for leniency. Further adding to their problems was the fact that part of the estate was occupied by the Revd Francis McMahon, the Catholic priest of Kinnitty, which had caused considerable unrest in the locality. McMahon refused to give up possession of the land after he had promised to do so, looking only to be allowed remove his crops. The priest had bought the goodwill to a twenty-five acre holding from an emigrating tenant in 1843. When McMahon's lease expired in 1850 it was decided to bring two farms together. Taking the commissioners to task because he had not been compensated for improvements, McMahon continued to agitate on the tenant's behalf, claiming that only farms of Catholic tenants had been brought under the 'rationalization' plan. Using the influence of the aforementioned John Sadlier, McMahon succeeded in having the commissioner dismissed.[32] Remarkably, the Kilcloncouse estate was later sold to Loftus Bland, MP for King's County, for £8,390 and the tenants who remained were in no better circumstances than they had been under the crown.[33]

While many evictions in the early 1850s were carried out as a result of the introduction of the Incumbered Estates Court, others may have been as a result of the keenly contested election of 1852. As the Famine drew to a close, landlords and agents in King's County were determined to regain control over local politics and reassert their dominance over the tenantry. The 1847 general

---

31 Eilish Ellis, 'State aided Emigration schemes from Crown estates in Ireland, *c.*1850', *Analecta Hibernica*, 22 (1960), p. 383.   32 *Correspondence with reference to drainage and valuation of lands of Kilcloncouse, in King's County*, HC 1862 [286] liii, 615.   33 *House of Lords debates*, 134, 599–605 (23 June 1854).

election, as we have seen, had been a considerable victory for Repeal candidates despite assumptions that the party was in decline. This was something that greatly angered landlords and their agents. Lord Palmerston believed that it was 'not natural' that the Irish population had given victory to the Repeal party after the British government and Irish landlords had prevented the starvation of over three million people.[34] His sentiments were widely reiterated, and it was not surprising that the general election of 1852 reverted to type in King's County, with the Catholic clergy vying with landlords for supremecy. Agents were once again cast into the firing line. For many tenants, the fate of being ostracized by the local Catholic clergy was at least as serious as being evicted by the landlord, and so they were left in a perilous position. Indeed, even after the elections the clergy were not content with their success and were reported to have continued to 'pour scorn on the renegades' who did not vote for Catholic candidates.[35]

Amid such heightened tensions, 1852 proved to be a year of continued agitation and eviction. A report from Parsonstown in July outlined the seriousness of election agitation: 'this town is the scene at this moment of the most frightful excitement and disorder that can be conceived. The landlords are utterly paralysed; all their efforts to protect their tenantry from the open and undisguised intimidation of the priests have been unavailing'.[36] A combination of a small electorate and public voting meant that landlords and their agents knew who the tenants voted for at election time. Ultimately, where tenants refused to vote for the landlord's candidate, eviction was threatened. On the day of the 1852 election, George Garvey had many of the Durrow tenants assembled at Lord Norbury's residence in a show of support for the Bernard candidature. However, the Revd O'Farrell of Durrow appeared 'with some empty cars and used all sorts of spiritual and physical threats to induce the tenants to accompany him to vote for O'Brien and Bland'.[37] This was despite the fact that in the lead up to the election both the Catholic clergy and land agents had promised to respect the rights of tenants and religion.[38] It is not clear just how many tenants were evicted in King's County in the aftermath of the election but the continued unrest would indicate that the numbers were quite substantial. In August 1852, a commentator using the pseudonym 'Rusticus', writing in the *Nation*, criticized King's County landlords who were 'of no repute or little character'. According to the writer, Lord Rosse had left his place 'in the world of science' to lecture on the management of land and local politics and had ordered his agent to recover the rent and arrears of all those who had dared to vote against his interest. Sarcastically, and playing on Rosse's scientific achievements, 'Rusticus' believed that the earl would soon be able to announce another discovery, that is in

34 Thomas P. O'Neill, 'The organization and administration of relief, 1845–52' in Edwards & Williams (eds), *The Great Famine*, p. 255. **35** *Times*, 31 July 1852. **36** Ibid., 25 July 1852. **37** *KCC*, 28 July 1852. **38** *Nation*, 19 Jan. 1852.

'screwing the very last farthing out of the mere Irish'. Rosse was not alone in retaliating after the election results and was joined by a number of landowners in clearing the land. Francis Valentine Bennett's 'crowbar brigade' impounded the cattle, corn and belongings of tenants depending on how they had voted at election time.[39]

Evictions in King's County continued unabated in 1853. Throughout the county over 100 families, consisting of over 600 or more people, were evicted. The evictors included Lord Ashtown, Andrew Gamble, the Revd J. Alexander, A.W. Maxwell, A. Burchal, Andrew Armstrong, Sergeant Green, Mrs Hutchinson, John Pilkington, J.H. Drought, J.C. Westenra, Lord Rosse and Henry Kemmis. Another landlord called Winter evicted thirty-one families, some of which subsequently emigrated to Australia.[40] These evictions, whether as a result of the election or not, were another facet in the complex relationship of landlord and tenant in King's County, something that would become even more prominent as the tenantry became politically more empowered with the rise of the Home Rule movement from the early 1870s, and when landlords and agents alike were held up as symbols of everything that nationalist Ireland wanted to overthrow.

* * *

In the wake of the Great Famine land agents were faced with the task of surveying and mapping a decimated landscape. In many cases this was simply to ascertain who was left and who held what land. For land agents and their team of surveyors who ventured across land, which for the most part had been inhospitable territory during the Famine, the full scale of the calamity was made known. One such survey undertaken in the post-Famine period by John Logan on the Rosse estate at Parsonstown took four years to complete and highlighted the scale of the problems at hand. The survey provides ample evidence of the impact of the Famine and the radical transformation of an estate in its aftermath. The survey challenges the social memory of the Great Famine in the Parsonstown area, and showed that eviction and clearance had, in fact, taken place on the Rosse estate. On the basis of Logan's work, George Garvey, who was appointed agent of the Rosse estate in 1853, believed that the Famine had caused a 'revolution in Irish landed property'. He noted in particular the 'confusion where small tenancies have been numerous and where immediate interests usually termed middlemen have ceased to exist'. This observation points to two separate issues: one, that the Famine had obliterated the middlemen and second, where that had happened, small holders who survived found themselves in a

---

39 Ibid., 28 Aug. 1852.   40 'Return of evictions during the quarter ended 30 September 1853 compared with the preceding quarter and the cases preceding quarter of the past year' (NAI, CSROP, 1853/701/3/623/5).

limbo, not knowing who to look to in the future. In all likelihood many of these same smallholders were later cleared from the Rosse estate as the 1850s progressed in order to make way for more viable holdings, for it became Garvey's primary objective to 'restore and establish order in the rent accounts as well as in the division's arrangements and valuations of the respective farms'. In addition, he was anxious to quell local feuding over access to land. For Garvey, all holdings on the estate were to be properly mapped and boundaries defined. The rules for the management of the Rosse estates 'so equitably, liberally and considerably framed' in 1847 were to be continued, albeit with some revisions and additions. These proveded for the ending of the rundale system, the drainage of all lands and the stipulation that all improvements needed prior sanction from the agent before they could be carried out. In overseeing these changes to estate manage-ment Garvey looked for the 'cordial cooperation' of all concerned. Significantly, tenants were warned that the 'return to extensive cultivation of potatoes' was strictly prohibited.[41] Garvey's sentiments were widely reiterated by agents elsewhere who were equally adamant that large-scale dependence on potatoes could not continue. Indeed, the editor of the *King's County Chronicle* summed up the feeling at large when he argued that 'such a person who does not heed advice from an agriculturalist is a pest to the land'.[42]

At Parsonstown and across the Rosse estate Garvey quickly moved to collect what rents he could and received over £11,134 in rent in 1854, although arrears still amounted to over £6,000.[43] As happened following the publication of the 1847 estate 'rules', a large clearance of tenants was undertaken by the agent in 1853 and 1854. These evictions resulted in the loss of over £1,400 in arrears, but both landlord and agent believed that for future progress this was necessary. As noted above, the evictees were mainly smallholders, who in the eyes of the agent were unlikely to improve themselves in the years ahead. They included James Towers of Carrigeen, Deborah Guinan at Clonbonniff and the Claffey and Malone families at Fadden. Most owed only trifling amounts of arrears. On the other hand, and further evidence of the discrimination against smallholders, larger tenants such as Nancy Scully and John Kennedy at Killeen owed arrears of over £350 and were allowed to re-enter their holdings as caretakers. Generally, and this applied to many King's County estates, the rationale was that the arrears of smallholders could be done without; it was more important to gain access to their lands so that it could be redistributed in the process of creating more viable farms, and in some cases, extensive ranches. One of the best examples of this was at Kinnitty where Colonel Bernard 'removed some smallholders for the enlarge-ment of his own monster farms'. The creation of these ranches were universally detested. In the late 1860s, the *Times* newspaper questioned why 'a single

41 'Address from George Garvey to the tenantry of the Rosse estate, April 1853' (BCA, J/ 7/1–26).   42 *KCC*, 4 Feb. 1852.   43 'Rental of the earl of Rosse's estates and cash account for one year beginning 1 Jan. to 31 Dec. 1854' (BCA, Q/106/B).

individual, an elderly gentleman [Bernard] without any family should hold in his own hands thousands of acres of arable land, while so many industrious people have to live by the cultivation of the soil and are unable to get a few acres to till'.[44] Bernard was among a number of landlords who turned to grazierism in the aftermath of the Famine. Among the most successful of these graziers were Nesbitt at Tubberdaly, near Rhode, and Atkinson at Cangort, near Shinrone. This shift to ranching was to cause its own problems in the years ahead when antigrazierism would come to dominate the land question in King's County in the late nineteenth and early twentieth century.[45]

Although many agents had adopted a more professional approach to estate management, one of the most significant problems that existed in King's County in the aftermath of the Famine was the quantity of land which remained in the hands of schools, colleges, charities and foundations, none of which was adequately managed and where the tenants lived in appalling conditions. In most cases tenants had not seen or had any assistance from an agent during the Great Famine period and the situation did not improve during the 1850s. The management of the estates belonging to the Erasmus Smith and Banagher Royal Classical schools were cases in point. In 1857 a highly critical report on the management of the Erasmus Smith Schools' estates was published, highlighting that at Banagher the agent could find neither a map nor a valuation of the estate. Moreover, the agent had failed to collect any rent from 1842 to 1849, there were no leases, and no investment had been provided for improvements. By 1849 arrears at the estate were reckoned to be 'lost'.[46] Indeed, so inept was the agent that there was some degree of doubt about what land the school actually owned.[47] As a result of the report findings it was deemed necessary to replace the agent at Banagher and take legal proceedings against him.[48] A similar situation of mismanagement, in this case remarkably over a period of sixty years, existed at the Banagher Royal Classical School estate. While further work remains to be done in relation to the management of these estates and how their tenants fared during the Great Famine, it would appear that in most cases tenants on lands held by trusts, colleges and the church fared far worse than those under management of an agent or active landlord.

Problems such as the aforementioned were widespread. Significantly, agents failed to prevent many of the problems which were inherent in previous decades from continuing. Overcrowding was still unresolved by the early 1850s. At

---

44 *Times*, 29 Oct. 1869. 45 For a more in-depth study of the Ranch War in King's County see John Noel McEvoy, 'A study of the United Irish League in King's County, 1899–1918' (MA, St Patrick's College, Maynooth, 1992). 46 House of Commons, *Evidence taken before Her Majesty's commissioners of inquiry into the state of the Endowed Schools in Ireland*, 2 (Dublin, 1857), p. 31. 47 House of Commons, *Endowed Schools Commission: Report of Her Majesty's commissioners appointed to inquire into the endowments, funds and actual condition of all schools endowed for the purpose of education in Ireland* (Dublin, 1858), p. 265. 48 *Ibid.*, p. 236.

Lisclooney, for example, on a townland of 474 acres on the Rosse estate, tenants had built thirty-eight houses and subdivided holdings among their families.[49] Some landowners continued to pursue the policies that had been adopted throughout the Famine in the hope that tenants would act accordingly when abatements and other relief were provided. In February 1853 Sir William Cox ordered his agent to reduce the rent at the next spring gale by 30 per cent to the tenants on his King's County estate at Tynnecross, near Tullamore, in the hope that they would improve their ways.[50] However, the reaction of local communities to such policies summed up the fate of the land agent in general. In most cases tenants were reluctant to change their old ways and habits, and so adopted every measure possible to prevent the implementation of improvements. Indeed, when Jonathon Darby of Leap tried to improve the farming methods of his tenantry and in turn relieve distress, he was warned to 'mind his own business' or he would 'end in a coffin'.[51] At Geashill a man who returned from America to the Digby estate was shot dead after he took over the farm of an evicted tenant.[52] These are but two examples that typified the struggle for land and the intimidation of those who dared to occupy holdings in the decade after the Famine.

Eviction was a daily threat for many tenants, and this ensured that the memory of the Famine and subsequent emigration loomed large in the Irish psyche. The clearances and assisted emigration helped create an Irish diaspora scarred by the Famine, and who later used this calamity as a backdrop to subsequent agitation. In King's County the resentment towards the clearance of estates lingered. Interestingly, the number who were evicted during the 1850s was far greater than it had been during the years of the Famine. This possibly points to one of the reasons why King's County was one of the most disturbed counties in the decades that followed. However, by the end of the 1850s there were some who believed 'the present happy state of King's County' was mainly due to the Famine, emigration and the consolidation of farms which had begun in earnest prior to 1845. Consolidation, it was claimed, 'was arranged amicably without hardship or outrage'.[53] Yet it was the Famine clearances that were more vividly recollected in social memory, or at least clearances associated with the Famine, rather than those of other decades. While hunger and disease as well as clearances and emigration led to a dramatic decrease in the population of King's County, particularly at the lower end of the social scale, it also represented an opportunity for landlords to address the middleman system and more specifically the management of estates. For example, on the Cox estate, near Tullamore,

---

49 For instance, the Dolan family had built three houses on twelve acres, while Peter and John Lally had four houses on sixteen acres. Heenan's report did not offer any solutions to the problem of overcrowding, nor did it indicate whether the tenants were solvent or in arrears. See 'Survey of the townland of Lisclooney, part of the Rosse estate carried out by George Heenan, *c.*1850 (BCA). **50** *KCC*, 2 Feb. 1853. **51** *Times*, 16 Aug. 1859. **52** Ibid., 5 Feb. 1861. **53** Ibid., 15 & 24 Aug. and 10 Nov. 1859; 8 Nov. 1869. See also Lloyd papers (NLI, Ms 44,810).

10 Edenderry, *c.*1858 (courtesy of Edenderry Historical Society)

new leases issued in the 1850s included covenants against subletting and middlemen.[54] Undoubtedly many middlemen disappeared but the system itself continued in parts of King's County well into the 1860s. Indeed, even as late as 1880 Toler Garvey told the Bessborough Commission that middlemen and the rundale system were still in operation in the county.[55] The continuation of such practices obviously angered land agents and it was little wonder that some of the old school became more stringent under new employers. When Charles William George Bury, third earl of Charleville, succeeded to his father's estate in 1851, its fortunes quickly improved.[56] From 1851 to 1854 Francis Berry was successful in collecting almost £9,000 in rent and arrears.[57] In doing so Berry hired a team of bailiffs and 'hut tumblers' to assist in the recovery of arrears and the levelling of cabins.[58] These evictions, as elsewhere, appear to have been selective, as Berry chose to allow a number of tenants remain despite being heavily in debt.[59]

Acting with renewed energy, a new generation of agents were often more professional in their training and approach, as well as being commercially more flexible: there were some who encouraged new estate ventures, including the

---

54 'Particulars of the sale of the estate of Sir William Cox, Knight of Tinnycross, Tullamore, May 1856' (ORC). 55 *Royal Commission of inquiry into working of landlord and tenant (Ireland) Acts. Report, digest and minutes of evidence, appendices*, HC 1881, [C.2779] [C.2779–I] [C.2779–II] [C.2779–III] xviii, 1, 73, xix.1, 825. 56 Ibid. 57 See *KCC*, 4 Feb. 1852. 58 'Rental to 25 March 1854 signed by Francis Berry (agent) for the earl of Charleville' (Charleville MS, ORC). 59 Ibid. They included, for example, William Hanley of Croghan Hill whose lease had expired and who owed £76 in rent.

mining of lead at Blundell Hill at Edenderry and copper in the Slieve Bloom Mountains at Kinnitty.[60] The Edenderry plan involved a Welsh mining expert named Pickering who established a lead and silver mining company in the early 1850s. Many of the town's shopkeepers and traders invested in the venture, which subsequently failed. In the 1880s, during the Land War, accusations were made that many local people had been defrauded in the mining project by the agent.[61] Thomas Richard Murray also had the foresight to realize that the vast bog of Allen, which surrounded the Downshire estate at Edenderry, could be utilized to the benefits of the estate and tenants, and organized a Peat Amelioration Society in 1851.[62] Others looked to alternative means for increasing estate income; Alfred Richardson, Lord Rossmore's agent, began a large-scale programme of siring horses at Sharavogue.[63] But equally, many tenants anxious to improve their lot were discouraged in their entrepreneurial endeavours by stringent agents. At the Lloyd estate, the agent William J. O'Driscoll frequently summonsed tenants for trivial misdemeanours, including the opening of sandpits without permission.[64] O'Driscoll was among a number of agents who watched meticulously for tenants who might emigrate while owing rent and arrears.[65] Elsewhere, those engaged in the manufacture of bricks were often rebuked by agents for damaging the soil or the bed of the river. A report compiled by the agent John O'Reilly in 1861 highlighted that although the manufacture of bricks in King's County had been profitable in the preceding decades, landlords could not permit any more brick making on their estates as resources were exhausted.[66]

This new generation of agents included William Steuart Trench who arrived at the Digby estate in 1857. Commencing the agency Trench stated that the estate was formerly 'one of the most wretched and discouraging in Ireland abounding in squatters, mud hovels and moors saturated with water'.[67] He quickly began to exert his influence and, in his own words, changed the estate 'from sterility and waste to rich and abundant pasture, well fenced and divided into fields of sufficient size and sheltered by belts of plantation'.[68] To surmount the pre-Famine problems Trench broke the existing leases and carried out

60 John Locke, *Ireland's recovery* (London, 1855), p. 79. See also John Beare, *Improvement of Ireland: a letter to the King on the practical improvement of Ireland* (London, 1827).   61 See Reilly, *Edenderry, 1820–1920*, pp 43–4.   62 *British Farmer's Magazine*, 1851, p. 56. This society had been first mooted as early as 1834 when Murray's father suggested a plan to Lord Downshire to reclaim the barren lands of the estate based on an English model and to harvest peat. See Thomas Murray to Lord Downshire, 23 May 1834 (DP, D/671/C/9/386).   63 *KCC*, 9 Nov. 1853. Colonel Westenra was among the leading owners and breeders in Ireland and won more prize money in Ireland than any other breeder in the period 1834–36 and in 1838.   64 Ibid., 10 Aug. 1853.   65 For other examples of this behaviour see 'Rent ledger of an estate in Banagher district, 1849–1874' (NLI, MS 12, 164).   66 'Report on brick building on the Rahan estate, 1861 by John O'Reilly agent' (NLI, Sherlock papers). See also 'Valuation of the estate of the reps of the late Oliver Plunkett Esq., Pollagh in the King's County' (Sherlock papers).   67 Trench, *Realities*, p. 330.   68 Breen, 'Landlordism in King's County', p. 638.

wholesale evictions. In total, over 260 families were evicted from the estate in his first year as agent. In January 1858 the *Nation* newspaper reported that Trench had raised the rents 'enormously' and now 'every new tenant is required under penalty of expulsion to put his name to a paper of rules and regulations of the most odious and grinding tyrannical character'.[69] Countering these claims Trench highlighted that nearly £100,000 was spent on improvements during his tenure as agent.[70] Of this figure some £32,795 was spent in the first ten years of his management, which included large sums expended on drainage and land improvement.[71] Nonetheless, as Mary Delaney highlights, Trench's memory in local lore is more associated with hardships caused by his estate policies than his improvements.[72]

The problem with social memory is that it is very selective and discriminatory. For example, it fails to record the deference shown to agents: in 1852 when George Heenan resigned as agent on the Rosse estate a banquet in his honour was attended by over 250 tenants at Dooley's Hotel, Parsonstown, 'to evince their gratitude for the great leniency with which they have been treated by him during the last few years of distress and depression'.[73] It is not hard to imagine who was present at his farewell banquet – undoubtedly those who had consolidated their position amid the calamity. Such sentiments towards Heenan were in contrast to claims by tenants in the months after his retirement that he had embellezed money belonging to the estate. These claims, however, did not stand up in court and Heenan was cleared of all charges.[74] Similarly, while agents in social memory bore the brunt of criticism from nationalists for their role in evictions and clearances during the Famine, little was said from Land League platforms about those who acquired land, and subsequently social and political status, as a result of these clearances.[75]

While many landlords were bankrupt and forced into the Incumbered Estates Court, the fortunes of some agents also suffered. First of all their income, based on their ability to collect rent, obviously declined. Second, the Famine changed perceptions about the professionalization of land agents, and, in turn, estate management policies, and so many of the old type of land agent's disappeared as professional agency firms came into vogue. However, from those in the case study, some individuals continued in the land agency business in the county for many years – the Garvey's, for example, as late as the 1940s.[76] Likewise, Richard

69 *Nation*, 30 Jan. 1858.   **70** Ibid., 15 June and 13 July 1861. See also Breen, 'Landlordism in King's County', p. 659.   **71** Trench, *Realities*, p. 330.   **72** See Mary Delaney, *William Steuart Trench and his management of the Digby estate, King's County, 1857–1871* (Dublin, 2012).   **73** *KCC*, 1 Dec. 1852.   **74** Ibid. George Heenan was also a member of the St Brendan's Masonic Lodge at Parsonstown. An address in his honour claimed that he was 'a man of business, distinguished by integrity and moderation, a willing contributor to every useful constitution, an unerring and devoted friend to the poor, and whatever might appear likely to improve their condition' and that he had won 'golden opinions from all sorts of people'. See *KCC*, 29 June 1853.   **75** Bew, *Ireland*, p. 214.   **76** George Garvey's son, Toler Roberts, was involved in the

Gamble continued as a land agent in the post-Famine period although he was preoccupied with other endeavours. A member of the Historical and Literary Society of Ireland, to whom he frequently presented lectures, he was also an accomplished writer and wrote about the major issues of the day, including landlord–tenant relations and the Land Act of 1870.[77] The longevity of agents was evident elsewhere. Thomas Murray was replaced in 1850 by his son, Thomas Richard, who remained in the position until 1893. In 1891 Murray was described as a 'fatherly figure' by the people of Edenderry and praised the town as a 'model of cleanliness'.[78] He was also 'an ardent sportsman' and was well known in Irish coursing circles.[79] The Manifolds continued to double as land agents and millers, and were among those who benefited from the Famine. In the 1850s they accumulated large tracts of land through the Incumbered Estate Court.[80] Their rise in the social world of King's County mirrored their counterparts and, that of the value of their wills is an indicator, the mid-nineteenth century proved to be a profitable time for many land agents.[81]

'Plan of Campaign' in the late 1880s. See Laurence M. Geary, *The Plan of Campaign, 1886–1891* (Cork, 1986), pp 155–7. See also Malcomson, *Calendar of the Rosse papers*, pp 141, 186.   **77** See Richard Wilson Gamble, *An address to the members of the Historical and Literary Society on 19 February 1855* (Dublin, 1855). A selection of the Gamble's writings include *Suggestions as to why the legislature should interfere to secure tenant compensation* (Dublin, 1866); *Compensation for improvements made by tenants in Ireland: When and how far should it be secured by law* (London, 1867) and *Fair rents? The only test is free contract… the report of the royal commission on the Land Act 1870: its errors as to fair rents* (Dublin, 1881). See also Byrne, *Legal Offaly*, pp 121–2 and Wright, *King's County directory*, p. 29.   **78** *KCC*, 28 May 1891.   **79** O'Leary, 'Notes on the collection of Irish antiquities lately at Edenderry', p. 325.   **80** The sons of other King's County land agents were also considerable landowners by the 1870s, including William Berry, son of Francis, who owned 800 acres. See U.H. Hussey de Burgh, *The landowners of Ireland: an alphabetical list of the owners of estates of 500 acres or £500 valuation and upwards in Ireland with the acreage and valuation in each county* (Dublin, 1876).   **81** For example when Francis Berry died in 1864 he left a will of £9,000; George Garvey died in 1879 and left £7,000; Thomas Richard Murray left £3,970 in 1901; Richard Wilson Gamble died in 1887 and left £4,915; while John Manifold who died in 1870 left £3,000 in his will. See NAI, Calendars of Wills and Administrations, 1858–1920.

Conclusion

> Black sheep disgrace any flock but it is unjust to characterize them all for
> the tyrannical and petty meanness of one individual.[1]

In King's County the impact that the end of the Napoleonic Wars had on the
rural economy – combined with a growing population put excess strain on land.
Whether, as R.F. Foster contends, the watershed year in the nineteenth century
was 1815 rather than 1845 is debatable.[2] Certainly, as William Crawford's study
of the Abercorn estates in Co. Tyrone has shown, when the transformation
occurred many landlords realized that they had lost control of the situation
because there were too many tenants on small holdings that were unviable.[3] The
simultaneous growth in agrarian agitation meant that land agents faced many
and varied challenges after 1815. As a body it appears that agents was were not
equipped to deal with these challenges, particularly when the Famine struck in
1845. Privately, land agents knew what their responsibilities were, but collectively they had no method, or at times even the will, to act in unison. There were
a number of factors that made such co-operation difficult, not least of these
religious and political tensions, which drove a wedge into local communities,
further isolating those who could have helped.

Moreover, land agents were not a homogenous social group. They came from
varying social backgrounds, though generally speaking they were connected
somewhere along the line to the landed class. Some were professionally trained,
others were appointed merely because they were related to the landlord, while
some rose through the ranks in an apprentice-like manner. Their varying social
backgrounds, education and training determined how, individually and collectively, they faced the numerous and challenging problems associated with estate
management. The education of King's County agents was too varied and incon-
sistent for them to act coherently when faced with crisis and change. Even if it
had been consistent, as Edward Hughes has noted, 'no professional training
could guarantee the essential qualities of tact, acceptance and integrity'.[4]
Neither Richard Gamble nor George Greeson, for example, who had been well
educated for land agency, were successful agents. On the other hand, there were
those who gained valuable experience in dealing with tenants through their
business interests who were arguably more successful. For many landlords it was
simply a case of agents having an aptitude to keep law and order among the lower
orders and to gather in their rents. When the political stability of the district or

---

1 *KCC*, 20 Oct. 1852. See also *KCC*, 1 Dec. 1852.   2 R.F. Foster, *Modern Ireland, 1600–1972*
(London, 1988), p. 318.   3 W.H. Crawford, 'Landlord tenant relations in Ulster, 1609–1820',
Irish Economic and Social History, 2 (1975), pp 5–21.   4 Quoted in Maguire, *The Downshire
estates*, p. 194.

county lay threatened, the agent became the enforcer of law and order and the cornerstone on which the tranquillity of the area rested. The clever land agent found the means to appease the tenantry, and thus was able to meet the requirements of the landowner, while also escaping the barrel of the blunderbuss.

The findings for King's County more-or-less substantiate Eric Richards' argument for the Victorian English case that 'some agents had the grace and tact of the landlord' while others 'were of a rougher breed, the kind of man who relished in authority'. There were both types in King's County: Francis Berry was patriarchal towards his tenants in contrast to George Garvey who mirrored Richards' 'rougher breed' and who 'managed to tyrannize entire rural populations creating riot and an undying legacy of hatred'.[5] When the Famine struck there were too many who were untrained or who lacked the necessary personal skills to cope with or alleviate distress among their tenantry. Indeed, agents such as the Manifolds too often put personal business interests first. They were not alone and many were enticed into the agency business in the first place because of the potential benefit it brought to their own endeavours. Despite their ineffectiveness in dealing with tenants, improving the estate and collecting rent, few were ever relieved of their position. While the claim by some agents that they knew every tenant on an estate was somewhat dubious, they did know the locality and knew which tenants were likely to default on the payment of rent. For these reasons many were retained in their positions despite their shortcomings. In the wider community the agent influenced social morals, maintained the power of the gentry and cultivated an attitude of deference towards them, even if deference is sometimes difficult to quantify. More importantly they were supposedly the point of contact between landlord and tenant. However, as the case of Thomas Murray shows, too often they simply reported to the landlord what he wanted to hear. Agents' letters to their employers were often manufactured to suit their own agenda. In addition, agents like Murray were given advance notice that the landlord was to visit the estate and so this time to prepare too often allowed for the reality to be marked. Did this mean that many landlords were ignorant of the plight of the tenantry or indeed the fortunes of their estate?

For many men the agency of an estate allowed for their rise within social circles. Their social status was also reflected in other positions that they held, but in some cases did not always mirror their stereotypical representation, or that retained in social memory. For example, James Devery was a prominent member of the Repeal party at Cloghan, as was Alfred Richardson.[6] The Murrays were actively involved in antiquarian pursuits and carried out numerous excavations around Edenderry. During drainage works of the river Boyne near the town, which were carried out to provide relief during the Famine, many Stone, Bronze and Iron Age artefacts were found, which Thomas Richard Murray later used to open a museum.[7] Likewise, George Garvey was a member of the Royal Society of Antiquarians and the Kilkenny and South East of Ireland Archaeological Society and was also responsible for the restoration of the medieval well of Saint Columcille at Durrow Abbey in the late 1830s.[8] It could perhaps be argued that these men saw themselves as custodians of the past, and it would make for an interesting study to determine what past they thought worthy of preserving. However, some land agents deemed local customs and traditions unworthy of preserving, although this may have been simply a means of exerting control over the local community. In 1838 the antiquarian, John O'Donovan, noted that the pattern at Durrow had been discontinued because of obstacles put in its way by the local landlord and his agent.[9] Likewise, the Manifold brothers were guilty of putting an end to the pattern of Saint Lugna at Kinnitty during the 1840s.[10] Arguably, had their community involvement been more active and had they involved themselves in pursuits of a much wider socio–economic nature, agents might have been more effective in stabilizing relations on their respective estates.

Regardless of their background or experience, agents faced numerous problems regarding leasing, subdivision, middlemen, overpopulation and a reluctance by tenants to embrace new farming methods, all of which hindered effective management. Agents reacted differently to each of these problems but generally speaking by the end of the 1830s, aided by the introduction of the Irish Poor Law Act of 1838, many resorted to clearances and assisted emigration. This study has shown that widescale clearance of estates was taking place in the late 1830s and early 1840s prior to the Famine. That the government saw it necessary to introduce a bill to protect tenants against ejectment in 1840 is further evidence that landlords had engaged in a widespread policy of eviction.[11] These clearances were often without compassion. At Edenderry on the Downshire estate, Thomas Murray had no regrets about the clearing of beggars and 'bad tenants' that he pushed to the edges of the bogs.[12] Similarly, George Garvey delighted in clearing tenants from the Norbury estate, which resulted in the murder of the earl, although it appears that the much-reviled agent was the intended target of the assassins. Although these clearances were not as frequent or numerous as those carried out during the Famine, particularly after the introduction of the

7 Reilly, *Edenderry, 1820–1920*, p. 53.   8 Michael Byrne, *Tullamore Catholic parish: a historical survey* (Tullamore, 1987), p. 15. See also *Journal of the Royal Society of Antiquarians of Ireland*, 1858 and T.L. Cooke, 'Wayside ancient monument at Drishoge, King's County', *Journal of the Kilkenny and South-East of Ireland Archaeological Society*, n.s., 1:2 (1857), p. 383.   9 Herity, *Ordnance survey letters Offaly*, p. 303.   10 Quoted in Elizabeth Fitzpatrick, Paddy Heaney & Alison Rosse, *The wet hillside of Saint Lugna* (Offaly, 1995), p. 95.   11 See *Ejectment and replevin (Ireland). A bill to amend the laws relating to ejectment and replevin in Ireland*, HC 1840 [13] ii, 391. 12 Thomas Murray to Lord Downshire, 21 Feb. 1840 (DP, D/671/C/9/625).

Gregory Clause and the Incumbered Estates Court, they acted as an important precursor for what was to come.

These clearances also provide another insight into the mindset of the agent, as often they were selective in who they chose for eviction. The accumulation of arrears did not always necessarily mean eviction. Agents, in many cases, took the opportunity to clear those they perceived to be useless, idle and troublemakers. It is little wonder then that agents and employees of landed estates carried out their duties in the face of constant threat and harassment. While agents might contend that evictions were based on sound business sense, tenants did not see it this way. This was equally true before the Famine when attacks on agents and their property prevailed. Indeed, a decade before the Famine agents were regularly attacked. For example, John Manifold had his house and barn at Annamore, Drumcullen, set on fire in April 1835 following a dispute with tenants, while Lord Bloomfield received threatening letters on account of him employing 'a devil for his agent'.[13] The litany of attacks on land agents underlined the perils of the profession, particularly in periods of economic crisis.

There was much however that was out of the control or remit of even the most able of land agents. Many were simply restricted or dictated in their policies by their employers' financial position. Mortgages, loose accounting, fire, murder, death, family charges and financial embarrassments all contributed to the demise of certain estates in King's County by the early 1840s. The case of the Charleville estate at Tullamore is instructive. The debt that the estate had accumulated by 1844 resulted in the second earl residing throughout the Famine in Germany in order to avoid debtors. As Lord Charleville leisured elsewhere, his creditors clamoured to be repaid money advanced in previous years. Indeed, his son, Charles William George Bury (see p. 156), had a number of accounts 'dishonoured from London to New York'.[14] With a reversionary company overseeing the finances of the estate, Francis Berry was severely curtailed in his duties and his correspondence and workload doubled as he served two masters. Naturally, because of such pressure, tenants on the estate suffered in a time of want. Other landowners had grossly overspent and were in a perilous position. Lord Downshire borrowed £185,000 in the period 1810 to 1840.[15] And there were agents like Thomas Murray who experienced his own personal hardship during the Famine. His daughter Caroline died in August 1846 aged twenty; his wife Margaret died in March 1847 aged fifty-nine, while a son William died in the early 1850s.[16] The impact of such personal tragedies should hardly be

13 Bernard Cummins to lord lieutenant, Dublin Castle 13 Apr. 1835 (OPKC, 1835). See also Alfred G. Richardson to Lord Rossmore, 29 Nov. 1838 (PRONI, Rossmore papers, T2929/4/65). 14 See, for example, John Ross Mahon to Lord Tullamore, 25 Aug. 1845; Mahon to Miss Cox and Co., London, 2 Mar. 1846 and Mahon to Messrs Manning & Dobson, Hertford Street, London, 2 Feb. 1846 (NLI, Guinness & Mahon Letter books, MS 32,013). 15 Dooley, *A research guide*, p. 24. 16 Edenderry Historical Society, *Edenderry then and now*, p. 54.

11 Fireworks at Birr Castle, 1851, to celebrate the end of
the Famine (*Illustrated London News*, 18 Feb. 1851)

minimized in assessing Murray's management of the vast Downshire estate.
Likewise, the destruction of Samuel Robinson's mill at Clara by fire in February
1840 had a considerable impact on his tenantry and the town of Clara. Prior to
the burning, almost 14,000 barrels of oats per week were brought to the mill.[17]
There is no legislating for an accident such as this, which undoubtedly impacted
upon a whole community and made all the difference between survival and
disappearance during the Famine. At Parsonstown, the third earl of Rosse was
preoccupied with his scientific endeavours and the building of the great
telescope. Despite ordering the reorganization of his 'estate rules' in 1847, Rosse
could have done more to ameliorate the plight of his tenantry in the late 1840s,
even if it can be claimed that the numerous building projects at Birr Castle
alleviated some of the distress caused by the Famine. Such failures on his part
are possibly best exemplified in the 'celebrations' held at Parsonstown to mark
the end of the Famine. In February 1851 Rosse provided an extravagant display
of fireworks for his tenants including the wheel piece, roman candles, rockets
and tourbillons. According to the *King's County Chronicle* 'no pains or expense
was spared in their procurement' for the celebrations which also included a
printed programme of events, the final bill estimated to be in excess of £400.[18]
The earl and countess of Rosse continued to entertain the gentry of the county

17 *FJ*, 17 Feb. 1840.   18 *KCC*, 5 & 12 Feb. 1851.

and surrounding areas throughout the Famine, hosting lavish balls where they received their guests with 'the usual urbanity and politeness'. In January 1852, for example, a ball at Birr Castle was attended by over three hundred guests, while in May of that year another 'soiree' at the castle was said to have been 'numerously attended'.[19]

For many landlords the choice during the Great Famine was simple: evict their debtors or be dispossessed by their creditors. These creditors were just as remorseless in pressing for their money as the landlords were in evicting tenants. The case of Robert Cassidy reflected this. Throughout the 1830s and 1840s Cassidy, a prominent member of the King's County Repeal party, was widely praised by his tenantry. However, by the late 1840s output from his distillery at Monasterevin, Co. Kildare, was severely affected by the Famine and thus greater emphasis was put into collecting rent and arrears on his King's County estate. In 1849 Cassidy began to evict tenants at Killyon, Drumcullen and Cullawaun for which he quickly incurred the wrath of the Catholic clergy. His eviction policy during this time determined his representation in the social memory of the area, which has depicted him as being among the 'merciless' landlord class. Had not the Famine intervened he may have been remembered very differently; his personal diaries of the 1830s and early 1840s show his involvement in the local community and his benevolence towards tenants at Killyon a view of him that may have been lost until now. Cassidy's actions mirrored those of Sir Andrew Armstrong at Gallen who was returned to parliament for the county throughout the 1840s. By 1849 he was bankrupt and forced to sell his estate in the Incumbered Estates Court, but not before he evicted his tenantry en masse. In his reminiscences of the Famine, William O'Connor Morris contended that the landlords of King's County were not a wealthy class, and many did not have the means to give employment or stem the tide of Famine.[20] However, as Tim O'Neill has argued, the wealthy landlords of the county could have done more to alleviate the plight of the poor, the case of Lord Digby who left more than a million pounds in his will when he died in 1856 being evidence of this.[21] Ironically, from 1857 onwards there were significantly more improvements carried out on the Geashill estate, with approximately £100,000 spent on the same, to make the estate more profitable. Such expenditure a decade previously possibly was not contemplated because of the existence of so many impoverished tenants on the estate. But where landlords were found wanting, some agents were not. Certainly the actions of individual agents highlight that many acted with great sincerity and kindness. On the other hand there were those such as Greeson, Gamble and Garvey who took what they could from the land and cared little for the tenant's plight. At Ferbane Robert Nugent was preoccupied with

---

19 Ibid., 28 Jan. & 2 June 1852. 20 O'Connor Morris, *Memories*, pp 98–100. 21 O'Neill, 'The Famine in Offaly', p. 710.

self-advancement and did little outside his routine estate duties. It was this type of inactivity that led to their later representation in Irish social memory but culpability was also shared by the land grabbers, gombeen men and the money lenders, described by Robin Haines as the 'merciless and rapacious ogres of the Irish village'.[22]

John Corcoran's statement quoted at the beginning of this chapter hides a myriad of exceptions and anomalies – as should be noted with all historical generalizations . On the eve of the Famine many land agents were endeavouring to improve the plight of the tenantry (and, of course, in turn to raise the estate rental capacity). Such efforts were most notably seen in the promotion of agricultural societies at Tullamore and Parsonstown, projects of drainage and land reclamation and the employment of Scottish agriculturalists to oversee the same. However, it must be remembered that modernization and the advance of agricultural knowledge and practice resulted in the clearance of tenants, and this became a more formidable social memory than improvement. Despite negative press during the Land War and after, the land agency business continued. Perhaps as a result of the negative portrayal of the profession, by the end of the nineteenth century there existed the need for an Irish Land Agents Association which represented members interests and offered protection to their much-maligned character.[23] Lamenting the implementation of the Wyndham Land Act in 1903, of which he was highly critical, Samuel Hussey declared that 'the agency class will soon be as extinct as the dodo'.[24] However, some land agents, such as the Garveys, continued representing the interests of landowners well into the twentieth century.

Undoubtedly, some agents were responsible for the negative image that pervades to this day. For many communities it was the interference of an agent in local affairs that made them detestable. This was exacerbated where the agent did not share the same religion as the majority of the local population and inter-fered in their worship and custom. While this may have been as a result of religious intolerance, such as that displayed by the Manifolds, others interfered as a means of preventing excessive drinking and violence, which usually followed patterns, fairs and pilgrimages. The stereotypical portrayal of the occupation

22 Haines, *Charles Trevelyan*, p. 23.   23 George F. Brunskill (ed.), *The Irish Land Agents Association: recent judicial decisions affecting the law of landlord and tenant* (Dublin, 1891–5). As early as the 1830s land agents met collectively at specially convened conferences to consider important issues of the day such as the tithes controversy. See, for example, Committee of Land Agents, Dublin to [H.L.] Prentice, Esq, Caledon (PRONI, D2433/A/1/370/15).   24 Hussey, *Reminiscences*, pp 40–1. Walter Walsh has estimated that the number of land agents in Kilkenny decreased from 1851 to 1871 by 50 per cent owing to the number of multiple agencies. See Walter Walsh, *Kilkenny: the struggle for the land, 1850–1882* (Kilkenny, 2008), p. 85.   25 At the Downshire (and formerly Blundell) estate in King's County, Thomas Murray deliberately portrayed the slovenly habits and absenteeism of his predecessors, Thomas Misset and the Hatches, Henry and his son John, as adding to the misfortunes of Edenderry, probably as a means of hiding his own inadequacies.

may have come from agents themselves who engaged in the character assassination of their predecessors.[25] Remarkably, in many cases the agent emerged from the Famine as a more influential figure than he had been before. A handful of men such as Francis Berry, George Heenan and John Corcoran retained their popularity, despite the policies that they implemented on their respective estates. While it remains to be seen whether agents in King's County were typical or atypical of the counterparts elsewhere, there were both good and bad, and, as John Corcoran's quote at the beginning of this chapter suggests, certainly not all should have been tainted with the same 'black sheep' image.

Appendix 1

Landed estates in King's County over 1,000 acres, *c.*1830

Landlord	Location	Acreage
Earl of Digby	Geashill	30,627
Earl of Rosse	Parsonstown	25,167
Earl of Charleville	Tullamore	23,370
Capt. Thos Bernard	Kinnitty	15,979
Marquis of Downshire	Edenderry	13,928
Garrett O'Moore	Cloghan	9,456
Henry Peisley L'Estrange	Moystown	8,000
Armstrong	Ballycumber	6,042
Col. J.W. Lloyd	Shinrone	5,481
F.V. Bennett	Thomastown	5,322
Thomas Mulock	Lemanaghan	5,200
R.J.E. Mooney	Doon	4,800
Francis L. Dames	Rhode	4,809
Lord Ashtown	Bracknagh	4,414
Lord Rossmore	Sharavogue	3,992
Revd Henry King	Ballylin	3,900
Trinity College	Endrim/Creggan	3,885
Earl of Norbury	Durrow	3,598
Robert Cassidy	Killyon	2,582
Sir George Gore	Ferbane	2,306
Dr Steevens' Hospital	Philipstown	2,237
Frederick Ponsonby	Cloghan	2,134
Mrs Dowdall	Clara	2,095
James Rolleston	Frankford	2,031
Lord Ponsonby	Philipstown	2,000
Andrew Gamble	Killooly	1,808
Lord Trimleston	Rhode	1,600
William O'Connor Morris	Pallas	1,423
Lord Mornington	Clara	1,360
Erasmus Smith School	Banagher	1,315
Sir William Cox	Tinnycross	1,240
Lord Bloomfield	Moneygall	1,230
George Rait	Rhode	1,200

Appendix 2

A sample of land agents identified as being associated with the management of
landed estates in King's County, 1830–60

Name	Estate	Location
Ashton, John	W.H. Turpin	Forelock
Baker, Arthur	Sir Andrew Armstrong	Gallen
Bailey, Daniel	Dr Belton	Lumpcloon
	Earl of Mornington	Clara
Bagnall, Abraham	Revd Henry King	Ballylin
Barnes, Joseph	Charles C. Palmer	Edenderry
Bennett, Frederick P.	Francis Bennett	Thomastown
Berry, Francis	Earl of Charleville	Tullamore
Berry, Thomas	Capt. Nesbitt	Tubberdaly, Rhode
Blunden, Mr	Earl of Glandore	Unknown
Boland, James	W.B. Buchanan	Glynn
Bracken, Edward	Court of Chancery	Lumpcloon
Briscoe, Edward	William Briscoe	Ballycowan
Bryant, John	E.J. Briscoe	Ross, Tullamore
Butler, Gerard Villiers	Col. Westenra	Sharavogue
Cage, Charles Trench	Chris St George	Ferbane
Colgan, Michael	Mrs Colgan	Durrow
Connolly, Mr	Dean Laufane	Ballinamere
Cooper, Samuel	Erasmus Smith Schools	Banagher
Corcoran, John	Robert Cassidy	Killyon
Cox, Capt. Charles	Sir Charles St George	Coolestown
	Sir William Cox	Clara
Crampton, George	William Carter	Eglish
Dennis, Edward	Trinity College Dublin	Killmurryley
Devery, James	Frederick Ponsonby	Cloghan
	Earl of Fitzwilliam	Cloghan
Doorly, Terence	Richard Malone	Pallas
Drought, Philip	John A. Drought	Lettybrook
	Cmmrs of Education	Banagher
Dunne, James	John O'Brien	Rahan
Fallon, Robert	Mrs Dowdall	Clara
Fawcett, Paul	Revd Ralph Coote	Rahan
Fitzgerald, David	Chris St George	Ferbane
Fitzgerald, Revd Henry	Revd Henry King	Ferbane
Fitzmaurice, Arthur	W.F. Burton	Unknown
French, Dawson	William Johnson	Tullamore
Gamble, Andrew	W. O'Connor Morris	Mount Pleasant
Gamble, R.W.	Andrew Gamble	Killooly
	N. Biddulph	Rathrobin

Name	Estate	Location
Garvey, George	Bassett W. Holmes	Moneygall
	John A. Drought	Whigsborough
	R.J.E. Mooney	Doon
	Earl of Norbury	Durrow
	O.F. Toler	Parsonstown
	Valentine Bennett	Thomastown
	Earl of Rosse	Parsonstown
	R. Tyndall	Ballymeely
Gatchell, John	Mrs Gardiner	Coolestown
Gibbs, George	Garrett Tyrell	Warrenstown
Greeson, George	Mrs Armstrong	Kilcoursey
	Mrs Holmes	Ballycumber
Going, Caleb	Johanna Going	Ratheshill
Greer, Thomas	Mathew Higgins	Gurteen, Kilcoursey
Haire, Mr	Viscount Ashbrook	Shannonbridge
Hamilton, Charles	Garrett Tyrrell	Rooske, Edenderry
	Sir Duke Gifford	Castlejordan
Handcock, Charles	Lord Castlemaine	Tubber
Heenan, George	Earl of Rosse	Parsonstown
	Garrett O'Moore	Cloghan
Hopkins, Edward	Lord Ponsonby	Philipstown
Howard & Palmer	Court of Chancery	Kyle, Kinnitty
Hunt, E.L.	Royal Classical School	Banagher
Joly, Jasper Robert	Sir Duke Gifford	Castlejordan
Jones, Robert Lloyd	Rev Henry King	Co. Leitrim
Maher, Mr	Mrs Minnitt	Annabeg
Manifold, Daniel	Capt. T. Bernard	Kinnitty
Manifold, John	Capt. T. Bernard	Kinnitty
Manifold, Thomas	Capt. T. Bernard	Kinnitty
	Capt. Valentine Bennett	Thomastown
Manifold, William Ross	W. O'Connor Morris	Mount Pleasant
Matthews, Edward	Joseph Gough	Lurgan, Kilcoursey
Mayne, John	St George Gore	Ferbane
McDonald, John	Revd W. Minchin	Moneygall
	R. Going	Moneygall
	Revd J.C. Walker	Moneygall
	W. Harding	Moneygall
Minchin, Stephen W.	William Minchin	Busherstown
Moore, John H.	Garrett O'Moore	Cloghan
Moore, R.L.	Marquis of Drogheda	Dovehill
Moylan, Michael	Christopher Haughton	Banagher
Murray, Thomas	Marquis of Downshire	Edenderry
Murray, Thomas R.	Marquis of Downshire	Edenderry
O'Connor Morris, W	Revd O'Connor Morris	Mount Pleasant
O'Hara, Mr	F.L. Dames	Warrenstown
	Sir Duke Gifford	Castlejordan

Name	Estate	Location
O'Reilly, John	Oliver Plunkett	Tubber
O'Reilly, Philip	Robert Blosse Lynch	Banagher
Owen, Mr	Erasmus Smith Schools	Banagher
Pim, John	John Sabatier	Portarlington
Price, John Robinson	Marquis of Lansdowne	Killnagall, Ballyboy
Pyke, Robert	Robert Cassidy	Killyon
Reamsbottom, W.J.	Benjamin Humphrey	Ballycumber
	John Emerson	Ballycumber
	Arthur S. Bride	Ballycumber
Redden, Patrick	Major Jackson	Emmel West
Reynolds, E.	Lord Rossmore	Clonscara
Richardson, Alfred	Lord Rossmore	Sharavogue
Ridgeway, Samuel	Court of Chancery	Kilcooney
Robinson, John	Lord Milltown	Shinrone
Rutherford, John	Nicholas Biddulph	Rathrobin
	C.R. Baldwin	Lisduff
Sadlier, John	Earl of Portarlington	Portarlington
Sands, Charles S.	Sir Charles Coote	Ballycowan
Sharpe, Richard	James Banks	Banagher
Sheane, Henry	Revd Ball	Banagher
Sherrard, Mr	Rodolph de Sales	Eglish
	Sir R. Robinson	Eglish
	Smith Berry	Eglish
Smith, John	Sandford Palmer	Parsonstown
	T.F. Golding	Parsonstown
Smith, Robert	John Smith	Glasshouse
Spunner, Henry	Francis E. Mooney	Doon
Stewart & Kincaid	Lord Ponsonby	Philipstown
Stoney, Robert J.	Mr Oakley	Parsonstown
Tarleton, Robert	Earl of Digby	Geashill
Telford, John	Capt. Telford	Ballycowan
Thompson, George	Earl of Digby	Geashill
Thompson, Thomas	Peter Thompson	Garrycastle
Trench, Henry	Francis Hastings Toone	Shinrone
Walpole, George	Thomas Bergin	Ettagh, Drumcullen
Walsh, Thomas	William Longworth	Ballyboy
Warburton, Henry	William Kemmis	Ballycowan
White, William	Earl of Rosse	Parsonstown
	Capt. L'Estrange	Moystown

Appendix 3

A sample of land stewards and other estate personnel identified as being involved in the management of landed estates in King's County, 1830–60

Name	Position	Estate	Location
Allen, James	Clerk	Downshire	Edenderry
Bagnall, Robert	Bailiff	Charleville	Clonminch
Baker, Arthur	Land steward	M. of Drogheda	Portarlington
Beecham, Edward	Clerk	W. Reamsbottom	Ballycumber
Bermingham, John	Bailiff	John A. Burdett	Coolfin, Ferbane
Butler, J.C.	Rent collector	Col. Westenra	Sharavogue
Butler, Mr	Land steward	William Trench	Cangort
Byrne, Mr	Land steward	Capt. Nesbitt	Tubberdaly
Cahill, Michael	Bailiff	Revd B. Savage	Shinrone
Carroll, Michael	Sub-agent	Col. Westenra	Sharavogue
Cathcart, James	Land steward	Thos H. Mulock	Ballycumber
Cavanagh & O'Hagan	Law agents	Robert Cassidy	Killyon
Chitson, Charles	Land steward	Lord Trimleston	Warrenstown
Cloran, Timothy	Land steward	Capt. Richardson	Rathbeg
Colgan, Michael	Driver	Court of Chancery	Kilcooney
Cope, William	Drainage expert	Downshire	Edenderry
Coughlan, Owen	Bailiff	Robert Cassidy	Killyon
Daly, Bernard	Watcher	Court of Chancery	Lumpcloon
Day, Thomas	Bailiff/rent warner	F.V. Bennett	Thomastown
Deegan, James	Land steward	Francis Berry	Eglish
Duffery, John	Land steward	John Ridgeway	Ballydermot
Dunne, M.	Herd	Roger North	Philipstown
Egan, Martin	Rent warner/driver	Robert Lauder	Ferbane
Ellis, George	Process server	Robert Lauder	Ferbane
Fagan, Michael	Bailiff	Earl of Charleville	Tullamore
Fawcett, Paul	Sub-agent	Downshire	Edenderry
Feltus, Francis	Land steward	Col. Westenra	Sharavogue
Gill, Mr	Land steward	Roger North	Croghan
Gleeson, Denis	Caretaker	William Wells	Ballycormack
Grogan, Joseph	Sub agent	Lord Ponsonby	Philipstown
Grogan, Michael	Sub agent	Lord Ponsonby	Philipstown
Grogan, Peter	Bailiff	Earl of Charleville	Croghan
Hinsey, Mr	Bailiff	Robert Cassidy	Killyon
Hogan, Thomas	Rent collector	Henry Trench	Banagher
Hume, Mr	Land steward	Col. Bernard	Kinnitty
Hynes, John	Rent warner	Unknown	Clonfanlough
Jackson, Mr	Agriculturalist	O.F. Toler	Parsonstown
Jordan, Michael	Land surveyor	Capt. T. Bernard	Kinnitty
Kemmy, Thomas	Bailiff	R.J.E. Mooney	Doon

Name	Position	Estate	Location
Kennedy, James	Receiver of rent	Court of Chancery	Lumpcloon
Keyes, Henry	Bailiff	Henry Kemmis	Ballicallahan
Killeen, James	Bailiff	Robert B. Lynch	Banagher
Larkin, John	Land steward	John Drought	Lettybrook
	Land steward	Miss Anne Burdett	Banagher
Lavin, Alexander	Caretaker	D.H. Vaughan	Shinrone
Leeson, John	Driver	Col. L'Estrange	Lusmagh
Little, Mr	Bailiff	Richard Malone	Pallas
Long, John	Sub-agent	Bassett Holmes	Clara/ Ballycumber
Lowe, John	Bailiff	Philip McCormick	Clonmacnoise
Lyle, Mr	Agriculturalist	Earl of Rosse	Parsonstown
Maffett, William	Rent receiver	Lord Bloomfield	Redwood
Malone, Edward	Bailiff	C. St George Gore	Ferbane
	Keeper of rent	Garrett O'Moore	Cloghan
McComb, Robert	Bailiff	Downshire	Edenderry
McCormick, John	Driver	Luke Loftus Fox	Kilcooney
McLoughlin, A.	Woodranger	W. Armstrong	Ballycumber
McLoughlin, Patk.,	Bailiff	Lord Mornington	Clara
Meara, Dinny	Bailiff	Lord Bloomfield	Moneygall
Mills, Kenneth	Land steward	William H. Magan	Philipstown
Mitchell, Daniel	Bailiff	Sir George Gore	Ferbane
Mitchell, Patrick	Bailiff	Sir George Gore	Ferbane
Molloy, Thomas	Land steward	William Trench	Kilcooney
Molloy, Mr	Bailiff	Sir George Gore	Ferbane
Neale, Edward	Herd	George Rait	Rathmoyle
Nugent, Robert	Land steward	Rev Henry King	Ferbane
O'Driscoll, W.J.	Receiver of rent	Col. H. Lloyd	Gloster
Perry, George	Bailiff	Robert Cassidy	Killyon
Potter, Mr	Land Steward	Col. Westenra	Sharavogue
Porter, Thomas	Bailiff	Earl of Charleville	Walsh Island
Quinn, Mr	Sub-agent	Mrs Dillon	Philipstown
Quinn Jr, Mr	Bailiff	Mrs Dillon	Philipstown
Reilly, Thomas	Bailiff	Earl Norbury	Durrow
Roberts, Michael	Sub-agent	Lord Bloomfield	Moneygall
Ross, Mr	Agriculturalist	Sylvester Rait	Warrenstown
Russell, Edward	Bailiff	Capt. T. Bernard	Kinnitty
Salmon, James	Bailiff	John Drought	Whigsborough
Saunderson, Adam	Land steward	Earl of Norbury	Durrow
Sheppard, Revd	Receiver of rent	Trinity College	Endrim/ Creggan
Sheppard, Thomas	Bailiff	Mrs Holmes	Clara
Sheppard, William	Bailiff	Mrs Holmes	Clara
Smith, Patrick	Bailiff	Revd B. Savage	Shinrone
	Receiver of rent	Smith Berry	Eglish
Stapleton, James	Sub-agent	Mr Pepper	Tipperary

Name	Position	Estate	Location
Tierney, Patrick	Bailiff	Sir George Gore	Ferbane
Toone, Francis H.	Receiver of rent	Trinity College	Endrim/ Creggan
Vancover, Mr	Agriculturalist	Lord Shelbourne	Rahan
Watson, John	Rent collector	Bassett Holmes	Clara/ Ballycumber
Williams, Thomas	Watcher	R.W. Gamble	Killooly
Willis, William	Bailiff	Maunsell Andrews	Rathenny

Appendix 4

Estates (or part thereof) in King's County sold under the Incumbered Estates Court, 1850–63

Name	Date of sale	Location of lands included in the sale
Andrew Armstrong	June 1852 & Nov. 1856	King's County & Kildare
Matilda Bagnall	Feb. 1855	King's County & Tipperary
Richard Bewley	July 1864	Edenderry
Robert Belton	Feb. 1856	King's County & Meath
Lt.-Col. Bernard	June 1857	King's County & Carlow
J.C. Bloomfield	June 1852	Banagher
Sir R Lynch Blosse	Dec. 1855 & Nov. 1858	Banagher
George Clarke	Jan. 1855	King's County & Tipperary
John G. Collins	July 1859	Belmont
Robert Cooke	Feb. 1856	Tullamore
Richard Damer	July 1850	Shinrone
Revd A.L. Dames	July 1862	Clara
Amos Doolan	May 1852	Shinrone
John A. Drought	Feb. 1857	Parsonstown
Robert J. Drought	Dec. 1855	Franckford
Trustee Lord Dunsany	Nov. 1863	King's County & Galway
Denis Egan	May 1852 & Mar. 1853	Moneygall
John Emerson	Nov. 1861	King's County, Westmeath & Dublin City
Anne Featherstonehaugh	May 1855	Tullamore
Earl Fitzwilliam	Apr. 1853	Cloghan
Adam Fuller	July 1851	King's County
J. Gatchell	Mar. 1860	Portarlington
B. Gerathy	Nov. 1861	Tubber
Robert Grace	May 1859	Parsonstown
Thomas Grattan	Nov. 1854	Edenderry
Eliz F. Gyles	Nov. 1863	Clara
Thomas Hackett	June 1856	King's County, Galway & Tipperary
Samuel Hanks	Feb. 1861	Parsonstown
Alex Hardy	May 1860	Tullamore
Henry Higgins	Feb. 1851	Tubber
Joseph Horne	June 1862	King's County
Gus R. Jones	July 1851	King's County
Arthur Judge	Dec. 1852	Parsonstown
John Judge	Mar. 1857	King's County & Westmeath
Bernard Kelly	July 1863	Ferbane
Revd J.G. Kelly	Mar. 1864	Geashill

Name	Date of sale	Location of lands included in the sale
Revd A.J. Labatt	July 1850	King's County & Meath
Gustave Lambert	July 1850	King's County & Meath
Robert Leeson	June 1855	Franckford
Count Magawley	Nov. 1852	Tubber
Revd James Matthews	Apr. & June 1864	King's County & Tipperary
Revd William Minchin	Nov. 1851 & June 1852	Tubber
Arthur Molloy	July 1857	Banagher
Thomas Mitchell	July 1857	Tubber
Trustees of Maloney	May 1851 & May 1855	Tullamore
Moloney	June 1854	Clonona
Elizabeth Moore	Mar. 1855	Tubber
Elizabeth Morris	June 1851	Tullamore
Garrett O'Moore	Oct. 1852	King's County, Roscommon, Mayo & Clare
Earl Milltown	Jan. 1856	King's County, Dublin, Wicklow, Kildare, Meath & Louth
Samuel Parker	Apr. 1852	Tullamore
William Poole	Dec. 1855	Portarlington
Taylor M. Read	May 1858	King's County
Simpson Robinson	July 1854	Parsonstown
Thomas Robinson	July 1853	King's County & Westmeath
Edward Shawe	Dec. 1850	Philipstown
John Smallhorn	July 1851	Portarlington
Joseph Smith	June 1851	King's County, Tipperary & Queen's County
W.A. Steele	Mar. 1858	Parsonstown
George Stoney	Dec. 1850	Ballybritt
Edward Synge	June 1850	King's County & Clare
John F. Thewtes	Nov. 1854 & June 1856	King's County, Cavan, Meath, Dublin City
Clifford Trotter	Mar. 1851	King's County & Galway
Francis Usher	June 1852	King's County & Meath
Samuel Walsh	Oct. 1855	Geashill
Secretary of War	May 1860	King's County, Dublin and Youghal
Helen Wybrant	July 1854	Edenderry

Bibliography

PRIMARY SOURCES

I. MANUSCRIPT MATERIAL

Bedfordshire and Luton Archives
Earl de Grey papers.

Cornwall Record Office
Armstrong papers (X/819/1).

Fingal County Library
Hely Hutchinson papers.

Liverpool Record Office
Derby papers (920 DER).

National Archives of Ireland
Bernard papers, M 3878; Constabulary returns of evictions 1850, no. 6482.117 (3/02/4); Gamble papers, M 3485–3535; Gill papers, M 5539–40; Kelly papers, M 5619 (1–42) ; King papers, M 3522–25; M 3551; M 4121; Lloyd papers, M 3098; Map of the Milltown estate 1802, M 3012; Molloy papers, M 6167; Office of Public Works papers, 24194/51; Outrage papers King's County, 1835–53; Philipstown estate papers, M 7093 (104); Police returns for evictions, King's County for the quarter ended June 1851 (Official papers, 1851/28); Quit Rent Office papers, 2B/39/29; Relief Commission papers; Spunner papers, M 5805 (1–5).

National Library of Ireland
Ashtown papers, MS 1764; MS 1765–8; Baldwin papers (unsorted collection); Ballybritt papers, MS 2025; Biddulph papers, MS 5082; Bellew papers, MS 27,475 (3); Bennett papers, MS 10,073; Bracknagh estate map 1841, 21. F. 67; Cassidy papers (unsorted collection); 'Diary of hunts made by the King's County Fox Hounds', MS 16,193; Dames papers, MS 21 F 79 (4–19); Dowdall papers, Drogheda papers, MS 9737–38; MS 12,734–12,756; Guinness & Mahon Letter books, MS 32,013; Hatch papers, MS 11,324; Joly papers, MS 17,035; King papers, MS 11,703; Magan of Clonearl maps, 14. A. 27; Minute book, register of members and accounts of the Killeigh Book Society, Co. Offaly, 1839–1867', MS 19,449; 'Notebook listing the daily activities of a land agent in Co. Longford 1848–9', MS 18,245; Rent Ledger of an estate in Banagher district 1849–1874, MS 12,164; Palmer papers, MS 14,284; Ponsonby papers, MS 13,020; Portarlington papers, MS 19,720; Ridgeway papers, MS 4896; Sherlock papers, PC 704 (1); St George papers, MS 4001–22; Trench papers, MS 2579; Vaughan of Golden Grove papers, MS 29806 (209); Walsh papers, 16. I. 11 (6).

National University of Ireland, Galway
Blake papers.

Offaly County Library
Hanley papers; Monaghan papers; Poor Law Union minute books: Edenderry, Parsonstown and Tullamore.

Offaly Historical Society Research Centre
Bury papers; Greeson papers (copies); 'Particulars of the sale of the estate of Sir William Cox, Knight of Tinnycross, Tullamore May 1856'; Papers of the River Brosna drainage scheme 1840s (unsorted collection).

PRONI
'A register of trees for King's County 1793–1913' (T/3617/1B); Blundell papers (MIC 317); Charleville papers (T3069); De Ros papers (D638); Donoughmore papers (D619); Downshire papers (D671); Leinster papers (D3078); Magawley papers (T2354); Molesworth papers (D1567); Rosse papers (T3030); Staples (D1567); Rossmore papers (T2929).

Private possession
Acres papers; Ballinderry papers; Ballindoolin papers; 'Rental of the estate of the Marquis of Downshire, Edenderry 1922'; 'Rental and particulars of part of the lands of Gageborough, called Cappadonnell, King's County to be sold in the Incumbered Estates Court, 9 July 1857'.

Roscommon County Library
Stewart & Kincaid papers.

Sheffield Archives
Ponsonby papers; Wentworth Woodhouse Muniments (79/68).

Trinity College Dublin
Diary of John W. Armstrong, 1792–1858 (MS 6409–10); Joly papers (MS 2299).

University College Cork
Ryan of Inch papers (IE BL/EP/R).

Westmeath County Library
Howard Bury papers.

II. NEWSPAPERS

Anglo Celt   *The Armagh Guardian*
Economist   *The Evening Packet*
Freeman's Journal   *Illustrated London News*

King's County Chronicle	*The Leinster Express and Midland General advertiser*
Morning Chronicle	*Nation*
Nenagh Guardian	*New York Times*
Offaly Independent	*Pilot*
Times	*Tipperary Free Press*
Tipperary Vindicator	*Tralee Chronicle*
Tuam Herald	*Waterford Chronicle*

III. CONTEMPORARY ACCOUNTS

Beare, John, *Improvement of Ireland: a letter to the King on the practical improvement of Ireland* (London, 1827).

Brown, Robert E., *The book of the landed estate* (London & Edinburgh, 1869).

Campell, Alexander, *The farmers and cottagers guide* (Dublin, 1848).

Carleton, William, *Valentine McClutchy the Irish agent or chronicles of the Castle Cumber property* (3 vols, London, 1845).

——, *The Black Prophet: a tale of Irish famine* (London, 1847).

——, *The Squanders of Castle Squander* (London, 1852).

Carlyle, Thomas, *Reminiscences of my Irish journey in 1849* (London, 1852).

Craig, E.T., *An Irish commune: the history of Rahaline* (Dublin, 1919).

Curwen, J.C., *Observations on the state of Ireland* (London, 1818).

Dutton, Hely, *Statistical survey of the county of Clare* (Dublin, 1808).

Fitzgerald, P.H., *The story of the Incumbered Estate Court* (London, 1862).

French, George, *The land question: are the landlords worth preserving? Or forty years management of an Irish estate* (Dublin, 1881).

Furlong, John S., *The law of landlord and tenant as administered in Ireland* (Dublin, 1843).

Gamble, Richard, *An address to the members of the Historical and Literary Society on 19 February 1855* (Dublin, 1855).

——, *Suggestions as to why the legislature should interfere to secure tenant compensation* (Dublin, 1866).

——, *Compensation for improvements made by tenants in Ireland: when and how far should it be secured by law* (London, 1867).

——, *Fair rents? The only test is free contract... the report of the royal commission on the Land Act 1870: its errors as to fair rents* (Dublin, 1881).

Godkin, James, *The Land War in Ireland* (Dublin, 1870).

Grenville, Charles Cavendish Fulke, *The Grenville memoirs: a journal of the reign of Queen Victoria from 1837–1852*, vol. III (London, 1885).

Hamilton, John, *Sixty years experience as an Irish landlord: memoirs of John Hamilton* (London, 1894).

Head, Francis Bond, *A fortnight in Ireland* (London, 1852).

House of Commons, *The county courts chronicle and bankruptcy gazette from January to December 1854* (London, 1855).

House of Lords, *The sessional papers, 1801–33*, vol. 141 (London, 1842).

Hussey, S.M., *Reminiscences of an Irish land agent* (London 1904).

Inglis, H.D., *A journey through Ireland during the spring, summer and winter of 1834* (London, 1834).

Johnston, James, *A tour in Ireland: with mediation and reflections* (London, 1844).

Jones, William Bence, *The life's work in Ireland of a landlord who tried to do his duty* (London, 1880).

Kennedy, John Pitt, *Irish Chancery Reports: Reports of cases argued and determined in the High Court of Chancery, Court of Appeal in Chancery, The Landed Estates Court and Court of Bankruptcy and insolvency in Ireland during the year 1857*, vol. xiii (Dublin, 1858).

Lambert, Joseph, *Observations on the rural affairs of Ireland* (Dublin, 1829).

——, *Agricultural suggestions to the proprietors and peasantry of Ireland* (Dublin, 1845).

Laurence, Edward, *The duty of a steward to his lord* (London, 1727).

Lewis, George Cornwall, *Local disturbances in Ireland, 1836* (London, 1836).

Locke, John, *Ireland's recovery* (Dublin, 1855).

Mackenzie, Robert Shelton and Richard Lalor Sheil (eds), *Sketches of the Irish Bar* (New York, 1854).

Marshall, William, *On the landed property of England: an elementary and political treatise containing the purchase, the improvement and the management of landed estates* (London, 1804).

McDonald, Duncan George Forbes, *Hints on farming and estate management* (10th ed., London, 1868).

McNevin, Richard Charles, *The practice of the Incumbered Estates Court in Ireland from the presentation of the petition of sale, to the distribution of the funds* (Dublin, 1854).

O'Connor Morris, William, *Memories and thoughts of a life* (London, 1895).

O'Neill Daunt, W.J., *A life spent for Ireland* (London, 1896).

Pim, Jonathon, *The conditions and prospects of Ireland and the evils arising from the present distribution of landed property: with suggestions for a remedy* (Dublin, 1848).

Queen's University, *Queen's Quarterly* (Ontario, 1843).

Report on the trial of John Dolan for the murder of Right Hon., Hector John, Earl of Norbury (Dublin, 1844).

Rosse, The earl of, *A few words on the relationship of landlord and tenant in Ireland* (London, 1867).

Ryan, Charles, *An essay on Scottish husbandry adopted for the use of the farmers of Ireland* (Dublin, 1839).

Scott, M. (ed.), *Mr and Mrs Hall's tour of Ireland* (London, 1840).

Somerville, Alexander, *The whistler at the plough: containing travels, statistics and descriptions of scenery and agricultural customs in most parts of England: with letters from Ireland* (Manchester, 1852).

The case of the old and respected Alice Delin … 'Done to death' on Christmas Eve in the barony of Geashill. No beggar! (Dublin, 1862).

Trench, William Steuart, *Realities of Irish life* (London, 1868).

IV. CONTEMPORARY WORKS OF REFERENCE

Anon., *Remarks on Ireland; as it is, as it ought to be and as it might be … by a native* (London, 1849).

Alcock, T., *The tenure of land in Ireland considered* (London, 1848).

The Annual Register, or, a View of the history and politics of the Year 1851 (London, 1852).

The Annual Register, or a view of the history and politics of the year 1852 (London, 1853).

Binns, Jonathon, *Miseries and beauties of Ireland* (London, 1837).

Blacker, William, *Prize essay on the management of landed property in Ireland* (Dublin, 1834).

Blackwood's Edinburgh Magazine (Edinburgh, 1846).

British Farmers Magazine (London, 1851).

Coote, Sir Charles, *Statistical survey of the King's County* (Dublin, 1801).

De Burgh, U.H. Hussey, *The landowners of Ireland: an alphabetical list of the owners of estates of 500 acres or £500 valuation and upwards in Ireland with the acreage and valuation in each county* (Dublin, 1876).

De Moleyns, Thomas, *The landowners and agents practical guide* (Dublin, 1860).

Dublin Almanac (Dublin, 1840).

Dublin Directory (Dublin, 1848).

Ferguson, W.D., and A. Vance (eds), *The tenure and improvement of land in Ireland* (Dublin, 1851).

Griffith, Richard, *Valuation of 1854. Parish of Monasteroris, Edenderry, King's County* (Dublin, 1853).

Hawley, M., M. Maxwell and J. Watshun (eds), *Practical suggestions for a national system of agricultural statistics* (London, 1854).

Irish Equity Reports, by the Irish High Court of Chancery 1841 (London, 1842).

Irish Quarterly Review (Dublin, 1856).

Journal of the Royal Society of Antiquaries of Ireland 1858 (Dublin, 1858).

Lavelle, Fr, *The Irish landlord since the revolution* (Dublin, 1870).

Lewis, Samuel, *A topographical dictionary of Ireland* (London, 1837).

Mitchell, John, *History of Ireland from the treaty of Limerick to the present time* (Dublin, 1869).

Morris, John Paine, *The valuation and calculations assistant containing various tables* (Dublin, 1850).

The Parliamentary Gazetteer of Ireland (3 vols, Dublin, 1845).

The Parliamentary Gazetteer of Ireland (Dublin, 1846).

Prendergast, John P., *Letter to the earl of Bantry or a warning to English purchasers of the perils of the Irish Incumbered Estates Court* (Dublin, 1854).

Royal Agricultural Improvement Society of Ireland, *Dialogues on improved husbandry with a practical instructor under lord Clarendon's letter* (Dublin, 1848).

Smiles, Samuel, *History of Ireland and the Irish people, under the government of England* (London, 1844).

Smyth, George Lewis, *Ireland: historical and statistical* (London, 1849).

Thom's Directory, 1850 (Dublin, 1850).

Vallency, Charles, *A report on the Grand Canal or southern line* (Dublin, 1771).
Wakefield, Edward, *An account of Ireland: statistical and political* (2 vols, Dublin, 1812).
Wiggins, John, *The monster misery of Ireland: a practical treatise on the relation of landlord and tenant* (London, 1844).
Woodlock, William, *The Irish Jurist* (Dublin, 1862).
Wright, John, *King's County directory* (Parsonstown, 1890).

V. PARLIAMENTARY PUBLICATIONS

Ninth report from commissioner of Board of Education in Ireland on schools founded by Erasmus Smith, HC 1810 (194).
Report from the select committee on the state of Ireland 1825 (129).
Royal commission to inquire into municipal corporation in Ireland, 1831.
Select committee on disturbed state of Ireland [1831–2] (677).
Second report from the select committee on tithes in Ireland (508) xxi.245.
Returns of Courts of Petty Sessions in Ireland, 1835.
Royal commission of poorer classes in Ireland, 1835.
Return of the names of deputy lieutenants and magistrates in Commission of Peace in Ireland, 1835.
Royal commission on condition of poorer classes in Ireland, 1836 [35] [36] [37] [38] [39] [40] [41] [42].
Return of amount of constabulary force in each county, city and town in Ireland, January 1836.
Bill for the relief of conacre tenants in Ireland, 1837–8 (85).
Select committee of the House of Lords on the state of Ireland, 1839.
Report of the commissioners appointed to take the census of Ireland for the year 1841 (1843) [503].
Returns of the number of cases of ejectment for trial, and of the number actually tried at quarter sessions before the assistant barristers of the several counties of Ireland during each of the last five years, 1843 (320).
Royal commission of inquiry into state of law and practice in respect to occupation of land in Ireland, Minutes of evidence, parts II and III (1845).
Correspondence explanatory of measures adopted by Her Majesty's government for relief of distress arising from failure of potato crop in Ireland, 1846 [735].
Abstract return of the number of persons employed on relief works in the under mentioned counties for the four weeks of July 1846.
Select committee of House of Lords on laws, relating to relief of destitute poor and operation of medical charities in Ireland [1846] (694).
A return of all murders that have been committed in Ireland since the 1st of January 1842, House of Commons papers; accounts and papers (220) xxxv.293 (1846).
Return of the total number of outrages reported in each county in Ireland in the years 1845 and 1846 (LVI .231).
Return of assaults, incendiary fires, robbery of arms, administering of unlawful oaths, threatening letters, malicious injury to property and firing into dwelling 1845–46 [1846] (369).

Returns relative to homicides (Ireland) 1846.

Report from the select committee of the House of Lords on the laws relating to the relief of the destitute poor and into the operation of the medical charities in Ireland, together with the minutes of evidence taken before the said committee, 1846 (694) (694–ii) (694–iii).

Correspondence relating to measures for relief of distress in Ireland (Commissariat Series), January–March 1847 [796].

Correspondence relating to measures for relief of distress in Ireland (Board of Works Series), January–March 1847 [797].

Tables of number of criminal offenders committed for trial in Ireland 1846, 1847 [822].

Abstract return of estates under management of Courts of Chancery and Exchequer in Ireland, 1844–5, 1847–8 [226].

Correspondence relative to expenditure of advances under Land Improvement Act (Ireland), 1847–48 [423].

Papers relating to proceedings for the relief of distress, and the state of Unions and Workhouses in Ireland. Seventh series, 1847–8 [919] [955] [999].

Return of Advance under 10 Vict., c.32. PP, 1847–8, lvii.

Return of orphan girls sent from workhouses in Ireland as emigrants to Australia under arrangements set forth in papers in the commissioners annual report, 1848.

Fourteenth Report from the Select Committee on Poor Laws (Ireland); together with the proceedings of the committee minutes of evidence, appendix and index, 1849 [572].

Return of all notices served upon the reliving officers of Poor Law Districts in Ireland by landowners and others under the act 11 & 12 Vict., c.47 'An act for the protection and relief of the destitute poor evicted from their dwellings' 1849 [1089].

An act to amend the law with regard to distress for arrears of rent in Ireland, 1850 (485).

Select committee on outrages (Ireland) report 1852 [438].

Select committee of House of Lords on operation of Acts relating to drainage of lands in Ireland by Board of Works [1852–3] (10).

Returns of the proceedings of the commissioners for the sale of incumbered estates in Ireland, from their commencement up to the 1st day of January 1852 (167).

Return of number of petitions, produce of sales, number of conveyances and estates sold in Incumbered Estates Court, Ireland [1852–3] (390).

Evidence before Endowed Schools Commission, HC 1857–8 (2336).

Return by provinces and counties (compiled from returns made to the Inspector General, Royal Irish Constabulary) of cases of evictions which have come to the knowledge of the constabulary in each of the years 1849 to 1880 inclusive, HC 1881 [185] lxxvii, 725, pp 3–23.

VI. SECONDARY WORKS

Adams, William Forbes, *Ireland and Irish emigration to the new world from 1815 to the Famine* (Dublin, 1980).

Andrews, J.H., 'The French school of Dublin land surveyors', *Irish Geography*, 5:4 (1964–8), pp 275–92.

——, *Plantation acres: a historical study of the Irish land surveyor and his maps* (Belfast, 1985).

——, 'The Longfield maps in the National Library of Ireland: an agenda for research', *Irish Geography*, 21 (1991), pp 24–34.

Asmundsson, Doris R., 'Trollope's first novel: a re-examination', *Éire-Ireland*, 3 (Fall, 1971), pp 83–91.

Barlow, J., *Bog land studies* (London, 1983).

Barnard, Toby, *A new anatomy of Ireland: the Irish Protestants, 1649–1770* (London, 2004).

Barry, John, 'The duke of Devonshire's Irish estates, 1794–7: reports of Henry Bowman, agent', *Analecta Hibernica*, 22 (1960), pp 269–327.

Beames, Michael, 'Rural conflict in pre-famine Ireland: peasant assassinations in Tipperary, 1837–47', *Past and Present*, 96 (Nov. 1981), pp 75–91.

——, 'The Ribbon Societies: lower-class nationalism in pre-famine Ireland', *Past and Present*, 97 (Nov. 1982), pp 128–43.

——, *Peasants and power: the Whiteboy movements and their control in pre-Famine Ireland* (Great Britain, 1983).

Bell, Jonathan, *People and land: farming in nineteenth-century Ireland* (Belfast, 1992).

Bell, Jonathan and Mervyn Watson (eds), *Irish farming: implements and techniques, 1750–1900* (Edinburgh, 1986).

——, *A history of Irish farming, 1750–1950* (Dublin, 2008).

Bellot, Leland J., 'Wild hares and red herrings: a case study of estate management in the eighteenth-century English countryside', *The Huntington Quarterly*, 56:1 (Winter, 1993), pp 15–39.

Bew, Paul, *Ireland: the politics of enmity, 1789–2006* (Oxford, 2007).

Boyce, D. George, *Nineteenth-century Ireland: the search for stability* (Dublin, 1990).

Brady, Ciarán (ed.), *Interpreting Irish history: the debate of historical revisionism, 1938–1994* (Dublin, 1994).

Breen, Grainne C., 'Landlordism in King's County in the mid-nineteenth century' in Nolan and O'Neill (eds), *Offaly history & society: interdisciplinary essays on the history of an Irish county* (Dublin, 1998), pp 627–80.

Breiden, Jacqueline, 'Tenant applications to Lord Farnham county Cavan, 1832–60', *Breifne: Journal of Cumman Seanchais Bhréifne*, 9:36 (2000), pp 173–224.

Brown, Thomas N., 'Nationalism and the Irish peasant, 1800–1848', *The Review of Politics*, 15:4 (Oct. 1953), pp 403–45.

Bull, Philip, *Land, politics and nationalism: a study of the Irish land question* (Dublin, 1996).

Burke, H., *The people and the poor law in nineteenth-century Ireland* (England, 1987)

Byrne, Michael, 'The development of Tullamore, 1700–1921' (MLitt, UCD, 1979).

——, *Tullamore Catholic parish: a historical survey* (Tullamore, 1987).

——, *Durrow in history: a celebration of what has gone before* (Tullamore, 1994).

——, 'Tullamore: the growth process, 1785–1841' in Nolan and O'Neill (eds), *Offaly history and society: interdisciplinary essays on the history of an Irish county* (Dublin, 1998), pp 569–627.

——, 'Judge William O'Connor Morris, 1824–1904, Gortnamona, Tullamore', *Offaly Heritage*, 5 (2007–8), pp 117–46.

——, *Legal Offaly: the county courthouse at Tullamore and the legal profession in county Offaly from the 1820s to the present* (Tullamore, 2008).

——, 'The Magawleys of Temora and the Banons of Broughall, county Offaly', *Offaly Heritage*, 6 (2010), pp 128–77.

Carr, Peter, *The big wind* (Belfast, 1991).

Carpenter, Andrew, *Verse in English from eighteenth-century Ireland* (Cork, 1998).

Casement, Anne L., 'The management of landed estates in Ulster in the mid-nineteenth century with special reference to the career of John Andrews as agent to the third and fourth marquesses of Londonderry from 1828 to 1863' (PhD, Queen's University, Belfast, 2002).

Chestnutt, Margaret, *Studies in the short stories of William Carleton* (Gothenburg, 1976).

——, 'Studies in the short stories of William Carleton', *Gothenburg Studies in English*, 34 (1976), pp 102–18.

Christianson, Gale E., 'Secret societies and agrarian violence in Ireland, 1790–1840', *Agricultural History*, 46:3 (July 1972), pp 369–84.

——, 'Landlords and land tenure in Ireland, 1790–1830', *Éire-Ireland: A Journal of Irish Studies* (Eanach, 1994), pp 25–59.

Clare, Revd Wallace (ed.), *A young Irishman's diary (1836–1847): the early journal of John Keegan of Moate* (Dublin, 1928).

Clark, Samuel, 'The Land War in Ireland' (PhD, Harvard University, Massachusetts, 1973).

——, 'The importance of agrarian classes: agrarian class structure and collective action in nineteenth century Ireland', *British Journal of Sociology*, 29:1 (Mar. 1978), pp 22–40.

——, *Social origins of the Irish land war* (Princeton, 1979).

——, 'The importance of agrarian classes: agrarian class structure and collective action in nineteenth-century Ireland' in Drudy (ed.), *Ireland: land, politics and people* (Cambridge, 1982), pp 11–36.

Clark, Samuel and James S. Donnelly Jr (eds), *Irish peasants: violence and political unrest, 1780–1914* (Dublin, 1983).

Clarke, Joe, *Christopher Dillon Bellew and his Galway estates, 1763–1826* (Dublin, 2003).

Clarkson, L.A., Margaret E. Crawford, Paul S. Ell and Liam Kennedy (eds), *Mapping the great Irish famine: a survey of the famine decades* (Dublin, 1999).

Cleary, Joe and Claire Conolly (eds), *The Cambridge companion to modern Irish culture* (Cambridge, 2005).

Cloghan I.C.A., *A history of Cloghan parish* (Cloghan, 1988).

Clyne, Owen, Paudge English, Brother Raphael Kinihan and Brendan Kenny (eds), *Clara: a pictorial record* (Tullamore, 1992).

Connell, Peter, *The land and people of county Meath, 1750–1850* (Dublin, 2004).

Conwell, John Joseph, *A Galway landlord during the Great Famine: Ulick John de Burgh, first marquis of Clanricarde* (Dublin, 2003).

Cooke, T.L., 'Wayside ancient monument at Drishoge, King's County', *Journal of the Kilkenny and South-East of Ireland Archaeological Society*, 1:2 (1857), pp 380–5.

Cousens, S.H., 'Regional death rates in Ireland during the Great Famine from 1846 to 1851', *Population Studies*, 14:1 (July 1960), pp 55–74.

——, 'The regional pattern of emigration during the Great Irish Famine, 1846–51' in *Transactions and Papers (Institute of British Geographers)*, 28 (1960), pp 119–34.

——, 'The regional variations in mortality during the Irish Great Famine', *R.I.A. Proc.* 63 C, 3 (Feb. 1963), pp 127–49.

Crawford, William H., *The management of a major Ulster estate in the late eighteenth century: the eighth earl of Abercorn and his Irish agents* (Dublin, 2001).

Cronin, Denis A., *A Galway gentleman in the age of improvement: Robert French of Monivea, 1716–79* (Dublin, 1995).

Cronin, Maura, *Agrarian protest in Ireland, 1750–1960* (Dundalk, 2012).

Crowley, John, William J. Smyth and Mike Murphy (eds), *Atlas of the Great Famine* (Cork, 2012).

Cullen, Fintan, 'Marketing national sentiment: lantern slide of evictions in late nineteenth-century Ireland', *History Workshop Journal*, 54 (2002), pp 162–79.

Cullen, L.M., 'Eighteenth century flour milling in Ireland', *Irish Economic and Social History Journal*, 4 (1977), pp 56–65.

Curtis, L.P., 'Incumbered wealth: landed indebtedness in post-Famine Ireland', *American Historical Review*, 85:2 (Apr. 1980), pp 332–67.

——, 'The battering ram and Irish evictions, 1887–90', *Éire-Ireland: A Journal of Irish Studies*, 42 (Spring, 2007), pp 207–28.

Cusack, Danny, 'Breaking the silence: the poets of north Meath and the Great Famine', *Riocht na Midhe: Records of the Meath Archaeological and Historical Society*, 19 (2008), pp 170–88.

Daly, Mary E., 'Historians and the Famine: a beleaguered species?', *Irish Historical Studies*, 30:120 (Nov. 1997), pp 591–601.

Dardis, Patrick, *The occupation of land in Ireland in the first half of the nineteenth century* (Dublin, 1920).

Davis, Graham, 'The historiography of the Irish famine' in Patrick O'Sullivan (ed.), *The meaning of the famine* (London, 1997), pp 15–40.

Delaney, Enda, *The curse of reason: the Great Irish Famine* (Dublin, 2012).

Delaney, Mary, *William Steuart Trench and his management of Lord Digby's estate, King's County, 1857–71* (Dublin, 2012).

Delany, Ruth, *The Grand Canal of Ireland* (Newtown Abbot, 1973).

Devoy, John, *Recollections of an Irish rebel: the Fenian movement. Its origin and progress. Methods of work in Ireland and in the British army. Why it failed to achieve its main object, but exercised great influence on Ireland's future. Personalities of the organization. The Clan-na-Gael and the rising of Easter week, 1916. A personal narrative* (New York, 1929).

Dickson, David, 'Middlemen' in Thomas Bartlett and David Hayton (eds), *Penal age and golden era* (Belfast, 1979), pp 162–85.

——, *Old world colony: Cork and South Munster, 1630–1830* (Cork, 2006).

Dolan, Liam, *Land War and eviction in Derryveagh, 1840–65* (Dundalk, 1980).

Donnelly, J.S. Jr, 'The journals of Sir John Benn Walsh relating to the management of his Irish estate 1823–64 [Part I]', *Journal of the Cork Historical and Archaeological Society* (July–Dec. 1974), pp 86–123.

——, *The land and the people of the 19th century Cork: the rural economy and the land question* (London, 1975).

——, 'The journals of Sir John Benn Walsh relating to the management of his Irish estates, 1823–64 [Part II]', *Journal of the Cork Historical and Archaeological Society* (Jan.–June 1975), pp 15–42.

——, 'The Kenmare Estates during the nineteenth Century', *Journal of the Kerry Archaeological and Historical Society,* 21 (1988), pp 5–41.

——, *The Great Irish potato Famine* (Stroud, 2001).

——, 'Captain Rock: ideology and organization in the Irish agrarian rebellion of 1821–24', *Éire-Ireland: A Journal of Irish Studies* (Fall/ Winter, 2007), pp 60–103.

——, *Captain Rock: Irish agrarian rebellion of 1821–1824* (London, 2009).

Dooley, Terence, *The decline of the big house in Ireland: a study of Irish landed families, 1860–1960* (Dublin, 2001).

——, *The big houses and landed estates of Ireland: a research guide* (Dublin, 2007).

——, *The murders at Wildgoose Lodge: agrarian crime and punishment in pre-Famine Ireland* (Dublin, 2007).

Dowling, Martin W., *Tenant right and agrarian society in Ulster, 1600–1870* (Dublin, 1999).

Doyle, Anthony, *Charles Powell Leslie II's estates at Glaslough, county Monaghan, 1800–1841* (Dublin, 2001).

Duffy, P.J., 'Assisted emigration from the Shirley estate, 1843–54', *Clogher Record*, 14:2 (1992), pp 7–62.

——, 'Management problems on a large estate in mid-nineteenth-century Ireland: William Steuart Trench's report on the Shirley estate in 1843', *Clogher Record: Journal of the Clogher Historical Society*, 16:1 (1997), pp 101–22.

Dunne, Oliver P., 'Population and land changes in Croghan District Electoral Division, 1841–1911' (BA thesis, NUI Maynooth, 2002).

Dunne, Tom, 'A gentleman's estate should be a moral school: Edgeworthstown in fact and fiction, 1760–1840' in Raymond Gillespie and Gerard Moran (eds), *Longford: essays in county history* (Dublin, 1991), pp 95–121.

Edenderry Historical Society, *Edenderry then and now* (Tullamore, 1991).

——, *Carved in stone: a survey of graveyards and burial grounds, Edenderry & environs* (Naas, 2010).

Edwards, R.D. and T.D. Williams (eds), *The Great Famine: studies in Irish history, 1845–52* (Dublin, 1956).

Eiríksson, Andrés and Cormac Ó Gráda (eds), *Estate records of the Irish Famine: a second guide to the famine archives, 1840–55* (Dublin, 1995).

Eiríksson, Andrés, 'Irish landlords and the Great Irish Famine', *Working Papers Series* (1996). Centre for Economic Research, Dept. of Economics, UCD.

Ellis, Eilish, 'State aided emigration schemes from crown estates in Ireland *c.*1850', *Analecta Hibernica*, 22 (1960), pp 329–95.

Enright, Flannan P., 'Pre-Famine reform and emigration on the Wyndham estate in Clare', *The Other Clare*, 8 (1984), pp 33–9.

Feehan, John, *Farming in Ireland: history, heritage and environment* (Dublin, 2003).

Fegan, Melissa, *Literature and the Irish Famine, 1845–1919* (New York, 2002).

——, 'Something so utterly unprecedented in the annals of human life: William Carleton and the famine' in Peter Gray (ed.), *Victoria's Ireland? Irishness and Britishness, 1837–1901* (Dublin, 2004), pp 131–41.

Feingold, William L., 'The tenants movement to capture the Irish Poor Law Boards, 1877–86', *Albion: A Quarterly Journal concerned with British Studies*, 7:3 (Autumn 1975), pp 216–31.

Fenning, Hugh, 'Typhus epidemic in Ireland, 1817–1819: priests, ministers, doctors', *Collectanea Hibernica*, 41 (1999), pp 115–17.

Finney, Revd Charles, *Records of Castro Petre; taken from the Representative Church Body* (Dublin, 1978).

Foster, R.F., *Modern Ireland, 1600–1972* (London, 1988).

Freeman-Attwood, Marigold, *Leap Castle: a place and its people* (Norwich, 2001).

Garvin, Tom, 'Defenders, Ribbonmen and others: underground political networks in pre-Famine Ireland', *Past and Present*, 96 (Aug. 1982), pp 133–55.

Geary, Laurence M., *The Plan of Campaign, 1886–1891* (Cork, 1986).

Gibbons, Stephen, *Captain Rock, night errant: the threatening letters of pre-Famine Ireland* (Dublin, 2004).

Girourd, Mark, 'Charleville Forest, County Offaly, the property of Colonel C.K. Howard Bury', *County Life* (Sept. 1962), pp 710–14.

——, 'Birr Castle, county Offaly – III', *Irish Country Life* (Mar. 1965), pp 468–7.

Goodbody, Michael, 'The Goodbody's of Tullamore: a story of tea, tobacco and trade', *Offaly Heritage*, 5 (2007–8), pp 173–87.

Goodbody, Rob, *Sir Charles Domville and his Shankill estate county Dublin, 1857–71* (Dublin, 2003).

Gore, David, 'Landlord liberality during the Great Famine', *Clogher Record*, 10:5 (1996), pp 157–8.

Grace, Daniel, 'Crime in pre-Famine north west Tipperary', *Tipperary Historical Journal* (1996), pp 84–96.

——, *The Great Famine in Nenagh Poor Law Union, county Tipperary* (Nenagh, 2000).

Gray, Malcolm, 'The Highland Potato Famine of the 1840s', *Economic History Review: new series*, 7:3 (1955), pp 357–68.

Gray, Peter, *Famine, land, politics: British government and Irish society* (Dublin, 1996).

——, 'Memory and the commemoration of the Great Irish Famine' in Peter Gray and Oliver Kendrick (eds), *The memory of catastrophe* (Manchester, 2004), pp 46–65.

——, *The making of the Irish poor law, 1815–43* (Manchester, 2009).

Gray, Peter and Oliver Kendrick (eds), *The memory of catastrophe* (Manchester, 2004).

Griffin, Brian, 'An agrarian murder and evictions in Rathcore', *Riocht na Midhe: Records of the Meath Archaeological and Historical Society*, 9:1 (1994–5), pp 88–103.

Guinan, Revd Joseph Canon, *The Famine years* (Dublin, 1908).

——, *History of the Great Famine* (Dublin, 1910).

——, *Annamore and the tenant at will* (Dublin, 1924).

——, *Priest and people in Doon* (6th ed., Dublin, 1925).

Guinnane, Timothy W. and Ronald I. Miller, 'Bonds without bondsmen: tenant right in nineteenth-century Ireland', *Journal of Economic History*, 56:1 (Mar. 1996), pp 113–42.

Gribben, Arthur, *The Great Famine and the Irish diaspora in America* (New Jersey, 2000).

Haines, Robin, *Charles Trevelyan and the Great Irish Famine* (Dublin, 2004).

Hamrock, Ivor, *The Famine in Mayo, 1845–50: a portrait from contemporary sources* (Mayo, 2004)

Hayley, Barbara, *Carleton's* Traits and Stories *and the nineteenth-century Anglo-Irish tradition* (New Jersey, 1983).

Heaney, Henry (ed.), *A Scottish Whig in Ireland, 1835–38: the Irish journals of Robert Graham of Redgorton* (Dublin, 1999).

Heaney, Paddy, *At the foot of Slieve Bloom: history and folklore of Cadamstown* (Birr, 2000).

Hickey D.J. and J.E. Doherty, *A new history of Irish history from 1800* (Dublin, 2003)

Higgins, Noreen, *Tipperary's tithe war, 1830–38: parish accounts of resistance against a church tax* (Tipperary, 2002)

Hill, Jacqueline and Cormac Ó Gráda (eds), *The visitation of God?: the potato and the Great Irish Famine* (Dublin, 1993).

Hill, Lord George, *Facts from Gweedore* (5th ed., Belfast, 1971).

Hogg, William E., *The millers and mills of Ireland about 1850* (Dublin, 1998).

Holmes, John, 'Monasterevin distillery: a brief outline of its history and background', *Journal of the Kildare Archaeological Society*, 14 (1964–70), pp 480–7.

Hoppen, K.T., 'Landlords and electoral politics in Ireland', *Past and Present*, 75 (May 1977), pp 62–93.

——, *Elections, politics and society in Ireland, 1832–1885* (Oxford, 1984).

——, *Ireland since 1800: conflict and conformity* (2nd ed., Essex, 1999).

Horner, Arnold, *Mapping Offaly in the early 19th century: with an atlas of William Larkin's map of 1809* (Bray, 2006).

Hughes, E., 'The eighteenth-century estate agent' in H.A. Crowe, T.W. Moody and D.B. Quinn (eds), *Essays in British and Irish history in honour of James Eadie Todd* (London, 1949), pp 185–99.

Hutton, A.W. (ed.), *Arthur Young, a tour through Ireland, 1776–1779* (Shannon, 1970).

Jackson, Alvin, *Ireland, 1798–1998: politics and war* (Oxford, 1999).

James, Dermot, *John Hamilton of Donegal, 1800–1884: 'this recklessly generous landlord'* (Dublin, 1998).

Jones, Mark Bence, *Twilight of the ascendancy* (London, 1987).

Jordan, Donald E., *Land and popular politics in Ireland: County Mayo from the Plantation to the Land War* (Cambridge, 1994).

Katsuta, Shunsuke, 'The Rockite movement in county Cork in the early 1820s', *Irish Historical Studies*, 33:131 (May, 2003), pp 278–96.

Keane, Edward, P. Beryl Phair and Thomas U. Sadlier (eds), *King's Inns admission papers, 1607–1867* (Dublin, 1982).

Kearney, John, *From the quiet annals of Daingean: articles on the history of a parish in north Offaly* (Daingean, 2006).

Kelleher, Margaret, 'Factual fictions: representations of the land agitation in nineteenth century women's fiction' in Heidi Hannsson (ed.), *New contexts: re-framing nineteenth-century Irish women's prose* (Cork, 2008), pp 78–91.

Kelly, Denis, *Famine: Gorta I Lusma* (Lusmagh, 1995).

Kelly, Jennifer, 'A study of Ribbonism in Leitrim in 1841' in Joost Augusteijn & Mary Ann Lyons (eds), *Irish history: a research yearbook*, 2 (Dublin, 2003), pp 42–52.

Kelly, John, *The graves are walking: the history of the Great Irish Famine* (New York, 2012).

Kerrigan, Colm, *Father Mathew and the Irish Temperance Movement, 1838–1849* (Cork, 1992).

Kieberd, Declan, *Irish classics* (United Kingdom, 2000).

Kinealy, Christine, *This great calamity: the Irish famine, 1845–52* (Dublin, 1994).

——, *A death dealing famine: the Great Hunger in Ireland* (London, 1997).

——, *Repeal and revolution: 1848 in Ireland* (Manchester, 2009).

Knightly, John, 'The Godfrey estate during the Great Famine', *Journal of the Kerry Archaeological and Historical Society*, series 2, vol. 5 (2005), pp 125–53.

Lambe, Miriam, *A Tipperary landed estate: Castle Otway, 1750–1853* (Dublin, 1998).

Lane, Padraig G., 'The Encumbered estates court, Ireland 1848–1849', *Economic and Social Review*, 3:3 (Apr. 1972).

——, 'Glimpses of the Famine in Mayo: the letters of a land agent 1843–1849', *Cathair na Mart*, 17 (1997), pp 134–9.

——, 'Rents and leases in eighteenth- and nineteenth-century county Mayo: an observation of the Lambert estate', *Cathair na Mart*, 18 (1998), pp 57–60.

——, 'James Thorngate – archetypal or atypical 1850s landowner?', *Journal of the Galway Archaeological and Historical Society*, 53 (2001), pp 137–43.

——, 'The Boys was up: Connacht agrarian unrest in fiction, c.1800–1850', *Journal of the Galway Archaeological and Historical Society*, 58 (2006), pp 42–52.

Large, Peter Somerville, *The Irish country house: a social history* (London, 1995).

Larkin, Emmet, *The pastoral role of the Roman Catholic church in pre-Famine Ireland, 1750–1850* (Dublin, 2006).

Logan, John, 'Robert Clive Irish estates 1761–1842', *North Munster Antiquarian Journal*, 43 (2003), pp 5–23.

Lowe, W.J., 'Policing Famine Ireland', *Éire-Ireland: A Journal of Irish Studies*, 29:4 (Winter, 1994), pp 47–67.

Lyne, Gerard J., *The Lansdowne estate in Kerry under W.S. Trench, 1849–72* (Dublin, 2001).

Lyons, Francis Stewart Leland, 'Vicissitudes of a middleman in county Leitrim, 1810–27', *Irish Historical Studies*, 9 (1955), pp 300–18.

Lyons, Mary Cecilia, *Illustrated Incumbered Estates Ireland, 1850–1905* (Clare, 1993)

MacArthur, E.W.P., 'Memoirs of a land agent', *Donegal Annual*, 46 (1994), pp 90–107.

MacDonagh, Stephen, *Barack Obama: the road from Moneygall* (Dublin, 2010).

MacIntyre, A., *The Liberator* (London, 1965).

MacPhilib, Seamus, 'Profile of a landlord in folk tradition and in contemporary accounts – the third earl of Leitrim', *Ulster Folklife*, 36 (1988), pp 26–40.

——, '*Ius primae noctis* and the sexual image of Irish landlords in folk tradition and in contemporary accounts', *Bealoideas*, 56 (1988), pp 97–140.

Maguire, W.A., *The Downshire estates in Ireland, 1801–1845: the management of Irish landed estates in the early nineteenth century* (Oxford, 1972).

——, 'Lord Donegall and the sale of Belfast: a case history from the Encumbered Estate Court', *Economic History Review*: new series, 29:4 (Nov. 1976), pp 570–84.

——, 'Banker and absentee landowner: William Tennant in county Fermanagh, 1813–32', *Clogher Record*, 14:3 (1993), pp 7–28.

——, 'Missing persons: Edenderry under the Blundells and the Downshires, 1707–1922', Nolan and O'Neill (eds), *Offaly history and society: interdisciplinary essays on the history of an Irish county* (Dublin, 1998), pp 515–43.

Malcolm, Elizabeth, 'The reign of terror in Carlow: the politics of policing Ireland in the late 1830s', *Irish Historical Studies*, 32:125 (May 2000), pp 59–74.

Malcomson, A.P.W., 'A variety of perspectives on Laurence Parsons, 2nd earl of Rosse' in Nolan and O'Neill (eds), *Offaly history and society: interdisciplinary essays on the history of an Irish county* (Dublin, 1998), pp 439–85.

Marnane, Dennis, 'Samuel Cooper of Killenure (1750–1831): a Tipperary land agent and his diaries', *Tipperary Historical Journal*, 6 (1993), pp 102–28.

——, 'Such a treacherous country: a land agent in Cappawhite 1847–52', *Tipperary Historical Journal* (2004), pp 233–47.

Martin, Laura A., 'The Irish land agent as a mediator of urban improvement at Banbridge, county Down and Edenderry, King's County (Offaly) 1790–1840' (BSc, University of Ulster, Coleraine, 1994).

Maume, Patrick, 'A pastoral vision: the novels of Canon Joseph Guinan', *New Hibernia Review/Iris Eireannach Nua*, 9:4 (Winter, 2005), pp 79–98.

Maxwell, Constantia, *Town and country under the Georges* (Dundalk, 1949).

McAtamney, Neil, 'The Great Famine in county Fermanagh', *Clogher Record*, 15:1 (1994), pp 79–89.

McAulay, Eve, 'Some problems in building on the Fitzwilliam estate during the agency of Barbara Verschoyle', *Irish Architectural and Decorative Studies*, 2 (1999), pp 98–116.

McCarthy, Robert, *The Trinity College estates 1800–1923: corporate management in an age of reform* (Dundalk, 1992).

McClaughlin, Trevor, *Barefoot and pregnant? Irish famine orphans in Australia*, vol. 2 (Victoria, 2001).

McCormack, W.J., *The Blackwell companion to modern Irish culture* (Manchester, 1999).

——, *The silence of Barbara Synge* (Manchester, 2003).

McCourt, Eileen, 'The management of the Farnham estates during the nineteenth century', *Breifne: Journal of Cumman Seanchais Bhréifne*, 4 (1975), pp 531–60.

McDermott, Joseph P., 'An examination of the accounts of James Moore Esq., land agent and collector of port fees at Newport Pratt, county Mayo, 1742–65' (MA, St Patrick's College, Maynooth, 1994).

McDermott, M., 'The Shirley estate in south Mongahan and the development of gypsum mining, 1800–1936' (MA, NUI Maynooth, 2005).

McEvoy, John Noel, 'A study of the United Irish League in King's County, 1899–1918' (MA, St Patrick's College, Maynooth, 1992).

McGrath, Thomas, 'Interdenominational relations in pre-Famine Tipperary', William Nolan (ed.), *Tipperary history and society: interdisciplinary essays on the history of an Irish county* (Dublin, 1985), pp 256–87.

McMahon, Bryan, 'Sixty years of estate management in Ardfert', *The Kerry Magazine*, 10 (1999), pp 48–51.

McMahon, Michael, *The murder of Thomas Douglas Bateson, county Monaghan, 1851* (Dublin, 2006).

McMahon, Noel, *In the shadow of the Fairy Hill: Shinrone and Ballingarry – a history* (Birr, 1998).

McMahon, Theo, 'The Rose estate Tydavnet, county Monaghan', *Clogher Record*, 18 (2004), pp 219–56.

McManamon, Sean P., 'Irish National Land League, county Mayo: evidence as to clearances, evictions and rack renting etc., 1850–1880', *Cathair na Mart*, 24 (2004–5), pp 86–127.

Meehan, Patrick F., *The members of parliament for Laois and Offaly, 1801–1918* (Portlaoise, 1972).

Melville, Patrick, 'The landed gentry of Galway, 1820–1880' (PhD, Trinity College Dublin, 1991).

Middleton, Charles R., 'Irish representative peerage elections and the Conservative Party, 1832–1841', *Proceedings of the American Philosophical Society*, 129:1 (Mar. 1985), pp 90–111.

Miller, Kerby A., *Emigrants and exiles: Ireland and the Irish exodus to North America* (New York, 1985).

——, 'No middle ground: the erosion of the Protestant middle class in southern Ireland during the pre-Famine era', *The Huntington Library Quarterly*, 49:4 (Autumn, 1986), pp 295–306.

Mingay, G.E., 'The management of landed estates' in G.E. Mingay (ed.), *English landed society in the nineteenth century* (London, 1963), pp 126–46.

——, *Rural life in Victorian England* (London, 1977).

——, *The Victorian countryside* (London, 1981).

Mokyr, Joel and Cormac Ó Gráda, 'Poor and getting poorer? Living standards in Ireland before the Famine', *Economic History Review*, 41:2 (May, 1988), pp 209–35.

Moran, Gerard, *Sending out Ireland's poor: assisted emigration to North America in the nineteenth century* (Dublin, 2004).

——, *Sir Robert Gore Booth and his landed estate in Co. Sligo, 1814–76* (Dublin, 2006).

Morash, Christopher (ed.), *The hungry voice: the poetry of the Irish Famine* (Dublin, 1989).

——, *Writing the Irish Famine* (Oxford, 1995).

Morash, Christopher and Richard Hayes (eds), *Fearful realities: new perspectives on the famine* (Dublin, 1996).

Mullowney, Peter, 'The expansion and decline of the O'Donnel estate, Newport, county Mayo, 1785–1852' (MA, NUI Maynooth, 2002).

Murphy, Gerard William, 'On his majesties orders: Social relations in west Offaly – the barony of Garrycastle 1801–1851' (MLitt, NUI Maynooth, 2009).

——, 'A case study of midland settlement in West Offaly: Clonona Village circa 1800–60 Part II', *Offaly Heritage*, 4 (2006), pp 170–98.

——, 'Magistrates, police and the downright unruly, social relations in West Offaly: Rockite "Muscle for hire", 1834–8', *Offaly Heritage*, 5 (2007), pp 147–73.

Murphy, James H., *Catholic fiction and social reality in Ireland, 1873–1922* (Westport, CT, 1997).

Murphy, Michael, *Tullamore workhouse: the first decade, 1842–1852* (Tullamore, 2007).

Murphy, Nancy, *Guilty or innocent: the Cormack brothers – trial, execution and exhumation* (Nenagh, 1998).

Nally, David, *Human encumbrances: political violence and the Great Famine* (Indiana, 2011).

National Inventory of Architectural Heritage, *An introduction to the architectural heritage of county Offaly* (Dublin, 2006).

Nolan, William and Timothy P. O'Neill (eds), *Tipperary history and society: interdisciplinary essays on the history of an Irish county* (Dublin, 1985).

Norton, Desmond, 'On Viscount Frankfort's Kilkenny estates in the 1840s', *Old Kilkenny Review: Journal of the Kilkenny Archaeological Society*, 54 (2002), pp 18–40.

——, *Landlords, tenants, famine: the business of an Irish land agency in the 1840s* (Dublin, 2005).

O'Brien, George, *The economic history of Ireland from the Union to the Famine* (London, 1921).

O'Brien, Gerard, 'The establishment of Poor Law Unions in Ireland, 1838–43', *Irish Historical Studies*, 23:90 (Nov. 1982), pp 97–120.

O'Brien, Richard Barry, *Dublin Castle and the Irish people* (London, 1909).

O'Carroll, Gerald, 'Diary of Mr Justice Robert Day of Kerry (1746–1841)', *North Munster Antiquarian Journal*, 42 (2002), pp 151–75.

O'Connell, K.H., 'Land and population in Ireland, 1780–1845', *The Economic History Review*, 2:3 (1950), pp 278–89.

O'Connor, J., *The workhouses of Ireland: the fate of Ireland's poor* (Dublin, 1995).

O'Donnell, Ruán, 'King's County in 1798', William Nolan and Tim P. O'Neill (eds), *Offaly history & society: interdisciplinary essays on the history of an Irish county* (Dublin, 1998), pp 485–515.

Offaly County Council, *The Great Famine commemoration committee: locations of Famine sites* (Tullamore, 1994).

Offaly Historical & Archaeological Society, *Farming in Offaly* (Tullamore, 1987).

Ó Gráda, Cormac, 'Agricultural head rents, pre-Famine and post-Famine', *Economic and Social History Review*, 5:3 (1974), pp 385–92.

——, 'The investment behaviour of Irish landlords, 1830–75: some preliminary findings', *Economic History Review*, 23 (1975), pp 139–55.

——, 'Irish agricultural history: recent research', *Agricultural Historical Review*, 38:2 (1990), pp 164–73.

——, *Ireland: a new economic history, 1780–1939* (Dublin, 1995).

——, 'Bankrupt landlords and the Great Irish Famine', Cormac Ó Gráda (ed.), *Ireland's Great Famine: interdisciplinary perspectives* (Dublin, 2006), pp 48–62.

O'Hanrahan, Michael, 'The tithe war in county Kilkenny 1830–1834', William Nolan and Kevin Whelan (eds), *Kilkenny history and society: interdisciplinary essays in the history of an Irish county* (Dublin, 1990), pp 481–507.

O'Leary, John, *Recollections of Fenians and Fenianism* (2 vols, London, 1896).

O'Leary, Revd E., 'Notes on the collection of Irish antiquities lately at Edenderry', *Journal of the Kildare Archaeological Society*, 3 (1899–1902), pp 325–33.

O' Mearain, Lorcain, 'Estate agents in Farney: Trench and Mitchell', *Clogher Record*, 10:3 (1979–81), pp 405–13.

O'Murchada, Ciarán, *The Great Irish Famine: Ireland's agony, 1845–1852* (Dublin, 2011).

O'Neill, Padraig, 'The Fortescue's of County Louth', *Journal of the County Louth Archaeological and Historical Society*, 24:1 (1997), pp 5–21.

O'Neill, Tim P., 'The Famine in Offaly', William Nolan and Tim P. O'Neill (eds), *Offaly history and society: interdisciplinary essays on the history of an Irish county* (Dublin, 1998), pp 681–733.

——, 'Famine evictions' in Carla King (ed.), *Famine, land and culture in Ireland* (Dublin, 2000), pp 29–70.

——, 'Doing local history', *Journal of the Galway Archaeological and Historical Society*, 53 (2001), pp 47–65.

O'Rian, Seamus, *Dunkerrin: a parish in Ely O'Carroll* (Dublin, 1988).

O'Shea, James, *'Prince of Swindlers': John Sadlier MP, 1813–1856* (Dublin, 1999).

O'Tuathaigh, M.A.G., *Thomas Drummond and the government of Ireland, 1835–41* (Dublin, 1977).

Owen, Gary, 'A moral insurrection': faction fighters, public demonstrations and the O'Connellite campaign, 1828', *Irish Historical Studies*, 30:120 (Nov. 1997), pp 513–41.

Palmer, Norman D., 'Irish absenteeism in the eighteen seventies', *Journal of Modern History*, 13:3 (Sept. 1940), pp 357–66.

Pelly, P. and A. Tod (eds), *Elizabeth Grant: the highland lady in Ireland – journals 1840 to 1850* (Edinburgh, 1991).

Pey, Brian (ed.), *Eglish and Drumcullen: a parish in Firceall* (Birr, 2003).

Pilkington, Mary, 'The campaign for rent reductions on the Digby estate, King's County, 1879–1882', *Offaly Heritage*, 5 (2007), pp 187–225.

Pomfret, J.E., *The struggle for the land in Ireland* (Princeton, 1930).

Póirtéir, Cathal, *Famine echoes* (Dublin 1995).

Powell, J.S., *Shot a buck: the Emo estate, 1798–1852* (Portarlington, 1998).

Power, Margaret M.C., 'Sir Richard Bourke and his tenants 1815–55', *North Munster Antiquarian Journal*, 41 (2001), pp 75–87.

Proudfoot, Lindsay, 'The management of a great estate: patronage, income and expenditure on the duke of Devonshire's Irish property, c.1816–1891', *Irish Economic and Social History*, 13 (1986), pp 32–55.

——, 'Landlord motivation and urban improvement on the duke of Devonshire's Irish estates, c.1792–1832', *Irish Economic and Social History*, 18 (1991), pp 5–23.

——, 'Placing the imaginary: Gosford Castle and the Gosford estate c.1820–1900' in A.J. Hughes and William Nolan (eds), *Armagh history and society: interdisciplinary essays on the history of an Irish county* (Dublin, 2001), pp 881–917.

Quinlan, Todd B., 'Big whigs in the mobilization of Irish peasants: an historical sociology of hegemony in pre-Famine Ireland (1750s–1840s)', *Sociological Forum*, 12:2 (June 1998), pp 227–64.

Quinn, Eileen Moore, 'Entextualizing Famine, reconstructing self: testimonial narratives from Ireland' in *Anthropological Quarterly*, 74:2 (Apr. 2001), pp 72–88.

Rayfus, Colin E., *The 1865 Rathcore evictions* (Trim, 2008).

Read, David Breakenrid, *The Canadian rebellion of 1837* (Toronto, 1896).

Rees, Jim, *Surplus people: the Fitzwilliam clearances, 1847–56* (Dublin, 2000).

Reilly, Ciarán, 'Rebellion and disturbance at the Downshire estate, Edenderry, 1790–1800' (MA thesis, NUI Maynooth, 2006).

——, *Edenderry, county Offaly and the Downshire estate, 1790–1800* (Dublin, 2007).

——, *Edenderry, 1820–1920: popular politics and Downshire rule* (Dublin, 2007).

——, 'The burning of country houses in Co. Offaly during the revolutionary period, 1920–23' in Terence Dooley and Christopher Ridgeway (eds), *The Irish country house: its past, present and future* (Dublin, 2011), pp 110–33.

——, 'Clearing the estates to fill the workhouse: King's County land agents and the Irish Poor Law Act 1838' in Virginia Crossman and Peter Gray (eds), *Poverty and welfare in Ireland, 1838–1948* (Dublin, 2011), pp 145–62.

——, *John Plunket Joly and the Great Famine in King's County* (Dublin, 2012).

——, 'A middleman in the 1840s: Charles Carey and the Leinster estate' in Patrick Cosgrove, Terence Dooley and Karol Mullaney Dignam (eds), *The rise and fall of an Irish aristocratic family: the FitzGeralds of Kildare* (Dublin, 2014).

——, 'Between choice and coercion: land agents, eviction and assisted emigration during the Great Famine' in Enda Delaney and Brendan MacSuibhne (eds), *Power and hunger: popular politics in Ireland's Great Famine, 1845–1852* (forthcoming, New York, 2014).

Richards, Eric, 'The land agent' in G.E. Mingay (ed.), *The Victorian countryside* (London, 1981), pp 439–56.

Richey, Rosemary, 'The eighteenth-century estate agent and his correspondence. County Down: a case study' in R.J. Morris and Liam Kennedy (eds), *Ireland and Scotland: order and disorder, 1600–2000* (Edinburgh, 2005), pp 35–45.

Rossa, Jeremiah O'Donovan, *Rossa's recollections, 1838 to 1898: childhood, boyhood, manhood. Customs, habits and manners of the Irish plunder. Social life and prison life. The Fenian movement. Travels in Ireland, England, Scotland and America* (New York, 1898).

Ryan, Brendan, *A land by the river of God: a history of Ferbane parish from the earliest times to c.1900* (Ferbane, 1994).

——, *The dear old town: a history of Ferbane in the 18th and 19th centuries* (Ferbane, 2002).

——, *Policing in West Offaly, 1814–1922* (Tullamore, 2009).

Scally, Robert James, *The end of hidden Ireland: rebellion, famine and emigration* (New York, 1995).

Shaw, Revd Andrew, *The history of Ballyboy, Kilcormac and Killoughy* (Killoughy, n.d).

Sheil, Helen, *Falling into wretchedness; Ferbane in the 1830s* (Dublin, 1998).

Siddle, Yvonne, 'Anthony Trollope's representation of the Great Famine' in Peter Gray (ed.), *Victoria's Ireland? Irishness and Britishness, 1837–1901* (Dublin, 2004), pp 141–50.

Simons, P. Frazer, *Tenants no more: voices from an Irish townland, 1811–1901 and the great migration to Australia & America* (Victoria, 1996).

Smith, Maire, *The Rahan boys and the Killoughy barracks affray* (Tullamore, 2007).

Smith, J.G., 'Some nineteenth century Irish economics', *Economica*, 2:5 (Feb. 1935), pp 20–32.

Smyth, William J., 'The role of towns and cities in the Great Irish Famine' in John Crowley, William J. Smyth and Mike Murphy (eds), *Atlas of the Great Famine* (Cork, 2012), pp 240–55.

Snell, K.D.M. (ed.), *Letters from Ireland during the Famine of 1847* (Dublin, 1994).

Spring, David, 'The English landed estates in the age of coal and iron: 1830–1880', *Journal of Economic History*, 11:1 (Winter, 1951), pp 3–24.

——, 'A great agricultural estate: Netherby under Sir James Graham 1820–1845', *Agricultural History*, 29:2 (Apr. 1955), pp 73–81.

——, *The English landed estate in the 19th century: its administration* (London, 1963).

——, 'English landed society in the eighteenth and nineteenth centuries', *Economic History Review*, 17:1 (1964), pp 146–53.

Strauss, E., *Irish nationalism and British democracy* (London, 1951).

Sullivan, Eileen A., 'William Carleton (1794–1869)', *Éire-Ireland: A Journal of Irish Studies*, 24:2 (Summer, 1989), pp 3–10.

Taatgen, H.A., 'The Boycott in the Irish civilizing process', *Anthropological Quarterly*, 65:4 (Oct. 1992), pp 163–76.

Taylor, Laurence J., 'The priest and the agent: social drama and class consciousness in the west of Ireland', *Comparative Studies in Society and History*, 27:4 (Oct. 1985), pp 696–712.

Thunete, Mary Helen, 'Violence in pre-Famine Ireland: the testimony of Irish folklore and fiction', *Irish University Review*, 15 (1985), pp 129–47.

Trant, Kathy, *The Blessington Estate, 1667–1908* (Dublin, 2004).

Trodd, Valentine, *Midlanders: chronicle of a midland parish* (Banagher, 1994).

Trotman, Felicity, *Irish folk tales* (Dublin, 2008).

Turner, Michael, *After the Famine: Irish agriculture, 1850–1914* (Cambridge, 1996).

Vaughan, W.E., *Landlords and tenants in mid-Victorian Ireland* (Oxford, 1994).

Vesey, Patrick, *The murder of Major Mahon, Strokestown, county Roscommon, 1847* (Dublin, 2008).

Walsh, Walter, *Kilkenny: the struggle for the land, 1850–1882* (Kilkenny, 2008).

Ward, Patrick, *Exile, emigration and Irish writing* (Dublin, 2002).

Webster, Sarah, 'Estate management and the professionalization of Land Agents on the Egremont estates in Sussex and Yorkshire 1770–1835', *Rural History*, 18:1 (2007), pp 47–69.

Whelan, Kevin, 'An underground gentry? Catholic middlemen in eighteenth century Ireland' in Andrew Carpenter, Alan Harrison and Ian Campbell Ross (eds), *Eighteenth-century Ireland: Iris and dá chultur* (Dublin, 1995), pp 74–87.

——, 'The revisionist debate in Ireland', *Boundary*, 2:31 (part 1) (2004), pp 179–205.

White, Robert William, *Provisional Irish Republican Army: an oral and interpretive history* (London, 1993).

Winstanley, Michael J., *Ireland and the land question, 1800–1922* (London, 1984).

Woodham-Smith, Cecil, *The great hunger: Ireland, 1845–1849* (New York and London, 1962).

Woodward, Nicholas, 'Transportation convictions during the Great Famine', *Journal of Interdisciplinary History*, 37:1 (Summer, 2006), pp 59–87.

Wylie, J.C.W., *A casebook on Irish land law* (Oxford, 1994).

Yager, Tom, 'Mass eviction in the Mullet Peninsula during and after the Great Famine', *Irish Economic and Social History*, 23 (1996), pp 24–44.

——, 'What was rundale and where did it come from?', *Bealoideas*, 70 (2002), pp 153–86.

Young, Liz, 'Spaces for Famine: a comparative geographical analysis of Famine in Ireland and the Highlands in the 1840s', *Transactions of the Institute of British Geographers:* new series, 21:4 (1996), pp 666–80.

Zimmermann, George Denis, *Songs of Irish rebellion: Irish political street ballads and rebel songs, 1780–1800* (2nd ed., Dublin, 2002).

Index